Volume 2

YALE STUDIES IN THE HISTORY OF MUSIC

Leo Schrade, Editor

Yale Studies in the History of Music

Beekman C. Cannon, *Johann Mattheson, Spectator in Music*

William G. Waite, *The Rhythm of Twelfth-Century Polyphony*

THE RHYTHM OF

Twelfth-Century Polyphony

ITS THEORY AND PRACTICE

BY WILLIAM G. WAITE

Assistant Professor of the History of Music, Yale University

GREENWOOD PRESS, PUBLISHERS
WESTPORT, CONNECTICUT

The Library of Congress has catalogued this publication as follows:

Library of Congress Cataloging in Publication Data

Waite, William G
The rhythm of twelfth-century polyphony.

Reprint of the ed. published by Yale University Press, New Haven, which was issued as no. 2 of Yale studies in the history of music.
The music is transcribed from the facsim. of Leonin's Magnus liber in J. H. Baxter's An old St. Andrew's music book, London, 1931.
Bibliography: p.
1. Organum. I. Leoninus Magister, fl. 1160-1170. Magnus liber organi de gradali et antiphonario. II. Title. III. Series: Yale studies in the history of music, v. 2.

[ML174.W14 1973] 781'.24 73-2648
ISBN 0-8371-6815-5

Originally published in 1954
by Yale University Press, New Haven

Reprinted with the permission
of Yale University Press

First Greenwood Reprinting 1973

Library of Congress Catalogue Card Number 73-2648

ISBN 0-8371-6815-5

Printed in the United States of America

Foreword

Friedrich Ludwig, the greatest medievalist among historians of music, once gave a sensitive description of the duplum in Leonin's organum as a product of the artist's fancy, free in rhythm, bold in the design of the melodic contours, with a rhythmically unfettered overflow of melismata—a jubilus, as it were, which at once calls to mind the characteristics St. Augustine spoke of in the Alleluja; and by deliberate and effective contrast to such total freedom of rhythm Leonin developed within his organum limited sections which became subject to the system of the rhythmic modes. But Ludwig saw Leonin's strength in the style of the rhythmically free duplum, while he regarded any of his rhythmically strict organizations merely as a first approach to the system of modes. This opinion has long been maintained, and the stylistic difference between Leonin and Perotin has for the most part been described as the contrast between the rhythmic freedom of the one and the elaborate modal system of the other. To judge from the few transcriptions of Leonin's organa Ludwig himself, however, must have been aware that even the duplum over a sustained tenor was often governed by recurrent regular patterns which had all the characteristics of modal rhythm. On the other hand, there were long passages in all the dupla seemingly without any detectable order. Students of the vexing problems of these passages had discovered what they supposed to be a totally free rhythm.

We have come now to realize that the complete absence of rhythmic order was an illusion, comprehensible, to be sure, in view of all the irregularities and inordinate difficulties in the notation, but nonetheless an illusion. It is the merit of the present study to have disclosed the principles of Leonin's organum. No doubt details will still be the subject of discussion; and the author will welcome such discussion. But the basic elements of the rhythmic problems seem to be established.

It was clear from the outset that a study such as this would hardly be satisfactory or useful without ample transcriptions of Leonin's organa. We had no hope of realizing the ideal and including in this book the voluminous transcriptions which the author presented with his Ph.D. thesis; the prohibitive expenses of publication made a selection mandatory. The most reasonable choice, that best justified on historical grounds, was suggested by the material itself; it could be nothing else nor anything less than that part which in the original sources is compiled as an entity by itself: the *Magnus Liber Organi* by Leonin.

But what we confidently took to be a sound choice still left us face to face with the stark realities of the costs of publication. Convinced of the importance of this study as a substantial contribution to scholarship in the history of music, Edgar S. Furniss, Provost of Yale University, made university funds available which enabled the Department of Music in the Graduate School to proceed with publication. It is with profound gratitude that we recognize a generosity which in the end, we are certain, will be of benefit to all historians of music.

LEO SCHRADE

Yale University
13 May 1954

Preface

When the author undertook the investigation of Notre Dame organum as the subject of a doctoral dissertation in the summer of 1946, he was aware to some extent of the difficulties that lay before him, but fondly hoped to isolate and analyze the musical style of Leonin and Perotin and the other anonymous composers of organum. Since that time he has come to a more realistic appraisal of the task before him and of his own limitations in achieving such a goal. The results of his research, which are embodied in this book, may only be described as a limited contribution to our knowledge of the Notre Dame epoch. At the same time it is obvious that the study of organum of the twelfth century will always be hampered until the repertory has been made available in transcription, and so it is with some sense of satisfaction that the *Magnus liber* of Leonin in the version of W1 is presented here for the first time in modern notation. It is to be hoped that the time will come when the remaining versions as well as the substitute clausulae will also appear in modern form.

The author wishes here to acknowledge the profound debt that he owes to his friend and teacher, Professor Leo Schrade, who first suggested this study and who has been throughout both a counsellor and an inspiration. He also desires on this occasion to express his gratitude for the many services rendered him by the staff of the Music School Library and its former head, Miss Eva Judd O'Meara, and to thank the staff of the Yale University Press for their painstaking efforts in the preparation of this book. He is furthermore deeply grateful to Mr. Easley R. Blackwood, Jr. who expended many hours and much care in copying the musical examples. A very special debt is owed to my wife whose patience and forbearance have sustained me throughout the years of preparation of this work.

WILLIAM G. WAITE

Yale University, May, 1954.

Contents

List of Abbreviations

Acta: Acta Musicologica

AfMF: Archiv für Musikforschung

AfMW: Archiv für Musikwissenschaft

CS: Coussemaker, Edmond de. *Scriptorum de musica medii aevi nova series*

F: MS Florence, Bibl. Laurenziana, pluteus 29.1

Gerbert, *Scriptores:* Gerbert, Martin. *Scriptores ecclesiastici de musica sacra potissimum*

JAMS: Journal of the American Musicological Society

JMP: Jahrbuch der Musikbibliothek Peters

KJ: Kirchenmusikalisches Jahrbuch

Ludwig, *Repertorium:* Ludwig, Friedrich. *Repertorium organorum recentioris et motetorum vetustissimi stili*

MfMG: Monatshefte für Musikgeschichte

MQ: Musical Quarterly

SIMG: Sammelbände der Internationalen Musikgesellschaft

Sowa: Sowa, Heinrich. *Ein anonymer glossierter Mensuraltraktat 1279*

VfMW: Vierteljahrschrift für Musikwissenschaft

W_1: MS Wolfenbüttel 677 *olim* Helmstadt 628

W_2: MS Wolfenbüttel 1206 *olim* Helmstadt 1099

ZfMW: Zeitschrift für Musikwissenschaft

ZIMG: Zeitschrift der Internationalen Musikgesellschaft

Introduction

In the history of human culture perhaps no century reveals a more remarkable quickening of intellectual life than the twelfth. In these one hundred years the scope of human thought and its modes of expression were so broadened and expanded that modern historians frequently refer to this epoch as the Renaissance of the Twelfth Century. It is indeed a marvelous record of achievement that confronts the student of this era:

> The complete development of Romanesque art and the rise of Gothic; the full bloom of vernacular poetry, both lyric and epic; and the new learning and new literature in Latin. The century begins with the flourishing age of the cathedral schools and closes with the earliest universities already well established at Salerno, Bologna, Paris, Montpellier, and Oxford. It starts with only the bare outline of the seven liberal arts and ends in possession of the Roman and canon law, the new Euclid and Ptolemy, and the Greek and Arabic physicians, thus making possible a new philosophy and a new science. It sees a revival of the Latin classics, of Latin prose, and of Latin verse, both in the ancient style of Hildebert and the new rhymes of the Goliardi, and the formation of the liturgical drama. New activity in historical writing reflects the variety and amplitude of a richer age—biography, memoir, court annals, the vernacular history, and the city chronicle.[1]

To this list one must add the achievements in musical art which are of inestimable importance for the history of European music.

The center of this world of intellectual ferment came to be Paris in the second half of the century. There, in the shadow of the great Cathedral of Notre Dame which was begun in 1163, the University of Paris was evolving and rapidly attaining the position of pre-eminence that it was to hold throughout the thirteenth and fourteenth centuries. The historian William of Armorica, writing of the Paris of 1210, has this to say of the university:

> In that time letters flourished at Paris. Never before in any time or in any part of the world, whether in Athens or in Egypt, had there been such a multitude of students. The reason for this must be sought not only in the admirable beauty of Paris, but also in the special privileges which King Philip and his father before him conferred upon the scholars. In that great city the study of the trivium and the quadrivium, of canon and civil law, as also of the science which empowers one to preserve the health of the body and cure its ills,

1. C. H. Haskins, *The Renaissance of the Twelfth Century* (4th printing, Cambridge, Mass., Harvard University Press, 1939), pp. 6–7.

were held in high esteem. But the crowd pressed with a special zeal about the chairs where Holy Scripture was taught, or where problems of theology were solved.[2]

It is Paris, furthermore, that becomes the center of the musical world in the second half of the century, for it is at Notre Dame that the two great composers, Leoninus and Perotinus, created a repertory of polyphonic music and a system of rhythm which penetrated all the countries of western Europe. The Cathedral of Notre Dame and the University of Paris are both of the utmost importance for the history of the music of the twelfth and thirteenth centuries: the first as the center of musical composition and the second as the transmitter of musical theory.

The greatness of the Notre Dame composers, Leoninus and Perotinus, can by no means be overestimated. When Leonin undertook the composition of his great cycle of polyphonic music for the major feasts of the church year some time around 1160, polyphony had already lived through three hundred years of recorded history. There was in fact a much increased activity in the writing of polyphonic works, known as organum, in the first half of the twelfth century, and yet none of these compositions seems to have been great enough to attain other than local recognition.[3] It was Leonin and his successor, Perotin, who first created polyphonic music of such artistry that their compositions were copied and performed not only in Paris but in England, France, Spain, Italy, and Germany. They are the first international composers of polyphonic music. Moreover their works were still being copied and presumably performed at the beginning of the fourteenth century. Not only did the organa of these two men enjoy long lives as independent compositions but, by the process of troping, from these same works issued the motet, the most important category of composition in the thirteenth century. Finally, the rhythmic innovations of the same two men mark one of the most decisive developments in the history of music,

2. Quoted in Achille Luchaire, *Social France at the Time of Philip Augustus,* E. B. Krehbiel, trans. (New York, P. Smith, 1929), p. 74.

3. Friedrich Ludwig, "Die geistliche nichtliturgische und weltliche einstimmige und die mehrstimmige Musik des Mittelalters bis zum Anfang des 15. Jahrhunderts," in Guido Adler, *Handbuch der Musikgeschichte,* zweite vollständig durchgesehene und stark ergänzte Auflage (2 vols., Berlin-Wilmersdorf, 1930), *I,* 176: "[Die Gruppe von zweistimmigen liturgischen Organa des 11. und beginnenden 12. Jahrhunderts] zeigt einerseits zwar die bereits ziemlich weite Verbreitung des mehrstimmigen Gesangs im Gottesdienst, andrerseits freilich nur ein sich in verhältnismässig engen Grenzen bewegendes, man möchte sagen: Tasten, dem noch kein vollendetes Kunstwerk gelingt, das über die lokale Bedeutung hinaus stärkeren Einfluss auch auf weitere Kreise auszuüben vermöchte, wie ein solcher dann schon in der zweiten Hälfte des 12. Jahrhunderts den Organa der Pariser Notre Dame–Schule in grösstem Ausmass beschieden war."

for not only was a consistent system of rhythm, the so-called "rhythmic modes," established in their works but an adequate method of notation as well, which provided the basis of our modern notation.

Despite the acknowledged eminence of Leonin and Perotin, little has been done to rescue their music from oblivion. In recent years Heinrich Husmann has published an edition of the three- and four-part organa of the Notre Dame school, but due to the difficulties of wartime publishing this work is almost unobtainable.[4] Furthermore certain features of the notation are transcribed in this edition in a manner that is not acceptable. Beyond this one work the available examples of Notre Dame organum consist of only a little more than a dozen transcriptions scattered through textbooks of music history and articles in musicological periodicals. In order to expand our knowledge of this vital period in the history of music, I have transcribed the entire corpus of Notre Dame organum in the principal manuscripts. In the course of transcription, however, it became increasingly apparent that a critical re-examination of the system of modal notation was required in order to resolve many perplexing problems of the notation and above all to provide an answer to the troubled question of the rhythmic nature of Leonin's two-voiced organum. The search for the origins of modal rhythm and modal notation opened fascinating byways which led to new discoveries and new interpretations. The results of this study are presented here as a preface to, and justification of, the transcriptions of the part of the Notre Dame repertory included in this volume. It is hoped that this investigation will dispel somewhat the obscurity surrounding the origins of measured polyphony and that it will prove helpful in transcribing conductus as well as organum.

Before proceeding to a detailed discussion of Notre Dame rhythm and notation, it is necessary to outline briefly the essential facts concerning the work of Leonin and Perotin. All that is known of these two men is a brief sketch of their compositions by an anonymous Englishman (ca. 1280), who wrote:

> Magister Leoninus was the best composer of organum, who made the *Magnus liber organi de Gradali et Antiphonario* in order to increase the divine service. This was in use until the time of the great Perotinus who shortened this book and made many better *clausulae* or *puncta* [substitute sections], since he was the best composer of discantus and better than Leoninus, although he cannot be said to reveal the subtlety of [Leonin's] organum. This Magister Perotinus wrote the best *quadrupla* [four-part organa] such as *Viderunt* and

4. Heinrich Husmann, *Die drei- und vierstimmigen Notre Dame–Organa. Kritische Gesamtausgabe* (Leipzig, 1940).

Sederunt with an abundance of "colors" in the art of harmonic music, as well as many most noble *tripla* [three-part organa] such as *Alleluia, Posui adjutorium; Nativitas,* etc. He also made conductus in three parts, such as *Salvatoris hodie;* and two-part conductus, such as *Dum sigillum summi patris;* and simple conductus together with many others, such as *Beata viscera; Justitia,* etc. The book or books of Magister Perotinus were in use both in the choir of the church of Notre Dame in Paris until the time of Magister Robertus de Sabilone, and from his time until the present day, . . .[5]

At a later point [6] this same author reports that these compositions are contained in more than six volumes, which for the sake of brevity may simply be listed. Each of these volumes, with the exception of the last, contains only works of the same category and of the same number of voices. These are:

1. Four-part organum, such as *Viderunt* and *Sederunt.*
2. Three-part organum, such as *Alleluia, Dies Sanctificatus.*
3. Three-part conductus with melismatic sections, such as *Salvatoris hodie* and *Religantur ab arca.*
4. Two-part conductus with melismatic sections, such as *Ave Maria, Pater noster commiserere, Hac in die regi nato.*
5. Conductus in two, three and four parts without melismatic sections.
6. Two-part organum, such as *Judea et Jerusalem* and *Constantes.*
7. Many other volumes of various contents.

These remarks of Anonymous IV make it possible not only to attribute certain works to Leonin and Perotin but also to determine approximately the date when these composers flourished. Two ordinances issued by the Bishop of Paris, Eudes de Sully, for the observation of special religious services disclose that the

5. Edmond de Coussemaker, *Scriptorum de Musica Medii Ævi Novam Seriem a Gerbertina Alteram Collegit Nuncque Primum Edidit* (4 vols., Paris, 1864–76), (hereafter cited as CS), *1,* 342a: "Et nota quod *Magister* LEONINUS, secundum quod dicebatur, fuit *optimus Organista,* qui fecit magnum librum organi de Gradali et Antiphonario pro servitio divino multiplicando; et fuit in usu usque ad tempus PEROTINI *Magni,* qui abbreviavit eumdem, et fecit clausulas sive puncta plurima meliora, quoniam *optimus discantor* erat, et melior quam LEONINUS erat; sed hic non dicendus de subtilitate organi, etc.

"Ipse vero *Magister* PEROTINUS fecit Quadrupla optima, sicut: *Viderunt, Sederunt,* cum abundantia colorum armonice artis. (In) super et Tripla plurima nobilissima, sicut: *Alleluia; Posui adjutorium; Nativitas,* etc.

"Fecit etiam triplices Conductus, ut: *Salvatoris hodie;* et duplices Conductus, sicut: *Dum sigillum summi patris;* et simplices Conductus cum pluribus aliis, sicut: *Beata viscera; Justitia,* etc.

"Liber vel libri *Magistri* PEROTINI erant in usu usque ad tempus *Magistri* ROBERTI DE SABILONE, et in choro Beate Virginis Majoris ecclesie Parisiis, et a suo tempore usque in hodiernum diem, . . ."

6. CS, *1,* 360a,b.

gradual for New Year's Day (1198) and the Feast of St. Stephen (1199) was sung in four-part organum.[7] The gradual for the first day is *Viderunt omnes* and that for St. Stephen's day is *Sederunt principes.* Anonymous IV attributes the four-part setting of both these chants to Perotin, and since only one four-part setting exists for each of these graduals, it is safe to assume that Eudes de Sully was referring specifically to Perotin's great works which must then have been composed some time prior to 1198–99. Another approximate date for Perotin's life can also be derived from his conductus, *Beata viscera.* The text of this conductus is by Philip the Chancellor, who died in 1236. The collaboration of Perotin and Philip indicates that Perotin must have still been active as a composer in the first part of the thirteenth century. On the basis of these dates Mme. Rokseth suggests that Perotin was probably born sometime between 1170 and 1175, that he began to compose around 1190, and that he died some time after 1220.[8] It is more difficult to ascertain the probable dates of Leonin. Anonymous IV, however, records that Perotin reworked portions of Leonin's *Magnus liber.* It is not very likely that Perotin would have undertaken such a task of revision while Leonin was still alive or even within a few years after his death. Given a suitable length of time between the death of Leonin and the revision of his compositions by Perotin, we may establish the decade between 1160 and 1170 as the probable date of composition of Leonin's *Magnus liber.*

The volumes described by Anonymous IV have come down to us in what must be nearly their original state in the great Florentine manuscript once owned by Piero dei Medici, now Pluteus 29.1 at the Biblioteca Medicea-Laurenziana (F). An earlier manuscript Wolfenbüttel 677 olim Helmstadt 628 (W_1), probably written at St. Andrew's in Scotland, contains essentially the same repertory though in lesser numbers, while the manuscript Wolfenbüttel 1206 olim Helmstadt 1099 (W_2) contains a collection of the same works though in a version even later than F. Individual pieces from this vast repertory are also to be found in numerous lesser manuscripts.[9] The three manuscripts, W_1, F,

7. The first ordinance is to be found in B. Guérard, *Cartulaire de l'Eglise de Paris* (Paris, 1850), *1*, 72–75. Both are published by Jacques Handschin in "Zur Geschichte von Notre Dame," *Acta Musicologica, 4* (1932), 7. Both are discussed in detail by Yvonne Rokseth, *Polyphonies du xiiie siècle* (4 vols., Paris, 1939), *4*, 42–43.

8. *Ibid.*, p. 51. Hans Tischler has recently questioned these dates on quite unconvincing grounds. See "New Historical Aspects of the Parisian Organa," *Speculum, 25,* No. 1 (1950), 21.

9. For bibliographical information concerning these manuscripts one must consult the indispensable work of Friedrich Ludwig, *Repertorium organorum recentioris et motetorum vetustissimi stili* (Halle, 1910).

and W_2, have been the basis of this study. W_1 is available in a facsimile edition by J. H. Baxter, *An Old St. Andrew's Music Book* (London, 1931), while F and W_2 were accessible to me only in photostatic reproduction. All three manuscripts contain fascicles of two-, three-, and four-voiced organa arranged, with but few exceptions, in the order in which they appear in the liturgical year. In addition to these complete works W_1 and F contain a large group of smaller compositions, new versions of sections of the organa designed to replace equivalent portions of Leonin's *Magnus liber*. These are the "clausulae sive puncta" which Anonymous IV attributes to Perotin. It is highly improbable, however, that Perotin alone could have composed all these clausulae, for the Florence manuscript contains no less than 461 of these pieces written in a wide variety of styles and with varying degrees of competence.

One of the astonishing features of organum as revealed by the manuscripts is the comparative uniformity of the repertory. In general the manuscripts contain the same compositions, although the Florence manuscript offers by far the largest number of works. This curious state of arrested growth contrasts strongly with the motet repertory in the same manuscripts, for W_1, F, and W_2 reveal a successively larger number of new motets. It appears then that after Perotin the composition of organum disappeared almost completely in favor of the new form of the motet, which had been spawned from organum. While the liturgical works of Leonin and Perotin continued to be performed, they did not, however, invite emulation by later composers, who rather turned their attention to the newer form of the motet. Indeed, in a strange reversal of their former roles, the motet in the thirteenth century became the source of new substitute clausulae to enrich the then stagnant repertory of organum. A manuscript of unknown provenance, Paris Bibliothèque Nationale f. lat. 15139, formerly St. Victor 813, contains no less than forty such clausulae drawn from the motet repertory, and the Florence manuscript contains numerous examples of converted motets in its enormous repertory of substitute clausulae.[10] Despite the

10. The St. Victor pieces have been the subject of much controversy. Ludwig believed that these were new clausulae outside of the Notre Dame repertory. (*Repertorium, 1,* 143 f.) Heinrich Husmann also accepted this hypothesis ("Die Motetten der Madrider Handschrift und deren geschichtliche Stellung," *AfMF, 2* [1937], 173); and recently Hans Tischler (art. cit.) has used this same hypothesis in support of his revision of the dates of Perotin. Yvonne Rokseth, however, suggested that these pieces were in reality motets stripped of their text to provide new clausulae for the organum repertory (*Polyphonies, 4,* 70 f.). Her brilliant arguments can now be confirmed by the discovery of many such converted motets in the clausula repertory of F. Concerning these pieces, see below, pp. 100–101.

static nature of the organum repertory, this does not mean that the individual pieces remained unchanged. On the contrary, the three versions of Leonin's *Magnus liber* contained in W_1, F, and W_2 reveal many radical alterations and recastings of Leonin's original work, to say nothing of the hundreds of substitute clausulae composed to replace portions of Leonin's music. To attempt a description of these manifold changes would be far beyond the scope of this introduction; hence only the most general characteristics of the style and achievements of both Leonin and Perotin will be pointed out.

To Leonin must be ascribed a position equivalent to that of Monteverdi and Haydn, men who almost singlehandedly created out of existing musical categories new styles and new forms that were to become the dominant characteristics of a new age. The relationship of Leonin to preceding schools of organum, notably that of St. Martial, is unmistakable. At St. Martial at Limoges in the first half of the twelfth century there flourished a school of composition in which the polyphonic setting of the responsorial chants of the mass and offices reached a new peak of development. In these organa two styles are apparent: a melismatic upper part over individual, sustained notes of the Gregorian tenor, and a style which, predominantly *nota contra notam,* has the tenor part and the upper part, i.e., the *duplum,* move simultaneously from one note to the next. The polyphonic setting of the chants is restricted to the soloistic intonations of the respond and versus, while the remainder of the chant is to be sung as always by the full choir in the original monodic version.

Leonin's organa are stylistically related to the St. Martial compositions, but with significant differences. Systematically Leonin set about to embellish the great feast days of the church year with elaborate polyphonic settings of the responsorial forms. Before his death he had accomplished a great cycle of liturgical organa, providing a uniform repertory for the major days of the church year. The boldness of this project has been matched only by his successor, Perotin, who created a smaller cycle of three-part organa, and by Heinrich Isaac in the early sixteenth century with his massive cycle, the *Choralis Constantinus,* and William Byrd at the end of the same century with his *Gradualia.* Like preceding composers of organum Leonin confined himself to two-voiced writing, but at the same time he refined the stylistic features of the St. Martial school into new subtleties of expressiveness and artistry. The relatively limited melismata of the St. Martial organum became in his hands vast melodic sweeps moving over greatly extended sustained tones in the tenor part. In the St. Martial compositions the melody of the upper part moves almost aimlessly, starting with a note forming a consonance with the tenor part and proceeding through an unprofiled melodic movement to a final consonance with the same tenor note or with the next note of the tenor.[11] Leonin, on the other hand, controls his greatly increased melisma by directing its melodic movement from one consonance to another and yet another over the same sustained note in the tenor, so that his flexible melodic line is subdivided into smaller phrases, beginning and ending with consonant notes. If at times Leonin abandons this procedure, it is only in favor of an equally artistic principle, the use of melodic sequence, in which the repetition of the melodic figures, instead of harmonic considerations, serves to unify the melodic movement of the upper part.

Even more significant is Leonin's development of rhythm. As far as one can ascertain, none of the polyphonic music prior to Leonin's work shows any evidence of a coherent rhythmic system. It was Leonin's incomparable achievement to introduce a rational system of rhythm into polyphonic music for the first time and, equally important, to create a method of notation expressive of this rhythm. These advances in musical art are so revolutionary that one hesitates to ascribe them to one man alone. It is possible that Leonin's work comes as the fruition of experiments by earlier generations, but as yet no evidence has been found of such a development. In his search for a rhythmic basis for his music Leonin turned directly or indirectly to the treatise on rhythm by St. Augustine, *De musica libri sex*. From this work he derived, with but slight modifications, the fundamental doctrines of rhythm that came to be known as the rhythmic modes, i.e., rhythmic patterns derived from metrical feet. Leonin himself utilized only one of these modes, the first mode, which is the metrical trochee, while Perotin expanded the system into its final form of six individual modes. The nature of the modal system and its notation is the main subject of this book and will be treated in detail in the following chapters. In the melismatic sections of his organum Leonin utilizes the first mode with the greatest freedom, the long and short values frequently being broken up into still smaller values so that the rhythm becomes extremely pliant, although the underlying modal pattern is still discernible. In the sections of the organum where the tenor itself has a melisma, Leonin speeds up the rhythmic progression of the tenor so that the duplum has only one or two statements of the modal pattern to each note of the tenor. In these clausulae, which are equivalent to the sections of the

11. So few examples of the St. Martial compositions have been published that the exact nature of the style and repertory of this school is still obscure. New investigations may substantially alter the stylistic picture presented by the few printed examples.

St. Martial organum written nota contra notam, Leonin adheres much more strictly to the simple values of the modal pattern. The relative rhythmic simplicity of these clausulae, in contrast to the rhythmic elaborations of the other sections of the organa, is undoubtedly due to the necessity of helping the singers to make their parts coincide with greater ease. This problem is not so pressing in the sections where the tenor performs only long, sustained tones. The difference in the treatment of the rhythm in the two styles creates a composition of great diversity, a contrast between melodic pliancy as well as rhythmic fluidity on one hand, and melodic simplicity and rhythmic rigidity on the other hand.

While Leonin was apparently content to work out his revolutionary innovations in only one type of composition, "organum duplum" or "purum" as it was later called by the theorists, Perotin was a much more diversified composer. Not only did he revise Leonin's two-part compositions but he created new organa for three and four voices and also composed conductus for one, two, and three voices. The title "optimus discantor" applied to him by Anonymous IV is an apt one, for Perotin excelled in the application of the strict rhythmic modes in a nota contra notam style, a form of writing which was called "discantus" by the thirteenth-century theorists. Perotin rewrote many sections of Leonin's organum in this stricter manner and created many new substitute clausulae in which the tenor as well as the duplum was treated modally in contrast with the rather amorphous rhythmic character of Leonin's tenors. Indeed, Perotin seems to have been obsessed with rhythm as a constructive force in music. His compositions reveal a remarkable clarity of structure obtained by the repetition of the same rhythmic phrases over and over again. This feature of his style is particularly apparent in the great four-part organa. Not only does he impose symmetry upon his compositions through the repetition of rhythmic phrases, but he strives toward the same goal by melodic repetitions and by the interchange of the same phrases among the voice parts. There is a directness of expression in Perotin's music achieved by these devices that brings to mind the repetitive rhythmic and melodic qualities of the Baroque.

The rhythmic modes, introduced into organum and conductus by Leonin and Perotin, soon spread into all forms of music and into all countries. The rhythmic principles of the modes, however, bore within themselves an expansive force that was exploited by the generations of motet composers who followed Perotin. Each decade of the thirteenth century saw the discovery of new rhythmic principles, which in turn brought about radical changes in the notation evolved by Leonin and Perotin. By the middle of the thirteenth century modal notation had already been displaced in favor of the mensural notation established by Franco of Cologne. The rapid changes in rhythmic styles and notation came to preoccupy the attention of thirteenth-century theorists almost to the exclusion of all other aspects of the art of music. It is unfortunate that no treatises of the time of Leonin and Perotin have come down to us, but this misfortune is in part made up for by the preservation of a number of treatises of the thirteenth century which deal with modal notation, though at the same time introducing many of the later rhythmic and notational innovations. These works were written almost exclusively by men of Paris or by men who were intimately acquainted with the Parisian repertory. Some of these writers were in fact teachers or students at the University of Paris, such as Johannes de Garlandia.

Although there are many treatises of the thirteenth century which deal with some aspects of modal rhythm and modal notation, by far the most important is a group of six works which deal with forms of notation prior to Franco's establishment of mensural notation. These premensuralist treatises were composed over a period of forty years and reveal successively more advanced stages of notation. The earliest of these works is the *Discantus positio vulgaris* included by Jerome of Moravia in his compendium of musical treatises. The relative simplicity of the doctrine contained in the *Discantus positio vulgaris* places it around 1240. This is followed by the slightly more advanced work of Anonymous VII. Of the greatest importance is the treatise of Johannes de Garlandia (ca. 1195–ca. 1272) which exists in two slightly different versions. This work was probably not written until after 1250, for in the list of his writings which Garlandia included in his *Ars lectoria ecclesie* (1249) he makes no mention of any musical works.[12] Garlandia's doctrines are the basis of two later but equally important treatises by Anonymous IV, writing around 1280, and by the St. Emmeram Anonymous, who completed his book in 1279. The last of these treatises, which at the same time anticipates the credo of Franco, is by Magister Lambertus (Pseudo-Aristotle) who probably was writing around 1275.[13]

The fact that these treatises are not contemporary with the Notre Dame

12. This list is printed by L. J. Paetow, *Morale Scolarium of John of Garland,* Memoirs of the University of California, *4,* No. 2 (Berkeley, 1927), 107.

13. All of these treatises with the exception of the St. Emmeram Anonymous are to be found in CS, *1*. The St. Emmeram treatise has been reprinted by H. Sowa, *Ein anonymer glossierter Mensuraltraktat 1279* (Kassel, 1930). Garlandia's treatise is also available in P. Dr. Simon M. Cserba, O. P., *Hieronymus de Moravia O. P. Tractatus de Musica,* Freiburger Studien zur Musikwissenschaft, 2. Reihe, Heft 2 (Regensburg, 1935).

organum and deal with more advanced stages of notation than exist in the three principal Notre Dame manuscripts makes the position of the modern transcriber a difficult one. To unlock the buried treasure of these manuscripts he must proceed with whatever clues have been provided by the theorists, and then work out the remainder of the system for himself. Up to the present day there has been no complete presentation of the rhythmic system and the notation of the Notre Dame manuscripts. The first [14] extended discussion of these problems is that of Friedrich Ludwig in his *Repertorium* (pp. 42 ff.) and his investigations have been used as a basis by succeeding musicologists. The most useful of these later works are the dissertation of Husmann,[15] the chapter on modal notation by Apel,[16] and the theoretical writings of Michalitschke.[17] More or less independent conclusions have been reached by Ficker [18] and Handschin.[19]

At many points these writers hold widely divergent views as to the proper method of transcribing certain signs of notation. These differences of opinion arise from a number of causes. All too often elements characteristic of the later mensural system are taken to be factors of modal notation. Furthermore, certain hypotheses advanced by Ludwig in his chapter on modal notation have been accepted uncritically by other writers who have then proceeded to conclusions that Ludwig himself did not draw. Yet another cause of misunder-

14. I exclude G. Jacobsthal's *Mensuralnotenschrift des 12. und 13. Jahrhunderts* (Leipzig, 1871) and W. Niemann's *Über die abweichende Bedeutung der Ligaturen in der Mensuraltheorie der Zeit vor Johannes de Garlandia* (Leipzig, 1902) because their works were written without knowledge of the Notre Dame manuscripts and are therefore of little use for our present purpose. J. Wolf in his *Handbuch der Notationskunde* (Leipzig, 1919), *I*, 202–237, presents little more than the notation of the six rhythmic modes.

15. Heinrich Husmann, *Die dreistimmigen Organa der Notre Dame-Schule, mit besonderer Berücksichtigung der Handschriften Wolfenbüttel und Montpellier* (Leipzig, 1935). Also "Zur Grundlegung der musikalischen Rhythmik des mittellateinischen Liedes," *AfMW, 9* (1952), 3–26.

16. Willi Apel, *The Notation of Polyphonic Music 900–1600* (Cambridge, Mass., 1945). Also "From St. Martial to Notre Dame," *JAMS, 2* (1949), 145–158.

17. Anton Maria Michalitschke, *Theorie des Modus* (Regensburg, 1923); "Zur Frage der longa in der Mensuraltheorie des 13. Jahrhunderts," *ZfMW, 8* (1925–26), 103–109; "Studien zur Entstehung und Frühentwicklung der Mensuralnotation," *ZfMW, 12* (1930), 257–279.

18. Rudolf Ficker, *Musik der Gotik* (*Perotinus, Sederunt principes*) (Vienna, 1930); "Probleme der modalen Notation (Zur kritischen Gesamtausgabe der drei- und vierstimmigen Organa)," *Acta Musicologica, 18–19* (1946–47), 2–16.

19. Jacques Handschin, "Was brachte die Notre Dame-Schule Neues?" *ZfMW, 6* (1924), 545–558; "Zum Crucifixum in carne," *AfMW, 7* (1925), 161–166; "Zur Notre Dame-Rhythmik," *ZfMW, 7* (1925), 386–389; "The Summer Canon and Its Background," *Musica Disciplina, 3* (1949), 55–94; *5* (1951), 65–113; "Conductus-Spicilegien," *AfMW, 9* (1952), 101–119.

standing is the ambiguity of many of the statements of the thirteenth-century theorists, which have often been interpreted out of context or with only a superficial grasp of what the statements imply. (Perhaps no sentences have been more variously interpreted than Franco's "Et nota pausationes mirabilem habere potestatem; nam per ipsas modi ad invicem transmutantur" [CS, *1*, 126b] and Odington's "Longa autem apud priores organistas duo tantum habuit tempora, sic in metris" [CS, *1*, 235b]).

Since there are so many differing opinions about the proper manner of transcribing certain phenomena of the notation, I shall endeavor in the following pages to reconstruct the historical conception of modal rhythm and its notation. In order to do so, the following subjects will be taken up in order: 1) the theory of modal rhythm; 2) the notation of the modes; 3) the variations in modal notation caused by repeated notes or by the breaking up of the modal pattern; 4) notation *cum littera* and *sine littera;* and 5) the notation of the two-voiced organum.

1. The Rhythmic Modes

Music, like poetry, is an art which exists only in the succession of time and consequently an organization of temporal motion is a fundamental requirement of both arts. Such an organization can be achieved only through the establishment of some form of measurement. Music and poetry alike have found two methods of measuring time, quantitative and qualitative rhythm. Since the rhythm of the Notre Dame era is of a quantitative nature, while modern musical rhythm is qualitative, a clarification of the difference of the two methods is necessary. Perhaps no better explanation of modern rhythm could be offered here than the concise presentation made by Stravinsky in his series of lectures entitled *Poetics of Music.*

> The laws that regulate the movement of sounds require the presence of a measurable and constant value: *meter,* a purely material element, through which rhythm, a purely formal element, is realized. In other words, meter answers the question of how many equal parts the musical unit which we call a measure is to be divided into, and rhythm answers the question of how these equal parts will be grouped within a given measure. A measure in four beats, for example, may be composed of two groups of two beats, or in three groups: one beat, two beats, and one beat, and so on . . .
>
> Thus we see that meter, since it offers in itself only elements of symmetry and is inevitably made up of even quantities, is necessarily utilized by rhythm, whose function it is to establish order in the movement by dividing up the quantities furnished in the measure.[1]

The unit of measurement in modern music is then a measure which consists of a fixed number of beats of equal duration delineated through the stressing of the first beat of each measure. The basis of modal rhythm, on the other hand, is not a succession of beats of equal value but a succession of notes of *varying* value, as in the case of quantitative poetry.[2]

On this point the pre-Franconian theorists are in agreement. Anonymous VII writes, "Mode in music is the orderly measuring of time in long and short [notes]; or to put it in another way: mode is whatever proceeds in an appropriate measurement of long and short notes." [3] This statement is then clarified

1. Igor Stravinsky, *Poetics of Music, in the Form of Six Lessons,* Arthur Knodel and Ingold Dahl, trans. (Cambridge, Harvard University Press, 1947), p. 28.

2. With the exception of the fifth and sixth modes, which are not in reality, as will be shown later, independent modes in their own right.

3. "Modus in musica est debita mensuratio temporis, scilicet per longas et breves; vel aliter:

and its meaning expanded in the following sentences, which I shall quote directly since they are necessary for an understanding of what the term "modus" implies.

You must know that a certain mode is called correct [*rectus*]; another is said to be beyond measure [*ultra mensuram*], because it exceeds a correct *modus* or a correct measure. Moreover, that mode is said to be correct which proceeds in correct long [notes] and correct short [notes]. And a long [note] is correct when it contains only two times [*tempora*]. A correct brevis is that which contains one time. The first, second, and sixth modes are correct modes [*in recto modo*]. The third, fourth, and fifth are beyond measure [*in ultra mensuram*].

And you must know that there are six modes, that is, the first, second, third, fourth, fifth, and sixth . . .

The first mode proceeds by a long [note], a short [note], and another long.

The second mode proceeds in the opposite manner, a short, a long, and another short.

The third mode proceeds by a long, two shorts, and another long.

The fourth is just the opposite.

The fifth mode proceeds entirely in long notes.

The sixth mode proceeds entirely in short notes.[4]

From these sentences one can readily see that modal rhythm consists of a succession of notes of differing values arranged in a definite pattern. The first mode moves in an alternation of long and short notes; the second mode moves in an alternation of short and long notes, etc. The smallest component part of modal rhythm would be, then, one statement of any particular pattern. The

---

modus est quidquid currit per debitam mensuram longarum notarum et brevium." (CS, *1*, 378a.) Cf. Garlandia, "Maneries ejus appellatur quidquid mensuratione temporis, videlicet per longas, vel per breves concurrit." (CS, *1*, 175a.) Also Anon. IV, "Modus vel maneries vel temporis consideratio est cognitio longitudinis et brevitatis meli sonique" (CS, *1*, 327b); and Pseudo-Aristotle, "Modus autem seu maneries, ut hic sumitur, est quidquid per debitam mensuram temporaliter longarum breviumque figurarum et semibrevium transcurrit." (CS, *1*, 279a.)

4. "Notandum quod quidam modus dicitur rectus; alius dicitur in ultra mensuram, qui scilicet excedit rectum modum sive rectam mensuram. Dicitur autem ille modus rectus qui currit per rectas longas et per rectas breves. Et est recta longa que continet in se duo tempora solum. Recta brevis est illa que continet in se unum. Primus secundus et sextus sunt in recto modo. Tertius modus, quartus et quintus sunt in ultra mensuram.

"Et sciendum quod sex sunt modi, scilicet primus, secundus, tertius, quartus, quintus, et sextus . . .

"Primus modus procedit ex una longa et brevi et altera longa.

"Secundus modus e converso ex una brevi et longa et altera brevi.

"Tertius modus procedit ex una longa et duabus brevibus et altera longa.

"Quartus e converso.

"Quintus ex omnibus longis.

"Sextus ex omnibus brevibus." (CS, *1*, 378a,b.)

essential pattern of the first mode, for instance, is made up of the two notes ♩ ♪.[5] The sum of these two notes is, of course, three beats and it will be observed that the other modal patterns also add up to three beats, or twice three beats in the case of the third, fourth, and fifth modes. The modern mind will instantly jump to the conclusion that there is in reality but one type of rhythm in all the modes: all the modes are in triple time and therefore the six modes are nothing but the various possibilities of arranging time values within a given triple time measure. But such a conclusion is far from being the truth of the matter. The six modes are not dry abstractions made by pedantic theorists but the very life and blood of the Notre Dame music. These patterns not only determine the rhythmic flow of organa but also the melodic construction to an extent that has scarcely been equaled in the subsequent development of musical styles.

In order to understand the nature of the modes fully it is necessary to examine the statements of Anonymous VII more thoroughly and to explain several of the terms which he uses. He speaks of correct modes (modus rectus) and of modes which are beyond measure (ultra mensuram). What do these terms mean? The modus rectus, he says, is one which consists of a correct long note (longa recta) and a correct short note (brevis recta), and he states that these notes contain two times (tempora) and one time, respectively. Although he does not define the term "tempus," its meaning is made clear by other theorists. Anonymous IV gives this definition: "A tone of one tempus may be said to be a tone receiving a time value [tempus] which is not the smallest, nor yet the largest, but which can be produced in a moderately short time, so that it can be divided in rapid motion into two, three or four more [lesser values] by the human voice . . ."[6] Tempus is the equivalent of a beat taken at a tempo which would allow the human voice to execute several very rapid notes within the beat. Anonymous IV, however, wrote at a time (ca. 1280) when the brevis or tempus

5. Although Anon. VII gives three notes as an illustration of the first mode, the third note is in reality the beginning of the repetition of the pattern, long short. The theorists in their definitions of the modes usually present more than one statement of the pattern. Anon. IV, however, is careful to explain the limits of the pattern or foot, as he terms it: ". . . et pes primi modi in brevi terminatur, et pes secundi in longa terminatur . . ." (CS, *1*, 329b.) And the *Discantus positio vulgaris* describes the modes according to their essential patterns: "Primus scilicet constans ex una longa et alia brevi. Secundus scilicet ex una brevi et alia longa. Tertius ex una longa et duabus brevibus. Quartus ex duabus brevibus et una longa. Quintus ex omnibus longis. Sextus autem ex omnibus brevibus et semibrevibus." (CS, *1*, 96b.)

6. "Sonus sub uno tempore potest dici sonus acceptus sub tempore non minimo, non maximo, sed medio legitimo breviter sumpto, quod possit frangi veloci motu in duobus, tribus, vel quatuor, plus in voce humana . . ." (CS, *1*, 328a,b.)

was in practice divided into more notes of shorter duration than was the case in the twelfth century. An examination of the Notre Dame manuscripts will reveal that the brevis was rarely divided into more than two notes. (In transcription, I have represented the short note of one tempus as an eighth note, because the modern eighth note when taken at a moderate tempo is seldom divided into more than two sixteenth notes.) Thus for Anonymous VII correct and proper notes are only two in number: a short note of one tempus and a long note of two tempora. The short and long values are consequently in a specific mathematical relationship 1:2. The terms "brevis" and "longa" have been translated in the preceding paragraphs as short note and long note respectively, because of the possibility of confusion in terminology. Although the Notre Dame rhythm is based upon the two values of a short note of one tempus and a long note of two tempora, these values were not symbolized by any definite note form. But by the time of the earliest of the pre-Franconian treatises, the *Discantus positio vulgaris,* the short value (brevis) was represented by the specific form ■, the long value by ¶. From this time on the words brevis and longa mean specifically these note forms. For the sake of convenience these terms will be used from now on to mean a note of one tempus and one of two tempora, but unless so stated the names will not imply the specific note forms, since they are not endowed with definite rhythmic meaning in the manuscripts with which we are dealing.

To return to the question of the modes, it is seen from the statements of Anonymous VII that those modes which contain only notes of one tempus and two tempora are called proper modes (modus rectus), and that these are the first, second, and sixth modes. The remaining modes are said to be beyond measure (ultra mensuram). Upon examination it will be seen that the modi in ultra mensuram differ from the modi recti in that they include notes of three tempora (the perfect long of Franconian theory). But why should such modes be said to be beyond measure? Surely a note of three tempora can be measured as definitely as notes of one tempus or two tempora. It is here in this curious terminology, in this opposition of the terms rectus and ultra mensuram, that one can find traces of the origin and development of the modal system. Notes which contain either one tempus or two tempora are established as the absolutely normal values, the most fundamental of all values, and so are called correct or proper notes (notae rectae). Notes which have any other value, then, are said to be beyond measure because they represent values which are not the normal or proper values.

Magister Lambertus (Pseudo-Aristotle) was the first theorist to establish the ternary longa as the normal or perfect value, and the violent polemic of the St. Emmeram Anonymous[7] against this new theory throws much light upon the words rectus and ultra mensuram. This anonymous writer rejects the implications of the terms "perfecta" and "imperfecta" for long notes of three and two tempora. One should speak, he says, of a lesser longa and a larger longa, for perfection and imperfection are qualifications which pertain only to the physical appearances of notes.

That no note except the semibrevis may be said to be imperfect may be sufficiently explained in a rational manner in this way: perfection and imperfection are differentiated in the form of their notation just as in their effect, as can be seen in the case of the aforesaid breves and semibreves. [He has previously explained that the normal brevis is represented by the sign ■, while a short note of lesser value is represented by a different sign ♦.] Since, however, the lesser longa and the larger longa are drawn with the same form and not differently, although they differ in the quantity of their power, neither of them can be said de iure to be imperfect, because they retain and cause the form of perfection. Neither can one vary the nomenclature and speak of a *semilonga,* as one differentiates the semibrevis from the brevis, because we never believe this (lesser longa) to be imperfect, but say that it is a proper, true, superior, and perfect longa. Moreover, the larger longa is said to be more perfect in power and in an increase of time values, wherefore we call it beyond measure (ultramensurabilem) as will be explained in the chapter on modes.

Likewise it may be seen in the following explanation that a lesser longa must be said to be a proper, true, and perfect longa: for just as a recta brevis is that which will be seen to be no longer correct (recta), but on the contrary will be seen to be a deviation from its rectitude, if anything is added to or subtracted from it; so a minor longa is that which would lose its rectitude, if anything were added to or subtracted from it.[8]

Although these are the arguments of a scholastic and a nominalist, it is patent that the writer's beliefs are rooted in a rhythmic system in which notes of one

7. Heinrich Sowa, *Ein anonymer glossierter Mensuraltraktat (1279)*, pp. 23 ff.

8. "Item quod nulla figura preter semibreves dici debeat imperfecta potest satis rationabiliter declararj sic: perfectio et imperfectio differunt in forma protractionis quemadmodum in effectu, sicut patuit in brevibus et semibrevibus antedictis. Cum autem minor longa et maior in forma protractionis conveniant aliquo non abstante, licet in quantitate differant potestatis, nulla earum de iure dici poterit imperfecta, cum perfectionis formam retineant et importent. Item nec in variatione nominationis, quemadmodum semibrevis a brevi videlicet semilonga vocaretur, quare ipsam nonquam esse credimus imperfectam sed eam esse dicimus rectam longam et veram et insuper et perfectam. Maiorem autem longam in potestate dicimus esse perfectiorem et temporum ampliatione, quare ipsam ultramensurabilem apellamus sicut in capitulo declarabitur specierum.

"Item quod minor longa recta longa et vera dici debeat et perfecta, patet sic: quemadmodum recta brevis est illa cui si aliquid addatur vel sustrahatur iam non videbitur recta brevis, immo a sua rectitudine deviabit; similiter minor longa est illa cui si quid addatur vel sustrahatur iam sue rectitudinis inde amittit." (Sowa, pp. 24, 25.)

tempus and two tempora are the absolute measure. Any deviation from the values of these two notes must consequently be a deviation from normal measurement, and as a result notes of less than one tempus (i.e., the semibrevis) and notes of more than two tempora (i.e., the ternary longa) must be considered as aberrations from normal measurement and are to be designated as ultra mensuram or beyond true and normal measurement.[9] By extension of meaning those modes which contain only notae rectae are said to be modi recti, while those modes which admit notae ultra mensuram (i.e., the ternary longa) are said to be modi in ultra mensuram.

Since all the premensuralist theorists, with the exception of Lambertus, insist upon the distinction between rectus and ultra mensuram, one is led to suspect that at the inception of modal rhythm only the two rectae values were accepted and that consequently the first and second modes which admit only notae rectae must have been historically the first modes to be conceived. The sixth mode, although technically a modus rectus, will be shown later on to be nothing but a variation of either the first or second mode. The modi in ultra mensuram from their very name must have appeared after the modi recti had already been formulated, for their nomenclature indicates that these modes deviate from values which had already been accepted as the normal values of measurement. These conclusions drawn from the statements of the theorists are upheld by the evidence of the Notre Dame manuscripts themselves. In the two-voiced organa of the *Magnus liber,* which are presumably the earliest compositions of the Notre Dame school, the first mode is overwhelmingly in the majority. The first mode, it is safe to say, was chronologically the first mode to be devised by the Notre Dame composers, presumably by Leonin, and its preeminence is continued by tradition so that it always heads the list of the modes given by the later theorists, who undoubtedly were not aware of the historical correctness of the designation of this mode as the first mode.[10] Once the first mode had been created and crystallized into notational form, composers were free to invent other forms of the modes. A discussion of the historical development of the modes, however, should be postponed until all preliminary matters have been handled. For the moment it is necessary only to establish the point

9. The *Discantus positio vulgaris* says: "Those notes are beyond measure which are measured by less than one tempus and more than two tempora." CS, *1,* 94b: "Ultra mensuram sunt que minus quam uno tempore et amplius quam duobus mensurantur."

10. Handschin questions the priority of the first and second modes in a recent article without, however, providing any concrete reasons for his doubt. See Jacques Handschin, "The Summer Canon and Its Background. I," *Musica Disciplina, 3,* Fasc. 2, 3, 4 (1949), 74.

that the modal system must have begun with the creation of a mode or modes which contained only notes of one tempus, and two tempora, the brevis and longa, arranged in a specific pattern. From the direct evidence of the music itself, and from the indirect evidence of the theorists it is clear that the first mode is, as it were, the primary mode, the *fons et origo* of all modal notation.

If these conclusions are correct, and the compositions themselves irrefutably demonstrate that they are, we must accept the fact that from the very beginning of the Notre Dame school, rather than only in a later phase, a well-organized, rational system of rhythm existed. This system is completely unlike our conception of rhythm. It does not consist of a succession of beats of equal duration measured in binary or ternary meter by stressing every other beat or every third beat. On the contrary, the rhythmic system of the Notre Dame school is founded on the repetition of a given pattern of long and short notes. The pattern itself is an entity, the smallest component part, and only by the repetition of this unity is rhythm created. Odington's definition of rhythm corroborates this statement. "Rhythm," he writes, "is not regulated by a definite end, but nevertheless it moves rationally in properly organized feet." [11] In the modal system the pattern as the unit of measurement is always immediately apparent through the notation itself which consists of groups of notes representative of the pattern. At all times the form of the pattern is retained as the metrical unit, while the individual notes receive their values only as they lie within the pattern. In modern rhythm, on the other hand, the meter is only implicitly understood, while the actual temporal values are presented through individual notes having specific values complete in themselves.

To the modern mind it would appear that the pattern of the rhythmic mode was not itself meter, but that this pattern was in reality governed by triple time. But if we try to interpret the modes according to this conception we shall never be able to understand the essential quality of the modes themselves. If we persist in viewing the modal patterns in this way we shall be forced to the conclusion that modal notation is only an imperfect, fumbling attempt to express ternary rhythm and that modal notation was saved from its own inadequacies only by

11. "Rhytmus [sic] non est certo fine moderatus; sed tamen rationabiliter ordinatis pedibus currit." (CS, *1*, 211a.) Although in this section of his treatise Odington is not dealing with the modes, at a later point he equates metrical feet with the modal patterns (CS, *1*, 238b), so this definition accordingly is applicable also to the modal system. The definition, incidentally, is taken from St. Augustine, *De ordine*, Lib. II, cap. 39, "Musica et poetica," in J.-P. Migne, *Patrologiae cursus completus. Series latina, 32,* col. 1013.

the intervention of Franco of Cologne, who first established triple time as the basic meter and who first placed the various notes in their true relationship to this mystically perfect number three. This patronizing attitude toward modal notation is one which is held all too frequently, even by modern musicologists. The notation of the Notre Dame school was never intended to represent anything but the repetition of a pattern, and the system of notation which was evolved is a highly rational, completely adequate, even perfect expression of these patterns. And since the notation does, indeed, represent patterns of notes of differing values, we must assume that it was intended to represent these patterns and that the composers were not groping their way toward a ternary rhythm which they knew about, but could not devise a means to express. If the composers were rational enough to create a notation expressive of rhythmic patterns, they would certainly have been intelligent enough to have created a system of proportional notation if they had considered ternary rhythm the be-all and end-all of rhythm and if, above all, such a rhythmic organization had conformed to their basic understanding of rhythm in music. A pattern is, after all, something already more subtle, more stylized than a rhythm based on sounds of equal duration.

If the pattern is the *sine qua non* of the Notre Dame rhythm and Notre Dame notation, we must endeavor to establish the origin of these patterns. Did the Notre Dame organists invent them, or were such modal patterns to be found in some other form of music or in some other art? Certain facts in the history of music prior to the appearance of the Notre Dame school, as well as certain statements made by the theorists of modal rhythm, suggest almost beyond a doubt that modal rhythm developed out of the metrical system of the ancients. From the first appearance of notation in ninth-century manuscripts of Gregorian chant until the eleventh century there is unmistakable evidence that the note forms were intended to represent specific rhythmic values. And from contemporary treatises we know that the time values were a brevis note of one tempus and a longa note of two tempora. Moreover these treatises state that these time values are derived from or are analogous to the long and short quantities of classical metrics. A detailed discussion of Gregorian chant rhythm would instantly plunge us into the violent controversy which still rages between those who support the Solesmes theory of nonmensural chant and those who advocate a strict rhythmic interpretation. To avoid entanglement in this complicated problem I shall rely upon the dispassionate statements of Peter Wagner.

In his history of the neumes [12] Wagner gives a brilliant, condensed summary of the development of rhythm in the neumes.

> The oldest sources explain the neumes as rhythmic signs, and indeed neumatic notation employs both the longa and brevis values. The first is represented by the two forms of the *virga,* the other by the *punctum.* The "hook neume" [Haken] in its manifold combinations with other signs also fulfills the function of a short tone. These rhythmic values are combined according to the measures of the ancient verse feet, a fact attested by Alcuin. Many songs are strictly regulated by these feet and are called therefore "cantus metrici" (Guido) or "bene procurati" (Aribo); others are more free, either combining different meters or moving in a way which has nothing to do any longer with the ancient metrics. The relationship of the long and short notes was considered a mathematical one, so that the long was twice the value of the short, and strict attention to this rhythmic difference was always expressly enjoined. [Footnote: The terms "docta cantio," "docte canere," used by the *Musica Enchiriadis* and the *Commemoratio brevis* to designate a performance paying strict attention to the long and short values, justifies the conjecture that already in the 10th century the less "learned" singers were no longer placing much emphasis upon the exact observance of such rhythmic differences.] Performances corresponding to these rules were general into the eleventh century. At that time the rhythmic differentiation began to disappear and an interpretation of the neumes as of equal value came to be used. Some observations of the authors lead one to think that the practice of polyphonic music, which they expressly declare has evened the rhythmic lines, might be the cause of this. One must also take into account the carelessness of the scribes.[13]

Wagner also traces the disappearance of rhythmic values from the neumes to the use of diastematic notation and its gradual development into the square notation of the eleventh and twelfth centuries. He states that in the oldest neumes the note forms correspond exactly to the intended rhythm. Thus the long value is represented by the *virga* /, or the *virga jacens* —, while the brevis is represented by the *punctum* . . These signs were combined into composite figures, but still retained their rhythmic significance. The *scandicus,* for instance, is to be found in the form .·/ (two shorts and a long) and ≦ (three longs), etc. The physical appearance of these neumes, and so presumably their rhythmic significance, correspond to the theoretical discussions of these matters in the treatises of the ninth, tenth, and part of the eleventh centuries.

12. Peter Wagner, *Einführung in die gregorianischen Melodien. Zweiter Teil: Neumenkunde. Paläographie des liturgischen Gesanges nach den Quellen dargestellt* . . . Zweite, verbesserte und vermehrte Auflage (Leipzig, 1912). But see also the chapter on rhythmic notations in Dom Gregory Sunol, *Introduction à la paléographie musicale grégorienne* (Paris, 1935).

13. *Ibid.,* pp. 377–378.

If the authors since the time of the eleventh century report a change in the performance of the chant, evidence of this is also to be found in the chant books. In seeking a minimum expenditure of effort the scribes were led to disregard the different rhythmic variations of a sign. They contented themselves with a single form, or adapted the originally rhythmically different figures to new uses for the sake of convenience in writing. This was done by the scribes of the Longobard-Beneventine manuscripts that are in diastematic notation. The French and English manuscripts obliterate the difference between the *virga jacens* and the *punctum,* since they eliminate the former and always replace it by the latter; while the German scribes for a time follow the practices which were general in the books of their predecessors, but soon succumb to the general decline. This decline is reflected in the quadratic notation, which rhythmically at least represents an impoverishment of the rich nuances of neumatic notation. Quadratic notation recognizes only one single form for each sign, only one *pes,* one *flexa,* one *torculus,* etc. Since the writing utensil supposedly used makes ascending ligatures in quadratic form, but descending figures in a rhomboid form, from now on the *scandicus* and *salicus* have only the form  (i.e., the form corresponding to a short value has disappeared) and the *climacus* always appears in the form .[14]

From these statements, which are only a summary of Wagner's detailed investigations, the fact emerges that the development of disastematic notation and the growth of quadratic writing led to a system of note signs that are rhythmically indifferent. Square notation is incapable of expressing the value of each note in a ligature, since there are no longer any specific forms for the brevis and longa values.

The preceding paragraphs have introduced two points that are extremely important for our discussion of the origin of the modal system. First of all, it establishes the fact that a tradition of rhythm measured according to the quantities and feet of metrics existed for a number of centuries prior to the appearance of the Notre Dame school. Most authorities place the deterioration of this system in the eleventh century, but this is only a general statement, for in some localities measured chant lingered on into the twelfth century. Wagner points out that the "litterae significativae" (a system of letters used to indicate rhythmic values in manuscripts which center around St. Gall) were taught and written in Bamberg in the twelfth century and did not completely disappear until the fourteenth century.[15] In other words, the dividing line between the period when Gregorian chant was measured in poetic feet and the appearance of the Notre Dame modal system is a very narrow one, a century at the most. It appears to me highly probable that the tradition of such a rhythm was known to the first

14. *Ibid.,* pp. 379-380.
15. *Ibid.,* p. 246.

"organistae" of the Notre Dame school. It is also significant that the treatises which first discuss organum in any detail also contain references to a metrical rhythm in music. While it is possible that the Notre Dame composers did not know the *Musica Enchiriadis,* it is extremely unlikely that they did not know the famous *Micrologus* of Guido of Arezzo (ca. 995–1050).[16] In the fifteenth chapter of the latter treatise Guido says: One must beat time in the chant in the same manner as in metrical feet, and in their relationship one tone must be twice as long or twice as short as the other.[17] Later in the chapter he writes: "The similarity between chants and meters is by no means a small one, since the melisma corresponds to the foot, and the phrase to the verse. And, as is natural, this melisma proceeds in dactylic meter, this one in spondaic and that one in iambic; and one sees the phrase to be now in tetrameter, now a pentameter, or sometimes as if it were an hexameter." [18] In the light of such a passage, and this is only one of many similar passages which could have been and must have been known to the Notre Dame composers, it is quite safe to assume that they either knew or had heard of chant measured according to the metrical system, if they were not in fact still familiar with the practice of a rhythmic interpretation of the chant.

Furthermore, the thirteenth-century treatises suggest that metrics lie behind the rhythmic modes. Johannes de Garlandia at the beginning of his treatise states that "the subject in music is the joining of tones or rests in a necessary, properly observed manner. The predicate is the lawful art of adjusting this same music in suitable proportions by observing diligently all its modes, and for this art the *ars metrica* supplies the philosophical part." [19] Walter Odington makes a similar

16. These are only two of an impressively large list of treatises written before the twelfth century which contain references to metrical rhythm in the chant. For a summary of the most important passages concerning such a rhythm see Arthur Angie, "Die Tradition der Notenwerte im gregorianischen Choral," *Kirchenmusikalisches Jahrbuch, 29* (1934), 22 ff.

17. Gerbert, *Scriptores, 2,* 15a: ". . . ut quasi metricis pedibus cantilena plaudatur, & aliae voces ab aliis morulam duplo longiorem, vel duplo breviorem . . ."

18. *Ibid.,* p. 16b: "Non autem parva similitudo est metris & cantibus, cum & neumae loco sint pedum, & distinctiones loco versuum, utpote ista neuma dactylico, illa vero spondaico, illa iambico metro decurret, & distinctionem nunc tetrametram nunc pentametram, alias quasi hexametram cernes . . ." *Neuma* has two meanings: either it is a ligature or a melisma. The latter meaning is probably correct in this passage, for on the same page Guido says, "Sometimes one syllable has one or more neumae, sometimes one neuma is divided into several syllables." Neuma cannot mean ligature in this passage, for it is impossible for one ligature to have more than one syllable.

19. CS, *1,* 158a: "Subjectum in musica est aliquarum vocum seu pausationum conjunctio modo debito ac proprie observato. Predicatum est ipsius musice ars legitima proportionate omnibus suis modis diligenter observatis, cui partem philosophie supponatur ars metrice."

statement. The first sentence in the opening chapter of his treatise establishes metrics as the very foundation of the whole discipline of music. "Since the present treatise concerns music, and music consists of number related to sound, I believe that first of all the *ars metrica* must be explained, which concerns number per se without which no noble object could be discussed." [20] At a later point in this work Odington identifies the patterns of the rhythmic modes with poetical meters. Although his treatise, *De Speculatione Musice,* stems from such a late date (ca. 1300) that it cannot be used as prima facie evidence for twelfth-century theory, there is nevertheless in this book one remark of a historical nature that is relevant to our discussion: "The longa with the first composers of organum had two tempora, as in meters; but later it was brought to perfection so that it had three tempora . . . and a longa of this type is called perfect." [21] A number of musicologists, led by Hugo Riemann, have translated the word "metris" as songs with a poetic text, such as the conductus. Upon this misconception they have erected a theory of the existence of duple time prior to triple time. This position is untenable, if Odington's statement is carefully analyzed. Since the designation of the longa as perfect does not appear until the middle of the thirteenth century in the theory of Pseudo-Aristotle and Franco of Cologne, Odington's "priores organistae" must then be composers prior to this date, in other words the composers of the Notre Dame period. Duple rhythm is obviously impossible in compositions of this epoch since the longa of two tempora is always preceded or followed by a brevis. Hence ternary rhythm always results. Moreover, even if we accept the translation of the metris as meaning conductus, we cannot accept the implication that the conductus must then have been in duple rhythm, for the conductus too was modally measured.[22] Since Odington carries the identification of the modal patterns with metrical feet to absurd lengths, giving a metrical name to each *ordo* of all the modes, he probably employed the word "metrum" in the above quotation in its basic meaning

20. CS, *I,* 183b: "Quoniam de musica presens est pertractatio et ipsa quidem est de numero relato ad sonum, prius de arsmetrica arbitror expondendum que est de numero per se sine qua quicquid inclitum nequit pertractari."

21. CS, *I,* 235b: "Longa autem apud priores organistas duo tantum habuit tempora, sic in metris; sed postea ad perfectionem dicitur, ut sit trium temporum . . . diciturque longa hujusmodi perfecta." Handschin, "Summer Canon," p. 76, emends "dicitur" to "ducitur."

22. On the modal reading of the conductus, a much disputed point, see pp. 92 ff., below. M. Bukofzer has now come to the conclusion that the conductus is in modal rhythm. See Manfred Bukofzer, "Rhythm and Meter in the Notre-Dame Conductus," *Bulletin of the American Musicological Society,* Nos. 11, 12, 13 (September, 1948), p. 63.

and not its secondary meaning of a poetic text, such as the conductus.[23] Odington's statement would be paraphrased: the composers of the Notre Dame school employed a longa of two tempora analogous to the long syllable of metrics.

To the direct evidence of Garlandia and Odington may be added the indirect evidence of Anonymous IV. Although this author does not specifically state that the modes are derived from meters, he nevertheless makes use of metrical terminology when he calls the modal pattern a foot. "The basis [of the notation] of the third perfect mode is a longa and ternary ligatures without a rest. The foot is complete with the penultimate note of the ternary ligature, and the foot of the first mode ends in a brevis, and the foot of the second mode ends in a longa . . ."[24]

Still another relationship to metrics is revealed by the designation of the semibrevis and the ternary longa as notae ultra mensuram.[25] In their preoccupation with the problem of establishing the priority of duple or triple rhythm most musicologists have directed their attention exclusively to the problem of the longa recta and longa ultra mensuram as evidence for the existence of duple or triple rhythm. But the inclusion of the semibrevis as a nota ultra mensuram shows that the term ultra mensuram is not simply a synonym for triple rhythm. The semibrevis at first had one half the value of a brevis, which relates it to duple rather than triple rhythm, unlike the longa ultra mensuram which is a ternary value. Hence the term ultra mensuram as applied to the semibrevis and ternary longa must not refer to ternary rhythm as such, but rather it is to be applied to notes which deviate in duration of time from the normal measurement of the brevis recta and longa recta. Significantly the values of the brevis recta and longa recta are exactly those of the short and long syllables of classical metrics. Thus the normal note values are only those known to metrics, while the notae ultrae mensuram are those which have no counterpart in the metrical system. The inference to be drawn from this is, once again, that modal rhythm was created with metrical considerations in mind.

This inference is strengthened by the fact that the St. Emmeram Anonymous

23. Michalitschke also comes to this conclusion. See A. M. Michalitschke, "Zur Frage des longa in der Mensuraltheorie des 13. Jahrhunderts," *ZfMW, 8* (1925–26), 105.

24. CS, *1,* 329b: "Principium tertii modi perfecti procedit per longam unam et tres, tres, tres, etc., sed sine pausatione. Pes perficitur in penultima, et pes primi modi in brevi terminatur, et pes secundi in longa terminatur . . ." Anon. IV also uses the term "pes" in reference to the pattern of the sixth mode; cf. CS, *1,* 334b.

25. See p. 18, n. 9, above.

quite specifically relates the term ultra mensuram to notes which are smaller or larger than the values accepted in metrics. The term *musica mensurabilis,* he states,

is derived from mensura [measure], just as in grammar, metrica is derived from meter, that is, measure. Grammatical measure contents itself with and means two measures of accents, i.e., long and short, of which the long is of two tempora and the short of one . . . and thus we say that the measurement of music is correct and perfect under these two measurements.[26]

Whatever deviates from these two metrical quantities is to be called *ultramensurabile,* and as an example of such notes the anonymous author cites the brevis altera and triple longa of the third and fourth modes. "Whatever appears to exceed such a measurement of long and short is called ultramensurabile, as for example the longa of three tempora and the brevis of two tempora that appear specifically in this third and fourth mode." [27] It is not without significance that this treatise of St. Emmeram as well as that of Anonymous IV indicate a relationship to metrics, for both treatises are derived to a large extent from the writings of Garlandia who maintains that the philosophical part of the art of music is supplied by the ars metrica. Thus these three treatises, which are the principle sources of knowledge of modal rhythm and notation and which at the same time are closely related to each other, all agree in suggesting a metrical basis for modal rhythm.

On the one side we find that a tradition of a metrical rhythm in music existed prior to the Notre Dame school and perhaps extended up to the appearance of modal rhythm.[28] On the other side we find that theorists coming after the Notre Dame period speak of the modes in terms related to metrics. Under such circumstances I believe the conclusion to be justifiable that the Notre Dame com-

26. Sowa, p. 25, l.33 through p. 26, l.4: "Musica mensurabilis dicitur a mensura sicut gramatica, metrica a metris, quod est mensura, que inquam gramatica, duas mensuras accentuum desinet et importat scilicet longum et breuem, quorum longus est duorum temporum, breuis unius . . . sic rectam musice mensuram reperiri dicimus et perfectam sub illis duobus accentibus . . ."

27. Sowa, p. 84, ll.25–28: "Quicquid autem talem longitudinis mensuram ac etiam breuitatis excedere reperitur, ultramensurabile nuncupantes utputa longam trium temporum et breuem duorum, que in ista tercia specie et in quarta specifice reponuntur." Cf. *ibid.,* p. 76, ll.15–32.

28. It is, perhaps, not beside the point to mention that the first descriptions of organum occur in treatises which are primarily discussions of Gregorian chant. Apparently organum was considered to be not a different species of composition but merely another manifestation of Gregorian chant itself. Cf. Wagner, *Neumenkunde,* p. 371. By inference one might assume that the rules of rhythm applied to the monodic chant would naturally be extended to chant sung in the simple nota contra notam manner of parallel organum.

posers drew their modal rhythm from poetical feet.[29] This assumption will be strengthened when we consider at a later point in this section certain other terminology of the theorists.

If we accept the hypothesis that the Notre Dame modal system is based on metrics and that the idea of such a system was derived from a pre-existent tradition in Gregorian chant, it would seem at first glance that a necessary corollary of this hypothesis would be the conclusion that the Notre Dame composers introduced nothing new with their modal system. But here we must take into consideration the second important point made in Wagner's summary of the rhythmic neumes, namely the fact that by the time of the appearance of the Parisian school the signs of notation had become rhythmically indifferent. In the progressive advances in diastematic notation the neumes gradually lost their rhythmic significance with a consequent deterioration of the rhythmic tradition. Complaints about the debasement of the chant tradition are frequent in the eleventh century. Aribo, for instance, writing in the third quarter of the eleventh century, laments: "In the past not only the composers of chant but also the singers took great care to compose and sing everything in due proportion [*proportionaliter*]. But such a consideration has died not long since; indeed it has been buried." [30] By proportion Aribo quite evidently means rhythmic proportion, for his complaint follows immediately after a definition of the rhythmic values in chant: " 'Tenor' means the length of a tone, which is proportional if two tones are compared to four, and the length of these two tones is greater by as much as their number is less [than four tones]." [31] Other contemporary observations about the growing disorder in the chant must also be related to a deterioration in rhythmic practices, for the chant manuscripts reveal no degradations in the melodies as such. Although the development of diastematic notation had freed singers from the uncertainties of measuring the distance of the melodic intervals, at the same time it brought with it a new source

29. The troubadour songs might also be suggested as a possible source of modal rhythm. However, the interpretation of these songs according to modal principles depends upon an application of a rhythm known to exist in organum and motets to these songs. If the modal measure of organum is used to prove the modality of the troubadour songs, one cannot reverse the process and use the troubadours to prove the modality of organum.

30. "Antiquitus fuit magna circumspectio non solum cantus inventoribus, sed etiam ipsis cantoribus, ut quilibet proportionaliter & invenirent & canerent. Quae consideratio jam dudum obiit; imo sepultus est." Gerbert, *Scriptores, 2,* 227.

31. "Tenor dicitur mora vocis, qui in aequis est, si quatuor vocibus duae comparantur, & quantum sit numerus duarum minor, tantum earum mora sit maior." Gerbert, *Scriptores, 2,* 227.

of confusion in that the neumes no longer could indicate the rhythmic values. The singers were thus placed in a position where they would either have to know the rhythm of a given chant from oral tradition or would have to impose a completely subjective, improvised rhythm upon the chant. Under the circumstances it is not surprising to find that writers censure the singers for their neglect of rhythmic proportions.

By the last third of the twelfth century, when the Notre Dame school arose, the original rhythm of Gregorian chant must have disappeared completely, although knowledge that it was once measured proportionately in a system analogous to metrics must have been known to Leonin and his contemporaries.[32] Thus the return to exact rhythmic measurement in the Notre Dame organa has somewhat the appearance of being a renaissance or a reform of rhythm. But the return to a metrical system was hampered by a notation which no longer had exact symbols for long and short values. The composers were confronted with the problem of infusing rhythmically indifferent signs of notation with rhythmic significance. Their solution—modal notation—was a unique and entirely original one, having little or nothing in common with the previous rhythmic neumes. The originality of their solution is to be seen in three of the modes, the modi in ultra mensuram, which have no true, exact counterpart either in metrics or Gregorian rhythm, but which in their terminology and disposition reveal a certain affinity with the metrical system. It will later be demonstrated that these modes arose because of certain difficulties inherent in a notation which has no symbol for the longa and brevis values.[33] Because of these difficulties the third mode, which corresponds to the dactyl, came to have the rhythm ♩.♪♩ instead of the proper metrical measurement ♩ ♪ ♪. Despite the fact that the last note of the modal pattern is actually a longa recta containing two tempora, it is always referred to as a *brevis altera* (another kind of brevis, or a changed brevis). Such a discrepancy in terminology could have arisen only if this note were considered to be the final short value of a dactylic foot. If the modal system had been created without any reference to the metrical system, there would have been no need for this curious nomenclature: the brevis altera would simply have been called a longa recta. But the fact remains that it is indeed called a brevis and so we must conclude that in theory the pattern of the third mode is equiv-

32. It is interesting to find that Jerome of Moravia (ca. 1275) formulates a number of rules for the measurement of Gregorian chant in long and short values. See CS, *I*, 90 ff.

33. See below, the discussions of the fifth mode, pp. 62 f., and the third and fourth modes, pp. 69 f.

alent to the dactylic foot. The special terminology applied to the third mode—modus in ultra mensuram, brevis altera—provides us with indirect but quite striking evidence that this mode was conceived in relation to a certain metrical equivalent. The term modus in ultra mensuram implies that this mode deviates from normal values—values which are normal in metrics; while the term brevis altera implies that despite its abnormality this is still to be considered a dactylic foot. And so we find that the Notre Dame school, although ostensibly drawing upon the metrical system of the past for inspiration, created something entirely new. In this we are reminded of the Renaissance, which consciously turned to the art of antiquity for its model with the result not that the past was recreated but that a new art was born—a new art having, it is true, certain bonds with the past but essentially an independent art.

The belief that the modal system is somehow related to a metrical system has been attacked by Willi Apel. Concerning this matter he writes:

> Brief mention must be made of a nomenclature derived from the identification of the six modes with certain metric feet of Greek poetry, namely . . . : trochaic —◡, iambic ◡—, dactylic —◡◡, anapaestic ◡◡—, molossic ———, and tribrachic ◡◡◡. Although this terminology is widely used in modern writings, it has little historical significance and justification. The only mediaeval theorist to mention these terms is Walter Odington who also goes in for such scholarly terms as procoleumaticus and pyrrichius (*CS,* 1, 240 f.). It is perfectly clear that his references to Greek poetry are the result of personal antiquarian studies, and that, in contrast to a wide-spread opinion to be found in Wolf's *Handbuch der Notationskunde* (vol. 1, p. 202) as well as in many books on music history, they do not offer the slightest evidence of the rhythmic modes having developed from the poetic meters of the ancient Greek.[34]

Apel is in part correct in his judgment of Walter Odington, but the preceding paragraphs have indicated that there is evidence other than Odington's for the relationship of metrics and modal rhythm. To date no one has endeavored to relate modal theory to pre-existent metrical treatises or to ascertain the possible sources of this theory. But there exists a work, well known to the Middle Ages, containing a theory of rhythm based upon metrics which coincides almost exactly with the modal system. It is the *De Musica* of St. Augustine. It is this work, I suggest, that provided the Notre Dame composers with the necessary system for the re-establishment of precise rhythmic values.

The important doctrine of rhythm contained in the *De Musica* has received scant attention from grammarians and musicologists. In general, the first five

34. Willi Apel, *The Notation of Polyphonic Music,* p. 222.

books have been mistaken for a treatise on metrics.[35] The first and only detailed presentation of this work in its true light is the excellent study by Franco Amerio, *Il 'De Musica' di S. Agostino* (Torino, 1929). Amerio insists correctly that

> the Augustinian treatise is not a treatise on metrics but fundamentally a treatise on rhythm understood as the element common to all musical arts and examined in the particular light of poetry. . . . It is a true treatise on rhythm based upon that material most accessible to everyone, that is upon the word, which is not considered as such, but simply as a sound and motion; so that whatever is said about this, or better, the laws that are derived from this or which are applied to it are applicable to every sort of motion that has the same dimensions of motion as syllables or words.[36]

There can be no doubt that Augustine himself intended this work to be a treatise on rhythm as a part of music and not a treatise on metrics. In his letter to Memorius who had requested a copy of *De Musica,* St. Augustine states: "I have written six books solely about rhythm and, I confess, I was disposed to write perhaps another six concerning melody when I had future leisure." [37] The *De Musica* would thus appear to be the first half of a complete presentation of the art of music, which consists of rhythm and melody,[38] and is not a work dealing with metrics. More than once in the *De Musica* Augustine makes a clear distinction between the function of the musician, who treats the quantities of words as components of rhythm, and the grammarian, who simply discusses the quantities of syllables as they have been handed down by authority.[39] The

35. E.g., K. Westphal, *Metrik der Griechen* (Leipzig, 1867), *1,* 129: "Es ist dies aber nicht, wie der Titel besagt, eine Darstellung der Musik, sondern eine Metrik." The recent work of de Bruyne still maintains this misconception: "On peut considérer les cinq premiers livres du 'de Musica' comme un traité technique de métrique . . ." E. de Bruyne, *Études d'esthétique médiévale* (Brugge, 1946), *3,* 199.

36. Amerio, *Il 'De Musica',* pp. 40, 45.

37. Epistola CI, Migne, *Patrologia Latina, 33,* col. 369: ". . . conscripsi de solo rhythmo sex libros, et de melo scribere alios forsitan sex, fateor, disponebam, cum mihi otium futurum sperabam."

38. ". . . quidquid numerose servatis temporum atque intervallorum dimensionibus movetur . . ." *De Musica,* I. 3. 4.

39. "At vero musicae ratio, ad quam dimensio ipsa vocum rationabilis et numerositas pertinet, non curat nisi ut corripiatur vel producatur syllaba, quae illo vel illo loco est secundum rationem mensurarum suarum. Nam si eo loci ubi duas longas syllabas poni decet, hoc verbum [cano] posueris, et primam quae brevis est, pronuntiatione longam feceris, nihil musica omnino succenset: tempora enim vocum ea pervenere ad aures, quae illi numero debita fuerunt. Grammaticus autem jubet emendari, et illud te verbum ponere cujus prima syllaba producenda sit, secundum majorum, ut dictum est, auctoritatem, quorum scripta custodit." II. 1. Cf. I. 1. 1.

art of metrics, which is part of grammar, is for Augustine only a preparatory discipline for the higher arts of number, music, geometry, and astronomy[40] but at the same time the science of music presupposes a knowledge of the quantities of syllables as taught by grammarians. And so we find that Augustine presents his doctrine of musical rhythm in terms of metrics, because, as he informs Memorius, "it is easier to discern in words whatever numbers prevail in all motions of things."[41]

It would be impossible to give here a detailed analysis of Augustine's treatise, but in the following brief outline an attempt will be made to present the salient features of his doctrine of rhythm. As the foundation of his system Augustine accepts two measurements of sound, a brevis of one tempus and a longa of two tempora—measurements which are also to be found in metrics.

> It is not absurd then that the ancients called one tempus that sort of minimum space in time occupied by a short syllable . . . , [and] since just as in numbers the first progression is from one to two, so in syllables, as we progress from a short syllable to a long syllable, the long must have a double tempus. Accordingly if the space that a brevis occupies is called correctly [recte] one tempus, the space that a longa occupies is to be called correctly two tempora.[42]

These two quantities are combined in feet of from two to four syllables, making in all twenty-eight possible combinations, ranging from the pyrrhic foot of two short syllables to the dispondee of four syllables. Every foot is understood to be capable of division into two parts which are in some proportion one to another.[43] And these two parts are represented by motions of the hand, a practice known in metrics as the *plausus*.[44] The plausus is the beating of the time of the metrical foot with an upward motion of the hand (*levatio*) and a downward motion (*positio*). No matter how many syllables are contained in a foot and no matter how many tempora are contained in the foot, the total value of the foot will be

40. See Amerio, *Il 'De Musica'*, pp. 16 f., "Le discipline in particolare."

41. Epistola CI, Migne, *Patrologia Latina, 33,* col. 369: "Verum quia in omnibus rerum motibus quid numeri valeant, facilius consideratur in vocibus." St. Augustine uses *vox* to mean the sounding word. Cf. the usage in n. 39. Cf. also *De Musica,* II. 3. 3.

42. II. 4. 3: "Non absurde igitur hoc in tempore quasi minimum spatii, quod brevis obtinet syllaba, unum tempus veteres vocaverunt . . . quoniam ut in numeris ab uno ad duo est prima progressio; ita in syllabis, qua scilicet a brevi ad longam progredimur, longam duplum temporis habere debere: ac per hoc si spatium quod brevis occupat, recte unum tempus vocatur; spatium item quod longa occupat, recte duo tempora nominari."

43. II. 5. 6: "Nam omnem pedem propter illam numerorum collationem duas habere partes, quae sibimet aliqua ratione conferantur, necesse est . . ."

44. II. 10. 18.

indicated by only two motions of the hand, levatio and positio. For example, the dispondee would be indicated by a levatio equivalent to two longs or four tempora, while the remainder of the foot would be marked by an equal positio. The trochee would have a levatio of two tempora and a positio of one tempus, while the iamb would on the contrary have a levatio of one tempus and a positio of two tempora.

In combining feet to create a verse it is necessary that the feet contain the same number of tempora and have the same levatio and positio.[45] For example, the tribrach (◡◡◡) may be combined with either the iamb or the trochee, since all these feet contain three tempora and the tribrach may be divided into a levatio and positio corresponding to the plausus of either the iamb or the trochee. But the iamb and trochee, even though they contain an equal number of tempora, may not be combined since the plausus of one conflicts with the other.[46] The combination of feet of the same number of tempora and with the same plausus into an orderly series creates rhythm. But rhythm as such is understood to be such a series of equivalent feet having no end but extending into infinity. In poetry and music, however, this abstract rhythm is regulated by establishing a definite end to the series, so that one senses a conclusion and then a definite return to the beginning. This measuring of a rhythmic series by imposing a definite end upon it is meter (*metrum* = measure).[47] A meter must have a minimum of two feet, since at least two feet are required to establish a rhythmic series.[48] The final foot of a meter may, however, be incomplete. That is, the second half of a foot, the positio, may be replaced by a silence or rest equivalent to the quantity of the missing syllable or syllables. This *semipes*[49] together with the rest is the equivalent of a foot, so that a minimum meter may

45. With the exception of feet of six tempora which may be combined even though the plausus is irregular. See II. 11. 20–24.

46. II. 14. 26: "Iambo posset [accommodari] chorius; sed propter inaequalem plausum vitandum est, quod alter a simplo, a duplo alter incipit. Ergo tribrachus utrique accommodari potest."

47. III. 1. 2: "Nam quoniam illud pedibus certis provolvitur, peccaturque in eo si pedes dissoni misceantur, recte appellatus est rhythmus, id est numerus: sed quia ipsa provolutio non habet modum, nec statutum est in quoto pede finis aliquis emineat; propter nullam mensuram continuationis non debuit metrum vocari. Hoc [metrum] autem utrumque habet: nam et certis pedibus currit, et certo terminatur modo. Itaque non solum metrum propter insignem finem, sed etiam rhythmus est, propter pedum rationabilem connexionem. Quocirca omne metrum rhythmus, non omnis rhythmus etiam metrum est."

48. III. 8. 19: "Itaque cum aliquid canitur sive pronuntiatur quod habeat certum finem, et plus habeat quam unum pedem, et naturali motu ante considerationem numerorum sensum quadam aequabilitate demulceat, jam metrum est."

49. V. 13. 27: ". . . omnes ergo isti non pleni pedes semipedes nuncupantur."

consist of a foot and a half with a rest replacing the remainder of the foot.[50]

The exact measurement of the rest or silence plays an extremely important part in Augustine's theory of rhythm. Almost all of Book IV is devoted to a study of the various meters and the various usages of rests in these meters. Augustine observes that poets and grammarians are accustomed to pay no heed to the quantity of the final syllable of a meter, whether it be long or short. But he maintains that such indifference is not to be condoned if one meter is to follow another as is the case in poetry. For if the length of the final syllable of a meter is not accurately measured according to the requirements of the chosen foot, the over-all rhythm will be disrupted in passing from one meter to another. When one meter follows another without the intervention of a rest, the final syllable of the first meter must conform to the laws of the meter in order that the flow of musical rhythm may not be disturbed.[51] When, however, a rest intervenes between the two meters, the final syllable may be indifferently a long or a short, since the ear judges the final syllable together with the pause to be a long quantity.[52] Nevertheless, the final syllable and pause together must add up to whatever quantity is necessary for the preservation of the meter and rhythm. Augustine establishes two rules for a final, incomplete foot.[53] 1) In feet of more than two syllables, the syllable before a rest must be long.[54] 2) The pause must not occupy more than the space of half a foot;[55] and at least the whole levatio must be sounded before the appearance of the rest. From these rules we draw the following important observation: In a poem consisting of a number of meters, or in a musical composition of a number of phrases, the established rhythm must be preserved; and so the individual meters and phrases must ter-

50. III. 8. 19: "Quanquam enim minus habeat quam duos pedes, tamen quia excedit unum et silere cogit, non sine mensura, sed quantum implendis temporibus satis est quae alteri debentur pedi; pro duobus pedibus auditus accipit, quod duorum pedum occupat tempora donec ad caput redeatur, dum annumeratur sono etiam certum atque dimensum intervalli silentium."

51. IV. 2. 3: ". . . nam in continuatione metrorum apertissime convincuntur aurium judicio, non se debere ponere ultimam, nisi quae ipsius metri jure atque ratione ponenda est."

52. IV. 1. 1: "Discipulus. Jam assentior, ultimam syllabam indifferenter esse accipiendam. Magister. Recte. Sed si hoc propter silentium fit, quoniam ita consideratus est finis, quasi deinceps nihil soniturus sit qui finierit, et ob hoc spatium temporis in ipsa quiete largissimum nihil distat quae ibi syllaba locetur; nonne illus est consequens, ut ipsa ultimae syllabae indifferentia, quae propter largum spatium conceditur, ad id proficiat, ut sive ibi brevis syllaba sive longa sit, eam sibi aures pro longa vindicent? Discipulus. Video plane esse consequens."

53. Amerio, p. 96.

54. IV. 8.

55. IV. 15. 29: ". . . non autem sileri oportere amplius quam pedis partem, quam levatio positiove occupant."

minate either with a complete foot or with a foot that consists of a complete levatio and an exactly measured pause or rest to complete the foot.

One other feature of the Augustinian system must be mentioned. Besides rhythm and meter poetry has the *versus* or verse. The verse is a meter characterized by the possession of two members separated by a caesura.[56] The two members must approach equality,[57] but there must be a difference between them in order to distinguish the beginning member from the concluding member.[58] In order to establish its position as final and in order to mark the end of the verse the final member must conclude with an incomplete foot.

For [Augustine says] I believe that the establishment of the end of a verse, so that it will not proceed further than necessary, pertains only to the measurement of time; and I believe that this mark can come from nothing but time. . . . Moreover, since time can have no difference here except that it be longer or shorter, do you not see that when a verse concludes, it is a question of not allowing it to proceed for a longer time [longius] and that the indication of the end must be a shorter time? [59]

The distinguishing characteristic of a shorter time (*nota brevioris temporis*) in a versus is, then, an incomplete foot, a semipes.[60] Every verse, therefore, will conclude with an incomplete foot, followed by a rest.

In addition to rests replacing the second part of a foot at the end of a meter or verse, Augustine admits the use of rests at the beginning of a meter and within the meter.[61] These rests are necessary when an incomplete foot occurs within a meter or to avoid a rest after a final brevis in the case of feet of more than two syllables. In all cases a rest may be introduced only at the end of a word. However, this restriction does not apply to music and rests may be employed there wherever necessary for the preservation of the rhythm.[62] Finally, there are also

56. III. 2; V. 1.

57. V. 2. 2: "At omnia quae recipiunt divisionem, nonne pulchriora sunt si eorum partes aliqua parilitate concordent, quam si discordes et dissonae sint?"

58. V. 3. 3.

59. V. 4. 6: "Ego enim, quoniam idispum finire versum ne longius quam oportet excurrat, non pertinet nisi ad temporis modum; non arbitror aliunde istam notam debere sumi quam ex tempore. . . . Videsne etiam illud, cum tempus hic differentiam habere non possit, nisi quod alius est longius, aliud brevius; quia cum versus finitur, id agitur ne pergat longius, in breviore tempore notam finis esse oportere?"

60. V. 4. 7: ". . . nota brevioris temporis, id est semipede . . ."

61. IV. 14. 19.

62. IV. 14. 24: "In iis autem numeris qui non verbis fiunt, sed aliquo pulsu vel flatu, vel ipsa etiam lingua, nullum in hac re discrimen est, post quam vocem percussionemve sileatur; modo ut legitimum secundum supradictas rationes intercedat silentium."

arbitrary rests that Augustine calls "voluntary" rests. These may be inserted anywhere within the meter and may even replace an entire foot instead of half a foot as is true of other rests. "In the case of those rests that we have called voluntary rests, it is permissible to sound a foot and to be silent for a foot, and if we should do this at equal intervals, it will no longer be a meter but a rhythm, . . ."[63] Augustine is obviously dealing here with a musical rather than a poetic practice, and his discussion of it, brief though it may be, makes it clear that his treatise was intended to be a presentation of rhythm in general and not simply of poetic rhythm.

The principles of the Augustinian system that have been outlined are applicable to any sort of motion, be it in poetry, music, the dance, or in the motions of objects.[64] Certain of the precepts, however, are applicable only to poetry. For example, if a meter should end with a complete foot, it is only possible to understand this as the end of the meter through the sense of the words, which have presented a complete thought. If we extract from these principles only those that have an application to music, we find that the following rules must be maintained in music. 1) Music will have a constant rhythm consisting of the repetition of a metrical foot or of feet which are equivalent to each other in the number of tempora and in their plausus. 2) This rhythm will be measured off into phrases (metrum or versus) by the introduction of rests, marking the ends of the phrases. 3) The end of each phrase will be marked by an incomplete foot (levatio) followed by a rest equivalent to the positio. 4) Arbitrary rests equivalent to a foot or to half a foot may be inserted within the phrase.

Although none of the modal theorists mention the *De Musica,* the resemblance of the modal system to the Augustinian doctrine is too striking to be ignored. One must keep in mind that the thirteenth-century treatises are dealing specifically with *musica practica* and to a large degree they ignore the theoretical side of music which occupied so large a part of earlier treatises. Nevertheless there is ample evidence that the *De Musica* was known and utilized by theorists and scholars from the earliest times. Both Cassiodorus [65] (ca. 485–ca. 580) and Isidore of Seville [66] (ca. 570–636) drew upon Augustine's definition of music as "scientia bene modulandi." Bishop Aldhelm (640–709) refers to the *De Musica*

63. IV. 15. 29: "Nam in iis quae voluntaria silentia nominavimus, licet etiam pedem sonare, et pedem silere: quod si paribus intervallis fecerimus, non erit metrum, sed rhythmus, . . ."

64. See I. 2; VI.

65. Gerbert, *Scriptores, 1,* 16.

66. *Etymologia, 3,* 15, in Migne, *Patrologia Latina, 82.*

in his *De metris et enigmatibus ac pedum regulis.*[67] The *Musica Enchiriadis* cites St. Augustine;[68] and Rudolph of St. Trond (1070–1138) repeats this passage.[69] Remigius of Auxerre (end of ninth century) in his *Musica,* which is a gloss of Martianus Capella, restates Augustine's definition of rhythm and meter without, however, citing Augustine.[70] Berno of Reichenau (d. 1048) paraphrases a large section from the *De Musica* in his *Musica Bernonis seu Prologus in Tonorum.*[71] Robert Grosseteste, bishop of Lincoln, (1175–1253) bases his theory of pleasure in music upon the sixth book of the *De Musica.*[72] St. Bonaventura erects his whole system of esthetics upon considerations drawn from the sixth book. As de Bruyne says, "A notre avis toute l'esthétique bonaventurienne gravite autour du principe tiré du VIe Livre du 'de Musica': la beauté est 'aequalitas numerosa,' c'est-à-dire un certain genre de rapport."[73]

For at least one important thirteenth-century scholar Augustine's *De Musica* is the only true exposition of the nature of meter and rhythm. Roger Bacon in his *Opus Tertium* (1267) states that for the interpretation of Scripture "it is necessary that one should thoroughly understand the laws of meters and rhythms . . . and it is impossible to comprehend these unless one knows the five books of Augustine's 'De Musica' . . . Only Augustine reveals the truth of this matter. It is impossible to know what is rhythm or meter or verse truly and properly except through these books."[74] Bacon's advocacy of Augustine's

67. *Monumenta Germaniae Historica* (Berlin, 1919), *15,* 81.

68. Gerbert, *Scriptores, 1,* 195b.

69. Rudolf Steglich, *Die Quaestiones in Musica,* Publikationen der Internationalen Musikgesellschaft, Beihefte, Zweite Folge, Heft X (Leipzig, 1911), p. 75.

70. *Remigius Altisiodorensis Musica.* Gerbert, *Scriptores, 1,* 68a: "Hoc interest inter rhythmum & metrum, quod rhythmus est sola verborum consonantia, sine ullo certo numero & fine, & in infinitum funditur nulla lege constrictus, nullis certis pedibus compositus: metrum autem pedibus propriis certisque finibus ordinatur: minimum autem metrum est, quod constat pede & semipede, & res est per ordinem usque ad octo pedes: octonarium autem numerum non transgreditur."

Cf. Augustine, *De Musica,* III. 7. 15: "Quia inter rhythmum et metrum hoc interesse dixisti, quod in rhythmo contextio pedum nullum certum habet finem, in metro vero habet: ita ista pedum contextio et rhythmi et metri esse intelligitur; sed ibi infinita, hic autem finita constat." The remainder of chapter VII and the next two chapters are devoted to the establishment of the minimum meter as a foot and a half, and the maximum as eight feet.

71. Gerbert, *2,* 77, par. 14: "Caeterum si quis cantus contra legem finalium ortus inceperit, etc." Cf. Augustine, II. 1. 1; I. 4. 5.

72. E. de Bruyne, *L'Esthétique, 3,* 146 f.

73. *Ibid., 3,* 199.

74. *Fr. Rogeri Bacon Opera Inedita,* ed. J. S. Brewer, in Rerum Britannicarum Medii Aevi Scriptores, *1* (London, 1859), 265: "Certe oportet quod bene intelligat rationes metrorum et

work is of particular interest because in this same volume he refers to the polyphonic music he had heard in Paris. It is interesting, furthermore, because of Bacon's close relationship with the grammarian, poet, and musical theorist, Johannes de Garlandia. These two men, both products of the Oxford school and kindred spirits in their defense of humanistic studies against the encroachments of the more practical disciplines, probably became acquainted in Paris around 1245, where Garlandia was teaching at the university.[75] Did Garlandia share Bacon's enthusiasm for St. Augustine's work? Due to the fact that most of Garlandia's works are still unedited, one can only speculate idly and inconclusively in this matter.

Not only was St. Augustine's treatise utilized by writers of all centuries but the principal libraries of Europe preserved copies of it. In catalogues prior to 1200 we find that this work was owned by the libraries of Reichenau, St. Riquier, St. Gall, Bobbio, Lorsch, St. Emmeram, Trier, Corbie, Michelsberg, Bec,[76] and also Cluny.[77] In Paris copies of the *De Musica* were in the possession of St. Germain des Pres [78] and the Couvent des Feuillantes.[79] It is impossible to ascertain when these two latter libraries came into possession of their copies, but the first is of the ninth century and the second is in a twelfth-century hand. The earliest catalogue of books in the Notre Dame library, dated 1297, does not list the *De Musica* among the nine volumes of St. Augustine owned by the cathedral,[80] but the number of books on this list is much smaller than that of earlier estimates of the library, so it is not impossible that the cathedral may once have owned a volume. In any case, the tradition of the *De Musica* is well attested in the Middle Ages.

If one compares the Augustinian doctrines of rhythm with the modal system of the Notre Dame composers, an almost perfect correspondence is apparent.

---

rhythmorum . . . et impossibile est eum haec intelligere, nisi sciat libros quinque De Musica Augustini . . . quia solus Augustinus hujus rei aperuit veritatem. Nunquam enim potui scire quid est rhythmus, nec metrum, nec versus, veraciter et proprie, nisi per illos libros."

75. Paetow, *Morale Scolarium,* pp. 95, 122.

76. Gustav Becker, *Catalogi Bibliothecarum Antiqui* (Bonn, 1895), Nos. 4, 11, 15, 32, 37, 42, 76, 79, 80, 127, 136.

77. Léopold Delisle, *Inventaire des manuscrits de la Bibliothèque Nationale. Fonds de Cluni* (Paris, 1884), Appendix, Catalogue de la Bibliothèque de Cluni. Milieu du XIIe siècle, No. 162.

78. L. Royer, "Catalogue des écrits théoriciens de la musique conservés dans le fonds latin des manuscrits de la bibliothèque nationale," *L'Année musicale, 3* (1913), No. 13375.

79. *Ibid.,* No. 17161.

80. Alfred Franklin, *Recherches sur la bibliothèque publique de l'église Notre Dame de Paris au XIIIe siècle d'aprés des documents inédits* (Paris, 1863). The catalogue is printed on p. 28.

Both systems accept a brevis and a longa of one and two tempora respectively as the basis of all rhythm. The modal theorists speak of a recta brevis and a recta longa; St. Augustine makes the following statement: ". . . ac per hoc si spatium quod brevis occupat, *recte* unum tempus vocatur; spatium item quod longa occupat, *recte* duo tempora nominari." [81] The modal patterns, furthermore, correspond to metrical feet. Apel has stated that there is no justification for the identification of the modal patterns with metrical feet except on the basis of Odington's late statements.[82] But it is particularly striking to discover that Augustine himself states that the feet could be named by their order in his list of twenty-eight feet, although it is not easy to give up the names bestowed upon them by ancient authority.[83] Accordingly, Augustine lists the feet as *primus, secundus, tertius,* etc., adding the conventional grammatical name for each foot. The first eight feet of this list are the pyrrichius, iambus, trochaeus, spondeus, tribrachus, dactylus, amphibrachus, and the anapaestus.[84] Of these eight feet, two cannot be combined with other feet to make a rhythmical series. The pyrrichius can only be joined to another pyrrichius, since no other foot has only two tempora. The amphibrachus also is excluded from forming a rhythm with other feet, since no other foot has the same plausus of one tempus in the levatio and three tempora in the positio. Thus we find that the first six feet which are capable of uniting with other feet to form a rhythm are the same six feet which appear in modal theory as the six rhythmic modes.

The Augustinian conception of the distinguishing characteristics of rhythm, meter, and verse are likewise fundamental to the modal system. In the first part of this chapter it has been demonstrated that modal rhythm consists in the repetition of a foot. A mode per se is simply the postulation of a given pattern repeated into infinity. It is rhythm in the Augustinian sense of the word. But in any piece of music the sounding rhythm will constantly be interrupted by rests. At the same time it is in the nature of rhythm that such rests cannot be of an irrational length. If any irregular time value were to be inserted within the regular flow of the rhythm, the rhythm would be deflected or destroyed so

81. II. 4. 4.

82. See p. 29, above.

83. "Sed num censes commode ista nos posse persequi nisi pedum nomina teneamus? Quanquam hoc ordine a nobis digesti sunt, ut possint ipsius sui ordinis nominibus nuncupari: dici enim potest primus, secundus, tertius, atque hoc modo caeteri. Sed quia non sunt contemnenda vetusta vocabula, nec facile a consuetudine recedendum, nisi quae rationi adversatur; utendum est his nominibus pedum quae Graeci instituerunt . . ." II. 8. 15.

84. *Ibid.*

that it could not be said that there is any longer a correct rhythmic succession. For this reason the absence of sound within a rhythmic succession must be measured as accurately as the sound itself, if the rhythm is to be maintained. Thus we find that rhythm will appear in a piece of music as a series of sounding phrases separated by rests that are measured according to the proportions of the chosen rhythmic pattern.

The rest, furthermore, is an essential factor in both the Augustinian and the modal system, for it is the rest which imposes an end upon the infinite progression of rhythm. It is the rest which changes rhythm into meter or into the musical phrase, which in the terminology of the modal theorists is called the ordo. The rest then is a determining factor in music, for it establishes and controls the length of a phrase. Anonymous IV recognizes this special power of the rest, when he applies to it the revealing adjective "regulative." [85] The rest, this adjective infers, regulates or controls the length and form of an ordo; the ordo depends for its existence upon the rest. Because of the intervention of rests a piece of music will be divided into groups or phrases of audible notes and it is only in these phrases or ordines that the rhythmic pattern can actually be heard. Since the rhythmic pattern never exists in sound except in such phrases, it is obvious that the mode will exist or be audible only in such phrases. For this reason we find that the modes are always discussed by the theorists in terms of the ordo (the Augustinian metrum). The ordo is thus the primal expression of the mode in practical music. This fact is of the utmost importance for our understanding of the notation of the Notre Dame school, for it will be seen that their solution to the problem of notating a rhythmic pattern was to provide a visual symbol of the pattern as it exists within an ordo.

The nature of the ordo must now be examined more thoroughly. An ordo consists of several repetitions of a modal pattern terminating in a rest. It must have at least one repetition of the pattern in order to be rhythm, so the minimum ordo will be two statements of a foot. The ordo may, like the Augustinian metrum, end either on a complete or an incomplete foot. If an ordo ends on the first part of the foot, it is said to be a perfect modus. If it ends on the second part of the foot, it is said to be an imperfect modus. But the definition of modus perfectus and modus imperfectus provided by the theorists is one which merely describes the phenomenon but does not explain the reason for it. A typical definition is that of Garlandia: "A modus is said to be perfect which ends with

85. CS, *I*, 348, 2: ". . . Omnis pausatio regulativa continuat modum precedentem . . ." (Every regulative rest continues the preceding mode.)

the same quantity as that with which it begins, for instance, longa, brevis, longa. An imperfect modus is that which ends with a quantity other than that with which it begins." [86] Such a definition explains what a perfect and an imperfect ordo are, but it does not explain why the one should be deemed perfect and the other imperfect. What is the reason then for this terminology? Obviously the terms "perfectus" and "imperfectus" cannot refer to the completeness or the incompleteness of the final foot, for it will be seen that a perfect modus ends with an incomplete, i.e., imperfect, foot, while an imperfect modus ends with a complete or perfect foot. Some other factor must be sought to account for the use of these terms.

The answer to this problem is a fairly simple one, but at the same time it enables us to gain further insight into the nature of the ordo. A minimum ordo, such as has been discussed thus far, does not in itself constitute a musical composition; it must be followed by other phrases or ordines, if we are to have a true piece of music. If the same rhythm is to be maintained throughout a composition, the following ordines must be in the same rhythm as the initial ordo. But what happens if an ordo in an imperfect modus is followed by another ordo?

Let us take for an example an imperfect ordo of the first mode:

♩♪♩♪|𝄽

The rest which determines the end of the first ordo also replaces the first part of the third foot. Consequently the second ordo will begin on the final short value of the third foot and will proceed in the order short, long, short long, etc., until a rest intervenes. The sound of this ordo—and it has been seen that an ordo consists of the measured sounds before a rest or between rests—will be the exact opposite of the pattern of the preceding ordo. It will be in reality the second mode (♪♩), and would receive an entirely different notation than that provided for the first mode. Franco of Cologne understood this phenomenon, for he wrote: "You must notice that rests have a wondrous power, for the modes are changed by them. . . . Whence, if the first mode, which proceeds by a longa, a brevis and a longa, should have a rest of two tempora after the brevis, the first mode will be changed into the second." [87] And he gives as an example of this the phrases:

86. CS, *I*, 97b: "Perfectus modus dicitur qui finit per talem quantitatem per qualem incipit ut longa, brevis, longa. Imperfectus est qui terminatur per aliam quam per illam in qua incipit."

87. CS, *I*, 126b: "Et nota pausationes mirabilem habere potestatem; nam per ipsas modi ad invicem transmutantur. . . . Unde si primus modus, qui procedit ex longa et brevi et longa,

However, the rest has this "wondrous power" of changing the modes only if it replaces the first part of a foot. For it is readily seen that if the rest replaces the last part of a foot, the following ordo will begin with a note of the same value as the opening of the previous ordo, and the mode will thus continue unchanged. The term perfectus, therefore, refers to a mode which ends in such a manner (i.e., on the first part of the foot) that, after the intervention of a rest replacing the remainder of the foot, the next ordo will continue the same modus. A modus is imperfect when it ends in such a way that it has not the power to cause a return to the same modus in the next ordo.

A rest is also said to be perfect if it is placed in such a way (i.e., on the second part of the foot) that the same modus will exist after the rest as existed before the rest.[88] The idea of "perfection" is the same for both the rest and the ordo: this term is reserved for rests and ordines which will allow the same modus to return after the rest. This conception is formulated by Anonymous IV in his definition: "Every rest within the first or second mode, etc., is said to be perfect, or must be said to be perfect, if it restores the same mode after it that exists before it." [89] This rule also applies to multiple rests, the voluntary rests of St. Augustine. It was a common practice in the polyphonic music of this era to employ rests at the end of an ordo with a value of more than half a foot.[90] Such rests occur primarily when the final note of the ordo is a ternary longa. Many ordines in the first mode, for example, end with a longa not of two tempora but of three. In other words, this final longa has incorporated in itself the temporal value of the following brevis, so that it stands for both the levatio and the positio of the final foot, and so it may be understood to be an imperfect modus in theory. Consequently it must be followed by a double rest in order that the

---

pausam post brevem habeat, longam imperfectam, ut hic patet: [example] variatur primus modus in secundum." This definition has led Ludwig, Sowa, and Husmann, among others, to the conclusion that there must be an upbeat form of the first mode.

88. Cf. Augustine, III. 8. 18: "Nam te sentire jam credo silendum esse, ut cum redimus ad caput, plausus non claudicet."

89. CS, *1*, 348b: "Unde regula: omnis pausatio primi modi, vel secundi, etc., si reddiderit talem modum post se sicut ante, perfecta dicitur, vel perfecta debet dici; . . ."

90. Although a silence equal to a foot would seem to call for two rests, one to replace each part of the missing foot, in practice this double rest was represented by only one sign. Only in a few cases in the Notre Dame manuscripts do we find two rests used to indicate a rest of a foot's duration. See, e.g., the triplum of *O sancte Germane,* W_1, f. 9, beginning with the syllable "ger"-[mane].

same modus may be continued. In such a case this multiple rest is termed a perfect rest.[91]

It has been shown that an ordo must consist of at least two feet, and that this combination of two feet will, in the case of a perfect modus, always contain an initial complete foot and a second foot that has a tone for the first part of the foot and a rest for the second part of the foot. A special situation arises in the case of the imperfect modes. It would seem that a single foot followed by a rest replacing the first half of the next foot would constitute a minimum ordo of an imperfect mode, but this would violate the first law of modal rhythm that a modal pattern must be stated at least twice in order to create rhythm. Consequently a value must be supplied to fill out the second foot. According to Anonymous IV an imperfect ordo is always completed by the addition of further notes, so that an imperfect ordo actually consists of a phrase ending on the second part of a foot followed by a rest occupying the first part of the next foot and a phrase of the same number of notes as the first, but beginning on the second half of the foot. In discussing the first imperfect mode he makes the statement that "the ordines of the first imperfect mode proceed in an even number of notes, but obviously with the addition of a phrase of like form." [92] Thus the first ordo of the first imperfect mode consists of a longa and brevis, followed by a long rest of two tempora, then a brevis and longa followed by a brevis rest [93]:

In this way the rhythm is established by the repetition of the foot and at the same time the second, balancing phrase provides a return to the normal form of the first mode. This means that an imperfect ordo, like a perfect one, must eventually terminate on the first part of the foot in order to preserve the characteristic rhythm and notation of the chosen mode.

From the preceding discussion it is apparent that the ordo, be it perfect or imperfect, is a musical phrase conforming to specific laws. The notes within the phrase are arranged in a definite order according to one or the other of the rhythmic modes and the beginning and ending of the phrase are determined

91. See Anon. IV, CS, *I*, 349a.

92. CS, *I*, 329a: "Iterato ordines primi modi imperfecti procedunt per numerum parem, videlicet cum adjunctione sub tali forma; . . ."

93. CS, *I*, 329a, b: "Et primus ordo sic procedit per longam brevem cum longa pausatione duorum temporum, cum adjunctione brevis longe, cum brevi pausatione unius temporis."

by a particular ordering of the notes. The term ordo is also extended to include the signs of notation which represent the particular pattern of the notes within the phrase. Anonymous IV defines the ordo in the following way: "The ordo of a mode is the number of notes before a rest. Any ordo is derived from its ordained principle. The arrangement according to the first principle of some modes is the arrangement of note-signs or melodic tones, which appear in a certain order of tones without a rest, and which are combined as much as possible into the form of ligatures." [94] The word, ordo, as used in modal theory quite evidently not only retains its primary meaning of series, the number of anything existing in succession, but also includes its figurative meaning, right order or regular succession.

The minimum ordo is called by the theorists the first ordo of a perfect mode (primus ordo modi perfecti). Ordines of the first mode, for example, which contain two, four, etc., more tones than the first ordo are designated as the second, third, etc., ordines. A rule was formulated by Anonymous IV for determining the number of an ordo from the notation itself. In the first mode the first perfect ordo is represented by a three-note ligature; the second ordo is represented by an additional two-note ligature; the third ordo adds another two-note ligature, etc. Anonymous IV's rule for computing the number of an ordo of the first perfect mode is this: "The number which gives an ordo its name is the sum of as many two-note ligatures as there are after a three-note ligature plus one." [95] The disposition of the various modes into ordines may be seen in the table on page 44. Only the ordines of perfect modes are given, because the imperfect modes seldom occur in Notre Dame organum, and when they do appear they are not organized in symmetrical phrases such as those outlined by Anonymous IV. Only the first and second ordines are given for each mode; other ordines would be constructed simply by adding another foot to the previous ordo.

Still another theoretical consideration must be taken into account before we proceed to the notation of the modes—namely, the equivalence of the modes. From the above table it may be seen that the modi recti (I, II, VI) have patterns equivalent to each other, for each pattern contains three tempora. The patterns of the modi in ultra mensuram are equivalent to each other in that they

94. CS, *I*, 328b: "Ordo modi est numerus punctorum ante pausationem. Qui quidam ordo sumitur a suo principio ordinato. Ordinatio principii primi aliorum modorum est ordinatio punctorum vel sonorum melorum que sine pausatione sumpta sub certo ordine sonorum punctorum figuris troporum plenius jungantur."

95. CS, *I*, 345a: "Unde regula: quot fuerint due ligate post tres . . . tot erit numerus nominis ordinis uno sibi addito."

each contain six tempora. How then can these modes be combined? In polyphonic music it is possible for each voice to proceed in a different modus. In fact this is usually the case in organum, for the tenor is generally in the fifth mode while the upper parts move in any one of the other modes. It also happens to be a general rule that in pieces of organum of extended length the modes may be changed within any one of the voices as well. For example, compositions

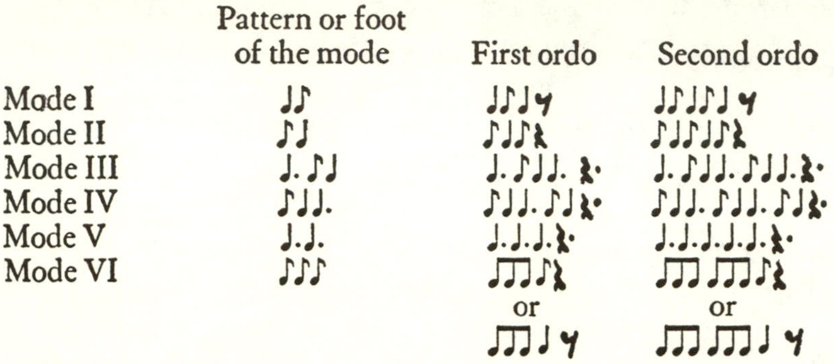

may have an opening section in the first mode, followed by another extended section in the third mode, and then perhaps another section once more in the first mode. But how can the feet of the modi recti which contain three tempora be combined with the feet of the modi in ultra mensuram which contain six tempora? Obviously a foot of the third mode cannot be equated with a foot of the first mode, because the former has a time value just twice that of the latter. On the other hand, the first mode and the second mode seem to be equivalent since they both contain three tempora, but nevertheless these modes are never combined in practice.[96] These seeming discrepancies are explicable only through a phenomenon which belongs properly to the art of metrics—the plausus.

Although we hear nothing about a plausus in organum from the thirteenth-century theorists, the music and the modal theory itself are tacit evidence that the early organistae preserved the metrical plausus in their modes. The plausus was quite evidently used in measuring the chant if we accept the statement of Guido which appears above on page 23, note 17.[97] That the plausus is not men-

96. The combination of these two modes is occasionally encountered in the later motets. But this is a development due to the particular stylistic qualities of the motet and it has no meaning for the organum. Such a combination could occur only when the original meaning of the modal system had been lost.

97. The *Musica Enchiriadis* has the sentence: "Veluti metricis pedibus cantilena plaudatur." Gerbert, *Scriptores, 1,* 182.

tioned by the thirteenth-century theorists is not conclusive proof that the plausus was not used in the Notre Dame organa. These theorists lived at a time when the style of the motet had brought about a division of the brevis into many more than two semibreves.[98] The multiple division of the brevis led to a slowing up of the tempo of the brevis and so it became the practice to beat time by marking each brevis. Such a method of marking time is not discussed by theorists prior to the thirteenth century. Since treatises prior to the Notre Dame school mention the plausus but not beating time by the brevis, and since treatises of the fourteenth century mention beating time by the brevis and do not mention the plausus, one may conclude that a change in the method of beating time occurred either when modal rhythm appeared or shortly thereafter. The music is proof that the change must have taken place after organum had reached the peak of its development (ca. 1225) or at just about this date.

If the modes had been beaten by the brevis value, there would be no hindrance to combining the first and second modes, either in succession in the same ordo or simultaneously in two different voices. But since the basic principle of modal rhythm is the repetition of the same pattern, it follows that feet of the second mode cannot be inserted within an ordo of the first mode, because the pattern and the plausus representing the pattern would be disrupted. Likewise the first and second modes cannot exist simultaneously in two different voices because the plausus would not coincide. The sixth mode, however, can be equated with either the first or second mode. This comes about because the sixth mode is made up of three equal notes and the plausus thus can be either a levatio of one tempus and a positio of two tempora, which corresponds to the plausus of the second mode; or it can have a levatio of two tempora and a positio of one tempus corresponding to the plausus of the first mode. (In practice the sixth mode is notated as a variant of the first or second mode, as well as having a special notation of its own. The latter form of notation is, however, a later historical development, as will be demonstrated below.) [99]

The modi in ultra mensuram can be equated with each other, for the feet of the third, fourth, and fifth modes are all marked with a plausus having an elevatio of three tempora and a positio of three tempora. But how can a modus in ultra mensuram be the equivalent of a modus rectus? The equation of these modes is a fact attested by almost any page of the organum manuscripts. The explanation of this apparent discrepancy is to be found in the historical develop-

98. As many as nine semibreves were used by Pierre de la Croix.

99. See pp. 64 ff.

ment of the organum and its notation. Modal rhythm was first applied to the upper voice of two-part organum. This voice moved in extended melismata measured at first almost exclusively in the first mode. The tenor sustained the individual notes of the Gregorian cantus firmus for long periods of time while the upper voice maintained its constant melismatic flow. The upper voice had so many tones for the one note of the Gregorian chant that the tenor note may be said to have no rational or proportional measure. Some parts of almost any chant, on the other hand, are themselves melismatic. These melismata were seldom treated in the sustained manner of the syllabic portions of the chant, for the organum would thus be protracted to an impracticable length. Therefore in such melismata the composer shortened the value of each note of the tenor melisma, so that usually there are only two to four notes in the upper voice for each note of the tenor.

Almost all organa contain sections in both manners of treatment. In themselves the notes of the tenor, usually written in the form of a longa, have no explicit temporal value. They derive their value from the number of notes placed above them in the duplum. In the sections where each foot of a rhythmic pattern is matched with a single note of the tenor, the individual note of the tenor will naturally be equivalent to the total value of the foot. The tenor note will thus have an exact value of either three tempora or six tempora, depending upon whether it is equivalent to a foot of a modus rectus or a modus in ultra mensuram. Since, however, the duplum in the organa of the earliest version of the *Magnus liber,* contained in fascicles 3 and 4 of W_1, is almost invariably in the first mode, it is obvious that these more rapid tenor sections will most commonly be measured in values of three tempora if the individual notes of the tenor are equivalent to a single foot of the upper part, or six tempora if the note is equivalent to two feet of the other part. It is in this phenomenon that the longa ultra mensuram came into existence. These notes of three tempora in the tenor are certainly long notes, but they are not the normal longa of the duplum rhythm. Therefore they are said to be long notes beyond the measure of a normal long. These successions of long notes were not originally thought of as a true mode. There was little, if any, attempt to arrange them in symmetrical ordines, which would have been the case had they been rationalized as a modus from the very start. Thus at first the so-called fifth mode was merely a series of long notes, whose values or measurement were entirely contingent upon the values of the modally measured duplum.[100]

100. The dependency of the tenor notes upon the value of the notes in the duplum is revealed

Since in many cases the tenor notes would have a value of three tempora, they offer the possibility of being rationalized as a modus. Such a rationalization was evidently made by Perotin. Anonymous IV informs us that Perotin created clausulae, sections of organum with rhythmically organized tenors, to replace equivalent sections in the organa of Leonin.[101] A comparison of Leonin's organum duplum in the third and fourth fascicles of W1 with the substitute clausulae contained in the fifth and sixth fascicles, which were presumably written by Perotin or his contemporaries, will provide a very illuminating picture of the development of the indeterminate succession of tenor notes of Leonin into the rational fifth mode of Perotin. In the third and fourth fascicles the undifferentiated series of single notes appears no less than 107 times. Although these tenor phrases are sometimes broken by rests, the rests are not employed to divide the tenor notes into symmetrical ordines but merely correspond with rests in the duplum or are introduced to allow the singers to take breath. On the other hand, tenor sections which are organized into either a definite fifth mode or some other mode occur only 17 times. Five of these sections at least are probably substitutions for Leonin's original work, since equivalent sections with undifferentiated series of notes in the tenors are to be found in the fascicles containing substitute clausulae in either W1 or F.[102] In these five cases Leonin's original work seems to have been consigned to the fascicles of substitute clausulae, while new clausulae have replaced them in the body of the original organa. It is quite possible that the remaining twelve sections are also substitutes for Leonin's work. In any case the number of strictly modal tenors in the organa dupla of the third and fourth fascicles is only a small fraction of the total. The proportion of undifferentiated tenors to modal tenors is six to one, if we count all the modal tenors as the work of Leonin; if we assume that at least in five cases the modal tenor is a substitute for an undifferentiated tenor, the proportion

---

by Anon. IV: "Iterato fuerunt quidam antiqui qui antiquitus solebant elongare illas tres longas conjunctim cum sua longa pausatione, quare ponebant juxta materialem signationem tres ligatas pro tribus longis, quamvis sit ista ligatura contra ligatas tres in aliis modis antecedentibus et postpositis; *sed nullus hoc poterit cognoscere, nisi juxta armonicam considerationem superius sibi attributam,* vel nisi superius fuerit longa brevis, longa brevis et longa brevis, pro pausatione secundum primum modum, vel brevis longa, brevis longa et brevis longa, pro pausatione secundum secundum modum; sed secundum tertium, longa et due breves, longa et due breves, longa, juxta ordines supradictos." (CS, *I,* 333b–334a.) In other words the single tenor note could be for the early writers of organum (antiqui) equal either to a foot of the first, second, or third modes.

101. CS, *I,* 342a.

102. *Tamquam,* f. 17′ = W_1, f. 49; *In seculum,* f. 31′ = W_1, f. 56′; *Torium,* f. 46 = W_1, f. 51; *Veritatem,* f. 41 = F, f. 183; *Dominabuntur,* f. 44′ = F, f. 182′.

rises to nine to one, (107 + 5) 112: (17 — 5) 12. In the fascicles of substitute clausulae this proportion is sharply reversed. Here we find 23 examples of an undifferentiated tenor and 54 examples of tenors in the fifth mode plus 30 examples of tenors in other modes. In other words, the proportion of undifferentiated tenors to modal tenors is now one to four. These statistics show quite conclusively that a nonmodal tenor is characteristic of Leonin's work, while modal organization of the tenor is characteristic of Perotin's composition. The inference is that modal organization of the tenor was first undertaken by Perotin.[103]

In the work of Leonin the tenor had been merely a succession of long notes having a value of three tempora or six tempora, depending upon the value of a foot of the duplum mode. Perotin, however, gave this tenor mode an independent status. Since the usual value assigned to an isolated note in a sucession of tenor notes was three tempora, this value was accepted for the notes of the fifth mode. Furthermore a pattern was established for the fifth mode—if there were no pattern or foot there could be no mode. Because it takes two ternary longs to equal a foot of a modus in ultra mensuram and because the ordines of the modi recti are most commonly to be found in multiples of two feet (two ternary longs), the pattern for the fifth mode was assumed to consist of two longs, a pattern which approximates the spondee of metrics. This pattern then became subject to the laws of the modes. It was organized into ordines which terminate on the first part of the foot, while the second part of the foot is filled by a rest equivalent to three tempora. In practice the first ordo of the fifth mode was employed almost to the exclusion of all other ordines, so that we find that the tenor moves in a precise succession of three longae followed by a rest of three tempora.

The fifth mode is obviously not the spondee of classic metrics which has only four tempora. The difference comes about, of course, because the simultaneous

103. This inference is substantiated by the statement of Anon. IV. In describing the use of a ternary ligature for the first ordo of the fifth mode, he says: "And this usage of a ternary ligature mentioned above is a method of notating in ligatures in the lower parts, above all in tenors, but the notes will be disjunct in all lower [i.e., the duplum of a three-voiced organum] and upper parts; and this was the case from that time on when men were beginning to understand such things, that is in the time of Perotinus magnus and from the time of his predecessors." (CS, *1*, 334a.) "Et iste modus trium supradictorum est modus notandi conjunctim in inferioribus, et in primis in tenoribus, sed disjunctim in inferioribus et in superioribus omnibus; et hoc ab illo tempore quo homines incipiebant talia cognoscere, veluti in tempore Perotini magni, et a tempore antecessorum suorum." The scarcity of modally organized tenors in the earliest version of the Magnus liber in W_1 would seem to exclude Leonin from the group of Perotin's "antecessores."

combination of meters is a phenomenon unknown to metrics. The longa ultra mensuram in the undifferentiated tenor series of Leonin's organum had been the equivalent of a foot of the upper voice and consequently had been marked by the plausus of this foot. Since a note of three tempora can, like the sixth mode, be measured by the plausus of either the first or second mode, this note can be combined with either a first, second, or sixth mode in the upper voice. Because of the pre-existence of this equivalence, when the longa ultra mensuram was organized into a mode with a pattern of two longs, the foot of the fifth mode became in practice and in theory equivalent to two feet of any of the modi recti and contained six tempora. Since the third mode (dactyl) and fourth mode (anapest) would be the equivalent of the fifth mode (spondee) according to the laws of metrics, it follows that the third and fourth modes would likewise contain six tempora and thus a foot of the third and fourth modes, like a foot of the fifth mode, would be equivalent to two feet of the modi recti. But because the breves of the anapest and dactyl were considered to have a value of one tempus and two tempora respectively, the third and fourth modes could be the equivalent of two feet of only the second or sixth modes since the same plausus must be retained in any rhythm.

It is evident that the law of the plausus has been violated in the modi in ultra mensuram, since the foot is beaten not as one levatio and one positio but as a levatio, positio, levatio, and positio. This is not the first time in history that theory has been forced to yield to practice. In this case, however, theory is not completely abandoned, because each part of the foot in these modes must have a plausus that is equivalent to that of the foot in the other voices sounding with it. One final observation may be deduced from the statements in this paragraph: in practice the plausus is restricted to only two varieties, corresponding either to the first mode or the second mode.[104] The other four modes will all be beaten in one of these two manners. A simple rule may be formulated from this: the first mode may be combined only with the fifth and sixth modes; any of the other five modes may be combined with each other.

The equivalence of the modes is a vital factor in the problem of transcribing modal notation into modern notation. In almost all modern transcriptions of the organa a 6/8 or 6/4 measure has been chosen as the most satisfactory expression of modal rhythm. I myself have chosen a 6/8 rhythm because an eighth note is a better expression than a quarter note for the value of a brevis which, if it is subdivided into lesser values, is never divided into more than two values

104. Garlandia, CS, *I*, 98b: ". . . omnes modi ad primum et ad secundum possunt reduci."

(i.e., sixteenth notes in modern notation). It has been suggested that a 3/4 or 3/8 measure would be a more exact equivalent of the feet of the modi recti, since these contain only three tempora. But such a transcription is contrary to the nature of the modes and to their notation. The foot of the rhythmic modes does not exist in isolation from other feet, but will always be grouped into a phrase or ordo. Modal notation was designed to express the rhythm within an ordo, not to express the individual foot. Since the minimum ordo consists of two feet, and since in practice larger ordines almost always exist in multiples of two feet, 6/8 rhythm, which is a compound measure of two three-beat units, is the best expression of this characteristic feature of modal rhythm.

Rudolf Ficker, however, advocates that a 3/4 (3/8) measure is the proper method of transcription. He has expressed this opinion in his edition of Perotin's *Sederunt*[105] and more recently in his review[106] of Heinrich Husmann's critical edition of the three- and four-voiced Notre Dame organa. In his review of Husmann, Ficker states that the third mode originally was only a more dynamic variety of the sixth mode (♩.♪♩ = ♩♩♩) and he bases this supposition on the quite negative testimony of the theorists and on the similarity of the notation of the third and sixth modes. In both cases, however, he has drawn erroneous conclusions from the evidence he cites as proof. Ficker begins his argument by announcing the well-known fact that the thirteenth-century theorists wrote at a time when the modal rhythm of the organa was already in a state of decline, and at a time when the brevis had become the measure of all other values and was established as the *tactus*. At this time the impossibility of combining a first and second mode no longer existed since time was measured by the individual brevis instead of by the foot as in organum. In the theorists who still have a faint understanding of the old modal system Ficker notes a "striking" lack of certainty in the evaluation of the third mode, and cites Anonymous IV and Garlandia.

> Both theorists[107] agree in explaining that the initial longa of three tempora of the third mode is to be understood by equivalence either as a longa and brevis (first mode) or as a brevis and longa (second mode). Garlandia adds, to be sure, that a reduction to the second mode is more correct than to the first mode because of the nature of the second half

105. Universal Edition (Wien, 1931).

106. R. Ficker, "Probleme der modalen Notation (Zur kritischen Gesamtausgabe der drei- und vierstimmigen Organa)," *Acta Musicologica, 18–19* (1946–47), 2.

107. See CS, *1*, 98 or 330; 338.

> of the measure[108] [i.e., short long]. This remark by both theorists is an unmistakable hint that in the preceding golden age of modal practice the third mode must have had quite another metrical meaning, that it is to be conceived neither as a first mode, nor a second mode, nor even as a mixture of both, but as an independent mode, valued for itself. The possibility here stated of the division of the initial longa in the sense of the first mode shows clearly that for Anonymous IV and Garlandia the memory was still living of the metrically indivisible character which the third mode, as a pure dactyl, containing only one measure, must have had originally. Had the third mode from the beginning been understood only as the metrical analogue of two measures of the second mode, then its postulation would have been at the very outset superfluous and completely senseless. In the golden age of the modes and therefore in organal style, the third mode is nothing other than the normal [!] one measure dactyl (𝅗𝅥.♩𝅗𝅥), therefore a 3/2 (3/4) measure and by no means a 6/4 (6/8) measure.[109]

It is only too evident from this quotation that Ficker has misunderstood the "unmistakable hint" of the theorists. In their declaration that the initial longa of the third mode is the equivalent of a foot of either the first or second mode Garlandia and Anonymous IV were stating a fact that is true for *motet and mensural notation*. The qualifying factor that it is better to reduce it to the second mode shows an understanding on their part of the true nature of the third mode in *modal* notation. Far from being uncertain about the nature of the third mode, they show a clear understanding of the difference between a modal and mensural interpretation of it. It is impossible from their statements to deduce a mysterious variant of the sixth mode. Ficker's "normal" dactyl is also somewhat startling. A normal dactyl in metrics consists of a long syllable and two short syllables, and the dactylic foot would consist of two equal halves, represented in notation by a compound measure 4/4 𝅗𝅥♩♩ and not as two 2/4 measures 𝅗𝅥|♩♩. The modal equivalent of the dactyl—if it is to be actually an equivalent—must then be understood also to have two equal halves. The only musical equivalent of this is a 6/4 or 6/8 measure, 𝅗𝅥.♩𝅗𝅥 or ♩.♪♩. It could not possibly be construed as 3/2 or 3/4 rhythm, since these divide a measure into thirds and not into two equal halves. Even if we accepted Ficker's belief that the third mode has the same time duration as the modi recti, we would be forced to transcribe the foot of this mode not, as in other modes, in 3/4 time but in 6/8 time.

108. CS, *I*, 98a: "Quare tertius modus et quartus potius reducuntur ad secundum, quam ad primum."

109. *Acta*, pp. 4–5.

Ficker then offers the notation itself as confirmation of his theory. In modal notation the third mode is represented by an isolated note followed by any number of three-note ligatures, but at times the initial note will be incorporated into the following ligature for the sake of convenience.

The sixth mode is also sometimes found in this latter form. The notation is the same in both cases, introducing an element of uncertainty into the transcription of them. Because these methods of notation are the same Ficker says that they represent either the sixth mode or his hypothetical variant of the sixth mode. But here Ficker has been led astray because he pays no heed to the historical development of the notation of the sixth mode. The first and most common method of notating the sixth mode was to write it in the form of either the first or second modes but adding a plica (a little line) to the end of each ligature, thus converting the final long note of the ligature into two equal breves rectae. For example, the sixth mode was written in the form of the first mode in the following manner:

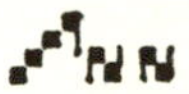

The lack of certainty in deciding the melodic interval intended by the plica led to the method of notation that resembles the third mode. Anonymous IV explicitly mentions this development of the notation of the sixth mode: "But because the plica [used in the sixth mode] sometimes greatly deceived all singers, unless they were the best singers of organum, because they did not know how much it [the interval] rose or descended; because of this, some wrote a four-note ligature at the beginning and followed it with three-note ligatures; . . ." [110] This method of writing the sixth mode was chosen not because it showed the essential similarity of the third and sixth modes but only to remove the uncertainty of indicating intervals inherent in the plica. In the next chapter it will be shown that if it were necessary or desirable to dispense with the plica in notating the sixth mode, only one alternative was possible—the alternative chosen by the scribes. Thus Ficker's theory of the equivalence of the third and sixth modes is supported neither by the notation nor by the statements of the theorists. We

110. CS, *I*, 347b: "Sed quia tractus ille quandoque decipit multum cantores omnes, quia nesciunt quandoque quantum que ascendit vel descendit, nisi fuissent optime organiste; propter hoc quidem posuerunt quatuor ligatas in principio sine tractu, et postmodum tres ligatas, tres, tres; . . ."

have no reason then to accept his method of transcription in 3/4 time, representing an equivalent time value for the feet of all modes; nor can we accept his hypothesis of the equivalence of the third and sixth modes.

The impossibility of the statements of Ficker indicates a fundamental misconception of the nature of the modes. The cause of his misunderstanding is visible from his table of the modes, all of which represent an equivalent value. He gives as metrical unities the following rhythmic values for all six modes: 𝅗𝅥♩, ♩𝅗𝅥, ♩.♪♩, (♪♩♩.), 𝅗𝅥., ♩♩♩. But the single ternary longa that he gives for the fifth mode does not represent a mode. No mode can exist except in a succession of time values. The other five modes conform to this fundamental law of the modal system, whereas the single longa does not. The single longa does not become a mode until it is combined with another longa. The true pattern of the fifth mode (two notes) will then be equivalent to two feet of the modi recti or one foot of the modi in ultra mensuram, the third and fourth modes. As the true fifth mode is equivalent to two feet of the modi recti, it will contain six tempora. Since the third and fourth modes are also equivalent to a foot of the fifth mode, it follows that the third and fourth modes must also have a total value of six tempora, i.e., a 6/4 or 6/8 measure. This is confirmed by the *Discantus positio vulgaris* (CS, *I*, 97a), where it is said of the combination of a tenor in the fifth mode with an upper part in the third mode, "then one long note of the tenor is the equivalent of another long in the motetus; the following longa of the tenor is the equivalent of the two breves of the motetus." Consequently one is justified in transcribing all modes in 6/8 time, for Ficker's theory of equivalence is completely untenable.

The achievement of the Notre Dame composers in creating a rhythmic system for polyphonic music cannot be praised too highly. Although the modal system is derived from metrics, it is not in any way dependent upon the prosody of the text being set to music. The musical rhythm is an independent one and thus the Notre Dame composers initiated the long development of purely musical rhythm which enabled music to free itself from its subservience to poetical rhythm and to develop rhythmic subtleties unknown to poetry. Even in its earliest stages modal rhythm permitted certain licenses in the treatment of the modes in a practice known as *fractio modorum* [111] or the breaking up of the modes. Essentially the fractio modorum implies nothing more than replacing the values of a modal pattern by other values.[112] The simplest example of this

111. Anon. IV, CS, *I*, 336b.

112. This is made clear by the St. Emmeram Anonymous who uses the term "equipollentia"

would be the substitution of two breves for the longa of the first or second modes. Such a substitution would create a foot of three breves and would be identical with a foot of the sixth mode. In this case we would have the substitution of a foot of one mode for another, an accepted practice according to the laws of rhythm. But even the theoretically indivisible brevis may be replaced by two or three lesser values known as semibreves, thus producing notes which are ultra mensuram. By this substitution of lesser values for any part of the modal pattern a very fluid rhythmic motion is attained. In this manner composers could create elaborate rhythmic lines by replacing the quantities of the modal pattern with other values. Nevertheless, the modal pattern is still considered to exist as the framework or skeleton upon which these freer rhythmic motions are erected. Anonymous IV, who alone of all theorists gives an extensive explanation of fractio modorum, makes it clear that the basic pattern of a mode is to be maintained no matter how extensively the individual quantities of the pattern are replaced by other values. He states that the second mode may be broken up in as many ways as the first mode, "but with this difference, that the first note [of the second mode] is usually a brevis and then follows a longa as it may be described; in contrast to the first mode which is a longa [followed by a] brevis . . ."[113] It is evident that the rigidity of the modal patterns is apparent rather than real and that the Notre Dame composers created a surprisingly flexible system of rhythm for their music.

To conclude this chapter on the modal system the following summary of the features of the modal system may be made:

1) Modal rhythm differs from modern rhythm in that it exists in the repetition of a pattern of time values. There are six such patterns or modes made up of combinations of notae rectae (one tempus and two tempora respectively) and notae ultra mensuram (a longa of three tempora, a brevis of two, and a semibrevis of less than one tempus).

2) The repetition of a pattern in actual tones is terminated by a rest. Rests thus divide a composition into groups of notes called ordines, which contain two or more repetitions of a given pattern.

3) An ordo will in practice usually end on the first part of the pattern and

instead of fractio modi. "Et nota quod equipollentia in omnibus modis intelligenda sunt. Equipollentia, dico ut si non sequitur longa vel brevis [primi modi], suo loco accipiatur illud quod loco earum reperitur."

113. CS, *I*, 338b: "Sed differentia talis est, quod prima est semper brevis, etc.; et tunc sequitur longa per descriptionem ejus per contrarium primi quod est longa brevis . . ."

will be followed by a rest completing the pattern. When a mode terminates in this fashion it is said to be perfect, because it allows the following ordo to continue in the same mode. An ordo which ends on the final part of the foot is said to have an imperfect modus, because the following ordo will appear to be in a different modus.

4) The equivalence of the modes is determined both by their total time value and by their plausus. In their total time value the modi recti are equivalent to each other, and the modi in ultra mensuram are equivalent to each other, but the modi in ultra mensuram are equivalent to two feet of the modi recti. Because of the plausus the first mode may not be combined with the second, third, or fourth modes, but only with the fifth and sixth modes. The other modes may all be combined with one another.

5) The quantities of the modal patterns may be replaced by other equivalent values.

6) Because an ordo must have at least two statements of the pattern, the modi recti are transcribed in 6/8 time (3 tempora + 3 tempora). Ordines with more than one repetition will usually repeat the pattern in multiples of two, so that these too are best expressed by a 6/8 measure. Since one foot of a modus in ultra mensuram is equivalent to two feet of a modus rectus, the foot of the former will also be transcribed in 6/8 time.

2. *The Notation of the Modes*

When the earliest composers of organum at Notre Dame took upon themselves the task of introducing rhythm into their compositions, they were faced with the almost insuperable difficulty of converting rhythmically indifferent signs of notation into rhythmically significant symbols. In the preceding chapter brief mention was made of the development of diastematic notation into its final form, the square notation which was incapable of signifying all the necessary rhythmic nuances. Presumably it was square notation in which Leonin wrote down his first rhythmic organa. It can only be assumed that Leonin used square notation, because we do not have the original manuscripts of the *Magnus liber* but only thirteenth-century copies of the original volume. But since these copies are all written in square notation and reproduce the same organa with only minor variants in the notation, it seems probable that they are based upon an original version which was also in square notation. In taking over quadratic notation the composers at first used the various symbols without any alteration of their physical appearance. This is not surprising in view of the fact that organum was based upon an original Gregorian chant, and the freely composed voices added to it were regarded only as a melodic troping of the chant. Consequently the original chant notation was retained for organum. Only later was the physical appearance of the notes altered in order to avoid ambiguity of interpretation and because of the exigencies of the new motet style. The normal form of the notational symbols was said by the thirteenth-century theorists to be with propriety (*cum proprietate*) and with perfection (*cum perfectione*). If the first part of a ligature were altered it was said to be without propriety (*sine proprietate*) or with opposite propriety (*cum opposita proprietate*). If the last part of a ligature were altered it was without perfection (*sine perfectione*). In the Notre Dame manuscripts the organa are notated almost entirely in normal note forms, although in a few instances the propriety of a ligature has been altered, presumably by the copyist, for the same ligature will be found in its normal form in the other manuscripts. (Although the number of ligatures sine proprietate or cum opposita proprietate is rather small, these ligatures are useful aids in deciphering the complicated notation of organum duplum.)

In the notation at their disposal the organistae had two forms of *notae simplices,* and , and a variety of ligatures. The principle ligatures are these:

Binaria *Ternaria* *Quaternaria*

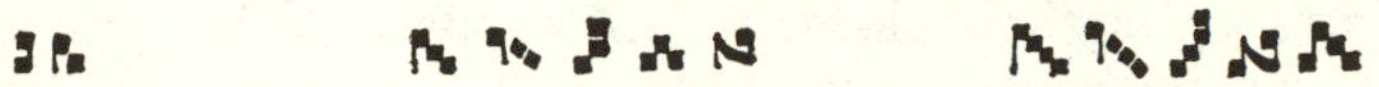

Two other signs were also employed. These were originally symbols of vocal embellishments, but were converted into rhythmic signs. The first of these is the plica, a small line added to the final note of ligature, (ex. a). If the plica were added to the final note of an ascending ligature, the head of the note would be turned to the right instead of to the left, as in example b. The latter method of writing, which alters the normal appearance of the ligature, was chosen for the sake of convenience, since it is almost impossible to add a plica to the normal form of an ascending ligature. The notae simplices may also have a plica added to them, (ex. c).

The other sign adopted by the composers was the *conjunctura* or *currentes,* rhomboid notes appended to a nota simplex or to the end of a ligature:

The conjunctura is used extremely often as a variant form of the descending ligature. The later innovations in the form of the ligatures, which occur but rarely in the Notre Dame manuscripts, are ligatures sine proprietate or cum opposita proprietate. (Ligatures with an altered final note are never to be found.) The lack of propriety is indicated in a descending ligature by the omission of the characteristic line added to the first note, while in an ascending ligature a downward line is added to the initial note:

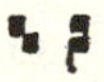

The sign of opposite propriety is an upward line added to the first note of any ligature,

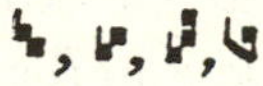

Together with the note forms of the Gregorian chant, the composers took over the fundamental rules of notation involving ligatures. 1) A ligature must not have more than one syllable. This rule arises from purely practical considerations. It is almost impossible to write more than one syllable under the compact form of a ligature, and furthermore there would be no way of ascertaining to what syllable a note of the ligature was to be applied if, for instance, two syllables were written under a ternary ligature. 2) If a syllable has a long melisma the notes of the melisma will be combined into various ligatures as much as possible. This rule also has a practical basis—to save parchment. 3) As a corollary of these rules it develops that a nota simplex will be used only when a syllable has only one tone or when a tone is repeated and consequently cannot be combined into a ligature. These rules are all valid for organum. Because organum is primarily a melismatic form of composition, it will be seen that it will be notated primarily in the form of ligatures.

Our problem now is to discover why the composers chose certain groupings of ligatures to represent the six modes. We know, of course, from the theorists what form of notation is used for each mode, but we find no explanation for the form. It is absolutely essential, however, that we uncover the reason why each form exists as it does. If once we understand the peculiar nature of the individual use of each ligature, we shall be able to reach sound conclusions about exceptional uses. Although each mode has a certain form of notation for itself, as often as not the rhythmic pattern of the mode is replaced by equivalent notes, either by lesser values (fractio modi) or by increasing the value of a long note (extensio modi). When the pattern is thus disturbed, the notation itself reflects this disturbance, making it difficult at times to ascertain what mode is intended. It is in these irregularities of notation that modern transcribers are most in disagreement. Most of such uncertainties can, however, be removed provided there is a fundamental understanding of the ligatures in their normal meanings. To this purpose we are going to reconstruct modal notation mode by mode, so that it may be understood why each mode necessarily is written in a certain pattern of ligatures and notes. The following reconstruction in its method owes much to the study by Michalitschke of the origin and development of mensural notation.[1] The premises from which Michalitschke starts are, however, different from those in this work, so that the results will be quite different. Michalitschke rests his theory upon certain assumptions concerning the normal reading of ligatures which were made by Ludwig in the discussion of modal rhythm and notation in his *Repertorium* (pp. 42 ff.)—assumptions which do not agree with the facts of the manuscripts and the premensuralist theorists. Since these assumptions cannot be accepted, our conclusions will be fundamentally different.

1. Anton Maria Michalitschke, "Studien zur Entstehung und Frühentwicklung der Mensuralnotation," *ZfMW*, *12* (1930), 257.

The reconstruction of modal notation will begin with the first mode, which was undoubtedly the first of all the modes to be given a definitive form of notation. The first mode is to be found on every page of the fascicles of organum duplum in the *Magnus liber* ascribed to Leonin by Anonymous IV, while other modes are extremely rare. The evidence of the music manuscripts that it was Leonin who created the first mode is corroborated by the explicit statement of the same Anonymous. After the definitions of ligatures with propriety and without propriety we find the following remark of a historical nature.

Those rules were used in many books of the old generation, and this was the case from the time of the great Perotin and in his time. But they did not know how to tell [formulate] these rules together with certain others that are written below, and always from the time of Leonin and for his part, because a binary ligature was placed then for a brevis and longa of time, and a ternary ligature likewise was placed for a longa, brevis and a longa, etc.[2]

It is Leonin, therefore, who first assigned specific values to the binaria and ternaria, the ligatures which are used to represent the first mode.

Because of the historical priority of the first mode, the notation of the other modes shows a dependency upon the notation of the first mode. In other words, they were built upon certain considerations that are inherent in the notation of the first mode. For this reason it is essential to understand the logic which lies behind the physical appearance of the notation of the first mode. When it was decided to impose a rhythm upon the long melismata of the duplum, the composer was confronted with two inescapable facts. 1) The rhythm was to be expressed in ligatures rather than in single notes, because of the accepted manner of notating melismatic song. Furthermore a notation employing only notae simplices would be meaningless because such notes were rhythmically indifferent. 2) The rhythm chosen consisted of the repetition of a pattern (long, short) which would exist within a phrase or ordo, necessarily terminating on the first part of the pattern, if the same pattern was to be continued in the following ordo. From these meager considerations the elaborate system of modal notation was constructed according to a plan of beautiful simplicity and logic.

Since an ordo, expressed in ligatures, could be of any length, only two of the notes within the series of ligatures would invariably have at the same time a

2. CS, *I*, 341b: "Iste regule utuntur in pluribus libris antiquorum, et hoc a parte et in suo tempore Perotini Magni; sed nesciebant narrare ipsas cum quibusdam aliis postpositis, et semper a tempore Leonis pro parte, quoniam due ligate tunc temporis pro brevi longa ponebantur, et tres ligate simili modi in pluribus locis pro longa brevi, etc." I have emended this passage from a microfilm of the original (British Museum, Royal 12.C.VI). In the first phrase "parte" must be read "tempore." At the end of the sentence "longa" must be added after "brevi."

definite time value and a definite position within the ligatures. The first note of the first ligature would of necessity be a long of two tempora and the last note of the last ligature would also be a long. Between these two extremes would lie a series of notes alternately short and long. But unless the ligatures were arranged in a meaningful way, these interior notes would be grouped into ligatures that would all be read in a different manner. This fact may be illustrated by a haphazard series of ligatures:

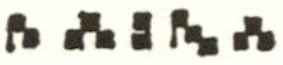

If we read these notes alternately long and short, it will be seen that the first binaria reads long, short; the second ligature long, short, long; the third short, long; the fourth short, long, short, and the last long, short, long. In this series the ligatures are meaningless since a binaria reads both long, short and short, long; while a ternaria is long, short, long as well as short, long, short.

The problem then is to establish a uniform meaning for the ligatures. If now we start with the end of an ordo, we find that the last note is a long and is necessarily also the final note of a ligature. The preceding note of the ligature must be short because of the pattern of the first mode. Since the pattern of the first mode includes only one long and one short, it is evident that a final two-note ligature will contain both parts of the modal pattern. A binaria at the end of an ordo would be read in the order short, long. To construct an ordo—still working backwards—it would then be necessary to keep prefixing binariae, each of which would always be read short, long. In this manner all but the first note of an ordo would be acounted for. Thus:

long *short long* *short long* *short long*

Because the initial long must not, according to the rules of melismatic writing, be an isolated note but must be part of a ligature, it follows that this note will be grouped with the following binaria into a ternary ligature reading long, short, long. The notation of the first mode as it exists within an ordo would thus consist of a ternaria followed by sufficient binariae to account for all the notes in the ordo. An ordo containing seven notes accordingly would be written:

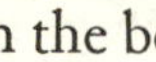

An ordo of only three notes would be represented by a single ternaria.

If we construct the first mode from the beginning instead of the end, we shall arrive at the same conclusions. The first ordo of the first mode which contains only three notes would be represented by a ternary ligature. Since the three notes have the order long, short, long, the ligature of necessity will read long, short, long. If we then construct the second ordo, the two notes added to the first ordo will also be grouped into a ligature and this binaria will read short, long. Since the ordines increase by adding a brevis and longa to the preceding ordo, one needs only to add a binaria to the preceding ordo to notate a larger ordo. It is in this manner that the binaria and ternaria come to have an explicit meaning. It will be seen that there is a close resemblance between the two ligatures. In both the binaria and the ternaria the final note is a longa and the preceding note is a brevis. While the binaria retains this fundamental meaning in other modes, the ternaria can have other readings as well. But it is necessary to recognize the fact that the most important reading of a ternaria is long, short, long. For the pre-Franconian theorists the ternaria cum proprietate et perfectione was to be read in this manner. The author of the *Discantus positio vulgaris* states: "Whatever two notes are joined in discant, the first note is a brevis, the second a longa, unless the first note is larger than the second, e.g. . When, however, three notes are joined together, if a rest precedes them the first note is long, the second a brevis, and the third a long." [3] Garlandia is even more explicit: "In every ligature with propriety and perfection, the penultimate note is said to be a brevis, and the final note a longa; if there are any notes preceding the brevis, they are all [in sum] equivalent to a longa." [4] The primary meaning of a ternaria is thus long, short, long and not brevis, brevis altera, perfect longa as it was for Franco of Cologne and all succeeding theorists.

The importance of this reading of the ternaria is attested by the fact that for the pre-Franconian theorists the ternaria representing long, short, long was always a normal or unaltered ligature. If a ternaria was to be interpreted in another manner, its physical appearance had to be altered. A ligature of which the appearance of the first note was altered (sine proprietate) signified a pattern just the opposite of the normal ligature: a ligature sine proprietate was to be read long, short in the case of a binaria, and short, long, short in the case of a ter-

3. CS, *1*, 94b, 95a: "Quecunque due note ligantur in discantu, prima est brevis, secunda longa, nisi prima grossior sit secunda, ut hic: . Quando autem tres, si pausa precedit, prima est longa, secunda brevis, tertia longa."

4. CS, *1*, 99b, 100a: "Omnis figura ligata cum proprietate posita et perfecta, penultima dicitur esse brevis, et ultima longa; si sint precedentes, tunc omnes ponuntur pro longa. . . ." Cf. Garlandia, CS, *1*, 178b; Pseudo-Aristotle, CS, *1*, 274a,b; Anon. IV, CS, *1*, 341b; Anon. VII, CS, *1*, 381b; Sowa, p. 36, ll.31–34.

naria.[5] In other words the normalcy of the reading long, short, long for a ternaria is confirmed by a normal ligature; a deviation from this primal meaning is indicated by an abnormal ligature. Although the various forms of the ligatures described by the theorists have little significance for the manuscripts of Notre Dame organum (since these were written almost exclusively in normal ligatures), the descriptions of these ligatures throw a strong light upon their evolution. The St. Emmeram Anonymous, in establishing the order of the modes, has this to say: "The first mode is said to be first because it is easier or smoother [*levior*] than all the others and it is first because it is more proper and more general than all the others. And this is because it has more general and nobler ligatures, to which other ligatures with propriety and perfection are to be reduced according to species and artifice." [6] According to this statement, it is the normalcy of its ligatures which gives the first mode its priority. We have already seen that the unaltered binaria and ternaria were assigned definite values in the first mode and so it is apparent that the "nobler" ternaria of the first mode corresponds to the "nobler and more general" reading of the ligature as long, short, long. It becomes very clear that the ternaria signifying long, short, long must have been the first of the various readings of the ternaria to be formulated.

The next step in modal evolution was the creation of the so-called fifth mode. In the preceding chapter it was shown that in all probability it was Perotin who first organized this mode out of the undifferentiated series of long notes in the tenor.[7] Leonin had made extensive use of sections in the organum wherein the tenor moved more rapidly so that each note of the tenor was equivalent to a foot of the first mode in the duplum and thus contained three tempora. But Leonin apparently did not treat this series of ternary longs according to the laws of a true mode. It was, according to Anonymous IV, Perotin who first organized this series of longs into the so-called fifth mode by establishing a foot of two longs, which was then presented in ordines according to the precepts of modal rhythm. In practice the fifth mode exists almost exclusively in the first ordo, so that we

5. Garlandia, CS, *1*, 178b: "Every ligature without propriety and with perfection has a value the opposite of a ligature with propriety." "Omnis figura sine proprietate et perfecta posita valet per oppositum cum proprietate." Cf. Anon. IV, CS, *1*, 341b: "Iterato omnis figura sine proprietate et perfectione [perfecta?] opposito modo se habet sic, penultima longa, ultima vero brevis."

6. Sowa, p. 74, ll.16–20: "Primus igitur dicitur primus, quia levior est et communior omnibus aliis, item primus quia dignior et generalior omnibus aliis est. Et hoc est quia in se generaliores et nobiliores figuras continet, ad quas cetere figure cum proprietate posite et perfecte sunt specialiter ac artificialiter reducende, . . ."

7. See pp. 47 f., above.

find that the tenor moves in a succession of three ternary longs followed by a rest of three tempora.

The notes of the fifth mode were already supplied with a form of notation since the long notes of the tenor were always written as notae simplices. The first ordo of this mode would be written as three notae simplices followed by a rest. To make this mode conform to the manner of notation of the upper parts, and also for the sake of convenience, it became the practice to join these three notes into a ligature, so that a ternary ligature assumed the additional meaning of ♩.♩.♩.. Such a reading for the ternaria is, of course, contrary to all rules for ligatures in either modal or mensural notation, and all theorists agree in condemning this usage as an abuse. Anonymous IV says that such a ligature is not correct, "but this use is to be found in the tenors of discant or motets for the sake of beautiful notation according to the rule: 'that which we may join is not to be separated.' "[8] However, a ligature was written only for the first ordo of the fifth mode. If any other ordo were employed all the notes would be single notes. Although this ligature used for the first ordo does not conform to the rules of ligature writing, there can be no possibility of misunderstanding its meaning. The fifth mode appears almost exclusively in the tenor and so this irregular ligature will be confined to the tenor part. If the fifth mode appears in the upper voices it will always be notated by single longae. The tenor thus was given a definite rhythmic pattern of its own by Perotin and also was assigned a ternary ligature having a time value to be found only in the ternariae of the tenor. The tenor consequently was enabled to move independently in phrases or ordines which may or may not coincide in length with the ordines of the upper voice.

That the fifth mode or tenor mode never quite freed itself from a contingence upon the upper voices is to be seen in a tenor formula that was a favorite among the successors to Leonin. Frequently in the clausulae one finds in the tenor two single notes followed by a rest and a ternaria followed by a rest. These notes are to be translated in 6/8 time:

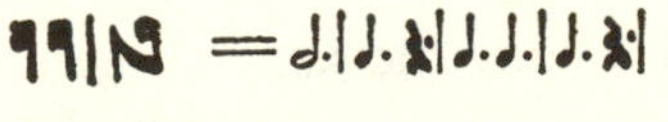

One may say that in a sense the first two notes are a variant of the fifth mode, in that the initial note incorporates both values of the foot of the fifth mode. There is nothing, however, in the notation itself to correspond to these values. The

8. CS, *1*, 347a: "Sed usus quidem est in tenoribus discantuum sive motellorum et hoc propter pulchritudinem punctandi propter regulam quamdam: *'quod possumus conjungere, non disjungatur.'* "

two initial notes are represented by the same sign, even though they actually are different values. One can only establish the value of these notes by noticing their relationship to the number of notes in the upper voices. Only in a few examples is the initial longa differentiated by being notated as a duplex longa. It is apparent then that the fifth mode never reached a status of independence comparable to that of the other modes which are written as successions of ligatures with unalterable values.

The sixth mode, or the rudiments of a sixth mode, appeared simultaneously with the introduction of the first mode, but it did not reach a completely independent status until the era of Perotin. Again it appears to be Perotin who rationalizes a phenomenon of the earlier organum into a modal pattern or metrical equivalent. One will search in vain for a true, systematized sixth mode in the organum purum; even the substitute clausulae reveal only a handful of examples of the sixth mode. But in the organum triplum one encounters numerous examples of an autonomous sixth mode, having a foot of three breves. The inception of the sixth mode is to be discerned in the practice of Leonin of replacing the longa value of the first mode by two breves. Leonin almost regularly enlivens the stiff pattern of a pure first mode by the occasional introduction of smaller values for the longa. The most common method of notating these shorter values is to add a plica to single notes or to the final note of a ligature, as the case may be. The plica had been originally the sign of a liquescent neume indicating some form of an embellishment of the note to which it was appended. Leonin, however, gave the plica a specific rhythmic value. It took half the time value of a brevis recta or longa recta and one-third the value of a ternary longa. At the same time the duration of the note to which the plica was added was shortened by the value assumed by the plica.[9] Thus the longa plicata, if it is a longa recta, is to be read ♪♪; if it is a ternary longa, it would be read ♩♪. A brevis plicata would equal 𝅘𝅥𝅯𝅘𝅥𝅯, if it were a recta brevis; or ♪♪, if a brevis altera. Although the plica actually diminishes the value of a note, the note itself is still considered to be a brevis or longa of whatever modal pattern. In other words, the note together with its plica will occupy the same amount of time as the note alone

9. Pseudo-Aristotle, CS, *I*, 273a: "[The perfect longa with a plica] has every power, rule and nature that a perfect long has, except that two tempora are retained by the body of the note and one by the plica, etc." "[Plica perfecta] habet autem omnem potestatem, regulam et naturam quam habet perfecta longa, nisi quod in corpore duo tempora tenet et unum in membris. . . . Secunda differentia est plica imperfecta . . . et continet unum tempus in corpore et reliquam in membris." Cf. Sowa, p. 19, l.28 ff.

would do.[10] As for the pitch, the plica represents an interval above or below the note to which it is added, depending upon whether the line is drawn upward or downward from the note itself. Most of the time it is the neighboring note that the plica stands for, a fact which can be substantiated by comparing variant readings in which the plica tone is written as a note instead. In transcription the plica is written as a note with an oblique line drawn through the stem of the note, not because it is to be thought of as a grace note, but merely because this is a convenient, visual clue to the original notation of this note.

Still another means of notation is needed if the initial longa of the first mode is to be supplanted by two breves. Since this longa is the first note of a ternary ligature it is impossible to add a plica to it. In this case the two brevis values are represented by an additional note within the ligature, so that we no longer have a ternaria opening the first mode, but a quaternaria, of which the first two notes are equivalent to the initial note of a ternary ligature. We see here the application of the rule of Garlandia: "In every ligature with propriety and perfection, the penultimate note is said to be a brevis, and the final note a longa; if there are any notes preceding the brevis, they are all [in sum] equivalent to a long." [11] An example of a quaternaria as well as a ligatura plicata used for the replacement of a long value by two breves is to be found in this ordo from *Sed sic eum.* (W_1, f. 27′, last brace):

It is evident from the appearance of the ligatures that this is still a first mode. The quaternaria replaces the opening ternaria ligature, while the following ligatures are the usual binaria of the first mode.

But the quaternaria and the plica are not the only method of notation used to indicate the breaking up of a long into two breves. At times the composer wishes to replace a longa at the end of a ligature with two breves of the same pitch. But the second of these notes cannot be written as a plica because a plica represents a tone either higher or lower than the note to which it is added. At the same time one cannot add this note to the ligature in a manner analogous to the use of a

10. Cf. Garlandia's rule: "In every ligature with propriety and perfection and with a plica the last note with the plica has the value of a long; because the plica is only a sign which divides a tone into another tone." CS, *1,* 178b: "Omnis [omnes] figure cum plica et proprietate, et perfecte, ultima cum plica, valet longam; quia plica nihil est, nisi signum dividens sonum in sono diverso."

11. CS, *1,* 99b, 100a.

quaternaria when the initial longa is broken. One cannot do this because it is impossible to include two repeated notes of the same pitch in a ligature. The only possibility then is to add this note to the beginning of the following ligature, thus:

The first ternaria represents the opening ternaria of the first mode. The final note of this ligature is understood in this case to be a brevis which is supplemented by the opening brevis value of the next ligature and so these two breves occupy the position of the usual longa of the first mode. The last two notes of the second ternaria conform to the rule: last note, longa; penultimate, brevis.

This irregular ternaria is also frequently to be found even in cases where no repeated notes are involved. Such a usage derives from the desire of the composer to avoid the ambiguity of the plica, which denotes no particular interval, but only a higher or lower interval. The choice of the interval depends upon the musical context. If the nota plicata is followed by a note a third higher or lower, the plica will be sung as the interval filling in this third. If the nota plicata is followed by a note a fourth or fifth higher or lower, it becomes more difficult to decide which of the intervening intervals is represented by the plica. Because of this uncertainty the plica is frequently not employed,[12] but instead the note which would have been written as a plica is added to the beginning of the following ligature. It could not possibly be added as a note to the ligature of which it is properly a partial value because of the absolute rule, the last note of a ligature is a longa, the penultimate a brevis. It is impossible, for instance, to represent the breaking of the final longa of a ternaria by writing a quaternaria instead, assuming that the final note of this quaternaria would then represent a brevis value subtracted from the previous note. The only alternative is to add this brevis to the following ligature. For example, in the series of ligatures:

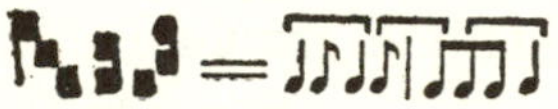

the third longa value of the ordo has been replaced by two breves and the second of these breves has not been written as a plica added to the final note of the ligature but has been added to the beginning of the last ligature. It will be seen that, despite the irregularity of the appearance of this ternary ligature within the proper ligature pattern of the first mode, all the ligatures still conform to

12. Anon. IV's explanation of this usage is quoted above, p. 52.

the rule for the final and the penultimate notes, for the binaria ligature in the above example is assumed to terminate with a long, whose "tone is divided into another tone" by the first note of the following ternaria.

All these methods of notating the breaking of a longa are to be found in the organa of Leonin. An examination of the music will reveal how common the practice is, and it will also make clear that such dissolutions occur for only some of the longae within an ordo of the first mode. Only occasionally will all the longae be replaced by breves, so that a true sixth mode appears. Moreover such breakings of the longa will always be notated in a manner that preserves the law of the penultimate and final notes of ligatures. Only one violation of this law is ever to be found and this violation is rare indeed, occurring only in the works of Leonin's successors. This infraction of the rule comes occasionally in the second mode, when the longa of the modal pattern is broken. In most cases the final long note of a binaria will be broken by means of a plica, but once in a while one finds this binaria plicata written instead as a ternaria. This ternaria of course disobeys the law of the final note of a ligature, since the final note is here a brevis. But this very infrequent practice is usually easily detectable, because of the context of the preceding and following ligatures.

Such breakings of the longa, whereby a foot of the first mode contained three brevis notes, offered the possibility of creating a new mode in which all feet contain three breves—i.e., the sixth mode or tribrach. All that was needed to create such a mode was to break all the longae of the first (rarely the second) mode, symbolizing this with one of the methods of notation described above. The theorists offer two forms of notation, one using plicae, the other replacing the plicae by adding the note represented by the plica to the succeeding ligature. The sixth mode may be written:

1) 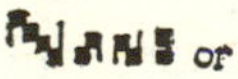 or 2) 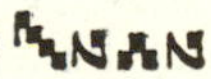

Both forms mean exactly the same thing. In practice we find both methods used within the same ordo and also simultaneously in different voices. Since both methods are variations of the notation of the first mode it was assumed that the final note would be read as a longa. When this mode is related to a second mode the final note is taken to be a brevis. A classic example of the use of the sixth mode is to be found in *Sed sic eum,* (F, last ordo of f. 18 and beginning of f. 19).

Both Ludwig and Husmann have misunderstood the significance of the ligatura ternaria inserted in place of a binaria plicata in the first mode. Ludwig says correctly that these ternariae are ornamentations of the straightforward rhythm of the first mode, but gives as an example [13] the phrase:

 = ternaria, ternaria, ternaria, binaria.

Such a reading is contrary to the rules for ligatures of the first mode with propriety and perfection, since the last note of the ligature does not stand for a long. Furthermore such a transcription does not make musical sense, since the final note of such ternariae is also a consonant note with the tenor and this consonance should coincide with the sounding of the tenor note. An examination of the manuscripts will reveal immediately that in such ternariae it is the final note which forms a consonance with the tenor. It is obvious then that the final note is intended to stand for a longa, which must form a musical consonance with the tenor according to the rule formulated by Anonymous IV: "Every odd note [1, 3, 5, etc.] of the first mode is a longa and must form a consonance with the tenor. The remaining even notes [2, 4, 6, etc.] are placed indifferently [in consonance or dissonance]." [14] If one attempts to transcribe by Ludwig's method one quickly perceives that the rule of consonance will be constantly disobeyed by placing the second note of such a ternaria where a longa would fall in the modal pattern. Husmann, on the other hand, transcribes these ternariae in another manner.[15] He advocates that such a ternaria is to be read ♫ 𝅗𝅥, assuming apparently that the first two notes of the ligature stand for a brevis. He arrives at this conclusion mostly from the evidence of the very late Montpellier manuscript, which employs mensural signs. Moreover, he completely ignores the evidence of the Notre Dame manuscripts, which in many instances will use a plica in one manuscript, while another manuscript will use a ternaria ligature, thus indicating that the first two notes of the ternaria are to be read as two equal breves. Husmann insists upon his reading because he will not admit the validity of the second manner of writing the sixth mode given above, for it resembles the notation of the third mode. In so doing he ignores Anonymous IV's direct statement that this manner of notating the sixth mode was created to avoid the equivocal melodic meaning of the plica.

Thus far we have examined the first, fifth, and sixth modes. It appears that the first mode with the consequent establishment of fundamental meanings for

13. *Repertorium,* p. 45.

14. CS, *I*, 356b: "Omnia puncta imparia primi modi sunt longa, et cum tenore concordare debent. Reliquia vero paria indifferenter ponuntur."

15. H. Husmann, *Die dreistimmigen Organa,* pp. 10–13.

the binaria and ternaria was the contribution of Leonin who at the same time paved the way for the creation of the fifth and sixth modes through his use of series of ternary longs in the tenor and his practice of breaking the long of the first mode into two equivalent breves. According to the evidence of the manuscripts it was Perotin and his successors who actually established these series of ternary longs or breves rectae as true modes. The completion of the modal system by the addition of the second, third, and fourth modes is somewhat more difficult to establish chronologically. In the case of the second and fourth modes it is safe to say that these must have been the creation of Perotin and his contemporaries for they are virtually nonexistent in the earliest version of the *Magnus liber* contained in W1. There are no examples of the fourth mode to be found and the second mode occurs so rarely that in all probability these isolated examples are substitutions for Leonin's original version. However, there are many clausulae in this same collection that are obviously in the third mode. At the same time the notation in these clausulae is somewhat equivocal, for sometimes it appears to be a variant of the first mode rather than a true third mode. In all, this earliest manuscript of the *Magnus liber* of Leonin contains twenty-four examples of the third mode, two of which however are identical.[16] The prevalence of this mode seems to indicate that it was Leonin who created it, an inference supported by the fact that in all but three instances the tenor is nonmodal.[17] Since the third mode apparently was evolved before the second or fourth modes, it is the next mode to be discussed.

In the modal system the third mode is a modus in ultra mensuram, for it consists of a longa of three tempora, a brevis recta, and a brevis altera. Despite the fact that the second half of the pattern contains a note of one tempus and one of two tempora, the second of these two notes is never referred to as a longa recta but is always called a brevis altera. The insistence upon this term reveals that the pattern of the third mode must have been regarded as the equivalent of a dactyl. Indeed we have already seen that the St. Emmeram Anonymous states that the third mode is called ultra mensuram because the longa of three tempora and the brevis of two tempora exceed the proper measure of the metrical longa and brevis.[18] The transformation of the dactyl of four tempora into a modal pattern of six tempora is one of the most curious phenomena of the modal

16. The first clausulae of *Ascendens Xristus,* f. 35 and *Judicabunt,* f. 44′.

17. The final clausula of *Assumpta est Maria,* f. 39′; "tudi" from *Vitam petit,* f. 45′; and "et exaltavi" from *Posui adjutorium,* f. 47.

18. See above, n. 26, p. 26.

system and is to be explained in part through the priority of the first mode and in part through the inability of the modal system to represent temporal values by specific note signs.

In the first mode it frequently happens that a brevis of the modal pattern is suppressed so that a ternary long replaces the usual pattern of a longa and brevis. It would be impossible for a binary longa to succeed another such without disrupting the modal rhythm. Hence Anonymous VII in his rules for the first mode states that "a longa before a longa equals a longa and brevis." [19] This same rule applies equally to the series of tenor notes each of which is equivalent to a foot of the first mode in the duplum, thereby coming to have a value of three tempora. The practice of substituting a ternary long for a foot of the first mode in the duplum, as well as the series of ternary longs in the tenor, led to the formulation of the rule that is stated in one form or another by all the theorists: "a longa before a longa has the value of three tempora." [20] An application of this rule is to be seen in the clausula "mus" of *Sicut audivimus* (W1, f. 29′, f. 30). This clausula is obviously in the first mode, but the first ordo consists of a nota simplex followed by a ternaria and another nota simplex. The initial note is a ternary longa replacing the first foot of the first mode. Since this longa precedes another longa, it has, according to the rule, a value of three tempora. Similarly, the final note of the ternary ligature, which is to be read as a longa, becomes a ternary longa since it precedes another longa. The series of long notes in the tenor of this same clausula also comes under this rule. It is apparent that the nota simplex used in this manner comes to be the equivalent of a foot of the first mode and consequently has three tempora. The single note when used in conjunction with the first mode thus receives an absolute value. (I do not, of course, include here the single notes used when a tone is repeated and which cannot be grouped in a ligature for this reason.) The nota simplex in modal notation becomes the symbol of a longa in ultra mensuram, of a long which deviates from the correct value of two tempora.

19. CS, *I*, 378b: ". . . longa ante longam valet longam et brevem."

20. Johannes de Garlandia, CS, *I*, 97b: ". . . longa ante longam valet tria tempora"; 176a: ". . . longa ante longam valet longam et brevem." *Discantus positio vulgaris*, 95a: ". . . si nota longa sequitur, tertia [nota ligaturae] erit longior longa."

Anon. VII, CS, *I*, 378b: ". . . longa ante longam valet longam et brevem."

Walter Odington, CS, *I*, 236b: "Longa perficitur cum longa precedit."

Pseudo-Aristotle, CS, *I*, 270b: ". . . quandocunque longa reperta est ante longam semper tria tempora tenet; . . ."

St. Emmeram Anon., Sowa, p. 24, l.24: "longa ante longam valet tria tempora . . ."

If one keeps in mind the fact that the nota simplex as well as the binary and ternary ligatures were assigned quite specific meanings in conjunction with the first mode, it is not difficult to see what problems arose when it came to finding a pattern of notation for the third mode. Although the pattern of the dactyl consists of a longa and two breves, these values could not simply be translated into a ternaria, for a ternaria at the beginning of an ordo had already been given the basic meaning of longa, brevis, longa. To read such a ligature as longa, brevis, brevis would violate the fundamental law that the final note of a ligature is a longa and would throw the whole modal system into a state of confusion. Only one solution was possible for the notation of an ordo of this pattern: the first longa could be represented by a nota simplex, while the remaining two breves and longa could be grouped together into a ternary ligature which would conform to the rule about the penultimate and final notes. But here again ambiguity would arise, for the nota simplex in the first mode, as well as in the series of tenor notes, had become the symbol for a tone lasting three tempora. Thus the composer was confronted with the choice of either admitting an element of uncertainty into modal notation by using the nota simplex as a longa of two tempora as well as three, or of transforming the nature of the dactyl. As we know, it was the latter alternative that was chosen and the third mode was given the value of a longa of three tempora plus a brevis of one tempus and one of two tempora. The levatio and positio of this variant of the dactyl would, however, have the same ratio of one to one as its original. At the same time, this new pattern would have the advantage of admitting combinations with other modes.

That the peculiar nature of the third mode depends upon factors derived from the first mode is to be seen in Garlandia's explanation of this mode. "The third mode," he writes, "consists of a longa and two breves; and two breves equal a longa." Here Garlandia is stating the fundamental relationship of the brevis recta and longa recta as they exist in metrics. "Likewise a longa before a longa equals a longa and brevis, and thus equals three tempora." This is, of course, a rule drawn from the practice of substituting a single longa for a foot of the first mode and from the succession of tenor notes which are equivalent to a foot of the first mode in the duplum. These two rules, one drawn from metrics and the other from a factor of polyphonic music, are then combined. "Therefore a longa before two breves has three tempora and thus equals a longa and brevis, or brevis and longa." The implication of this statement is then realized along lines familiar to all who are acquainted with scholastic reasoning. If two breves equal a longa, then these two breves when placed before a longa must be subject to the rule: longa ante longam valet tria tempora. Therefore two breves before a long "are the equivalent of a longa and brevis or brevis and longa." If two breves are equal to three tempora, one of these breves must be longer than the other, but which of the two will be longer? According to Garlandia it will be the second of the two breves, for "if there are several breves in modi ultra mensuram, the one nearest the end must be held longer. Therefore these two breves are the equivalent of a brevis and longa; and not a longa and brevis." [21] Although the logic of Garlandia's argument is not beyond reproach, it is perhaps the only way in which the relationship of the metrical longa and brevis can be reconciled with the longa ultra mensuram established as a practice in the first mode. The argument itself reveals that in the third mode metrical theory came into conflict with musical fact and that theory was forced to yield in order that a coherent, meaningful system of notation and musical practice could be retained.

The third mode, no longer a dactyl of four tempora but a modus in ultra mensuram, was thus given a notation of a nota simplex followed by as many ternariae as are necessary to represent the number of notes in the ordo.[22] Each ternaria has the meaning of brevis recta, brevis altera, ternary longa. This is yet another interpretation of the ternary ligature. Nevertheless, the pre-Franconian theorists obviously considered this simply as a variant of the normal ternaria, for all agree in notating this ligature with propriety and perfection. The St. Emmeram Anonymous admits that this ligature is an exception to the more usual reading of longa recta, brevis recta, longa recta,[23] but only because its values are ultra mensuram.[24] If the theorists had considered this ligature to be a deviation from the law of the penultimate and final notes, surely they would have altered the form of the ligature as they did in the case of the second mode.[25]

21. The whole passage runs in this way: ". . . quia tertius constat ex longa et duabus brevibus; et due breves equipollent longe; et longa ante longam valet longam et brevem, et sic valet tria tempora. Quare longa ante duas breves valet tria tempora, et sic valet longam et brevem, vel brevem et longam. Item due breves equipollent longe; ergo si ponantur ante longam valent tria tempora; ergo valent longam et brevem; vel e converso. Unde regula: si sint plures breves in modis obliquis, que magis appropinquatur fini, longior debet proferri; ergo ille due valent brevem et longam; et non longam et brevem." (CS, *I*, 98a)

22. At times the longa is grouped with the following ternaria to form a quaternaria.

23. Sowa, p. 36, l.37: "Hec est autem exceptio regule supradicte, eo quod in tercia specie et in quarta aliter se habent in effectu."

24. *Ibid.*, p. 84, l.15 f.

25. See below, p. 76.

We must assume therefore that this usage of the ternaria was sanctioned because the modal pattern was understood to end with two breves and not with a brevis and longa recta. The ternaria cum proprietate et perfectione, which ends with a brevis and longa, would thus be a perfectly satisfactory expression for the second half and first half of the pattern of the third mode.

There still remains some uncertainty about the order of the brevis and the brevis altera. The *Discantus positio vulgaris* is silent on this matter, but from Anonymous VII on, the theorists agree that the larger brevis should come at the end. On the other hand there is evidence that this order may originally have been reversed. Anonymous IV makes the statement that "there are some modes which are called unusual modes, as if they were irregular although they are not, such as in parts of England and elsewhere when they say longa, longa, brevis; longa, longa, brevis." [26] This would appear to be a variant of the third mode in which the values are to be read as ternary longa, brevis altera (longa) and brevis. That this irregular mode is related to the third mode seems to be confirmed by Anonymous IV in another passage dealing with the notation of this mode. Here he states: "Wherefore it follows that the first two notes of a ternary ligature after a longa are breves, but the English sing in a certain irregular manner. Concerning this same mode they say a binary ligature and a brevis, etc., and sometimes this suits them, sometimes not." [27] This passage as it stands does not make sense, but it does seem to be related to the previous, more lucid statement.

This casual reference to an irregular mode may possibly indicate that an earlier practice of placing the brevis altera before the brevis recta still lingered on in a country which was peripheral to the main tradition of Notre Dame. This same practice also suggests that the third mode may once have been nothing but a variant of the first mode in which every other foot has been replaced by a ternary long. The relationship of the third mode to the first mode is referred to by Anonymous IV in his presentation of the fractio modorum. In

26. CS, *I*, 328a: "Iterato sunt et alii modi qui dicuntur modi unisitati [sic], quasi irregulares quamvis non sint, veluti in partibus Anglie et alibi, cum dicunt longa, longa brevis; longa, longa brevis; . . ." Cf. Garlandia, CS, *I*, 97b: "Aliqui addunt modos alios . . . ut due longe et brevis . . ."

27. "Quare sequitur quod tres ligate post longam, due prime sunt breves, sed in quodam modo irregulari veluti canunt Anglici. Dicunt de isto modo duas ligatas, et unam brevem, etc., et quandoque eis competit, quandoque non." (CS, *I*, 346b.) In all probability "duas ligatas" should be emended to "duas longas."

speaking of the fractio of the third mode he states that it may be reduced either to the second mode or to the first.[28] The latter possibility could be true only if the first of the two breves was construed to be the longer. The manuscripts themselves seem to indicate that such is the case. In Leonin's *Magnus liber* there are numerous passages seemingly in the third mode in which the ternary ligatures frequently are broken up because of the appearance of a new syllable in the text. In this case the two breves are represented either by a binaria or by a longa plicata. Both practices are to be found in one and the same clausula, indicating that the binaria and the longa plicata are equivalent in meaning. An excellent illustration of this is to be found in the section of *Gabrielem archangelum* (W_1, f. 18′) beginning with the words "de spiritu sancto." But according to the theorists such a longa plicata is to be read as two tempora for the note and one for the plica.[29] Such a method of notation seems to indicate that the longer value precedes the shorter. Moreover, the binariae in this case are not necessarily to be read as brevis, longa, but are to be understood as forming a ternary ligature with the following longa, a ligature which is to be read as longa, brevis, longa.[30]

It is my belief that the passages in Leonin's work which have the appearance of being in the third mode are in reality nothing but a variant of the first mode. But at the same time this variant offers the possibility of being codified into a true mode in its own right. Just as the substitution of two breves for a longa of the first mode led to the creation of the sixth mode, so the substitution of a ternary longa for every other foot of the first mode led to the creation of the third mode. It may be conjectured that in the process of the transformation of this usage into the third mode after Leonin's time the need for a sharper differentiation between the first mode and the third mode brought about the reversal of the values of the second part of the foot. Since a dactyl concludes with two breves, it is more appropriate that the first of these, if they must be of unequal value, should be the shorter. Because the notation of passages seemingly in the third mode in the *Magnus liber* frequently appear to be not a true third mode but merely extensio modi, I have transcribed them as ♩.♩♪♩., etc. In the sub-

28. CS, *I*, 338b: "Quod si iste modus reducatur ad modum secundum, dividatur vel frangatur juxta ordinem fractionis ejusdem; si ad primum secundum ordinem primi frangatur . . . Frange igitur secundum possibilitatem vocis humane, et secundum quod melius competit juxta similitudinem modi secundi vel primi . . ."

29. Pseudo-Aristotle, CS, *I*, 273a: "[Longa perfecta plicata] habet autem omnem potestatem, regulam et naturam quam habet perfecta longa, nisi quod in corpore duo tempora tenet et unum in membris."

30. See Chapter 4.

stitute clausulae and in the three- and four-part organa, however, I have taken the notation to indicate a true third mode and have transcribed it accordingly.

The fourth mode is the next to last mode to be considered. It plays but a small role in the Notre Dame organa and seems to have been evolved merely to round out the modal system. As it is, the theorists pay scant heed to it. The fourth mode is the equivalent of the anapest and as such it has a pattern which is the opposite of the third mode. Like the third mode the fourth is a modus in ultra mensuram, consisting of a brevis recta, a brevis altera and a ternary longa. Since the pattern of the fourth mode is the opposite of the third, it was deemed satisfactory to notate it according to principles established for the third mode. Where the third mode was indicated by a nota simplex followed by a series of ternariae, the fourth mode is notated with a series of ternariae followed by a single binaria standing for the two breves of the first half of the pattern. The first ordo of such a mode would be represented by a ternaria followed by a binaria and thus would be identical in appearance with the second ordo of the first mode. It is this ambiguity which undoubtedly accounts for the scarcity of the fourth mode. When it is utilized, it most commonly terminates with a ternary longa instead of a binaria as, for example, in the concluding section of *Benedicta* (F, f. 29).

The fourth mode is not to be found in the fascicles of organum duplum in the *Magnus liber* and this would indicate that it was created by the successors of Leonin. The second mode is to be found in a few examples but these would seem to be replacements of Leonin's original version,[31] so that one may infer that the second mode is also of later genesis. This mode has the pattern of the iamb and so is the opposite of the first mode or trochee. To establish a form of notation for this new mode was a simple procedure, for the two notes, brevis longa, of the second mode had already been assigned a specific ligature, the binaria, by Leonin. Consequently it was only necessary to write a binaria for each foot of the second mode and to add a single note at the end for the first part of the incomplete foot which must terminate any ordo. But since it is a rule of melismatic notation to use ligatures whenever possible, the final note of the ordo was joined to the final binaria to form a ternaria. In this manner the pattern of ligatures for the second mode was established as a series of binariae followed by a ternaria.

The formula for the notation of the second mode is thus the opposite of the first mode, which has a ternaria at the beginning followed by a series of binariae.

31. See the opening of *Tamquam sponsus,* W_1, f. 17'.

The ternaria will be read differently in each of these two modes. In the first mode it equals long, short, long, while in the second it stands for short, long, short. In other words the same ligature is capable of representing values which are just the opposite of those assigned to it in the first mode. The ternaria receives this new meaning not through any physical alteration of its form but through its position. This is one of the most striking features of modal notation, that the same ligature comes to represent different values not because of an altered physical appearance as in mensural notation but because of its position relative to other ligatures in a modal series. In the final analysis it is the particular arrangement of ligatures, the order in which they appear, that establishes a mode in notation. Hence one can easily understand the preoccupation of the theorists with the ordo, the regular succession of ligatures. "In every mode," states Anonymous VII, "the order must be maintained, for each mode has its own order." [32] It is upon this proper order of the ligatures that the modal system ultimately depends, for the first and second modes, for example, utilize the same ligatures which attain modal meaning only through being arranged in a certain order.

When a ternaria appears as the final ligature after one or more binariae, one instantly recognizes this succession of ligatures as the second mode. However, when the first ordo of the second mode is to be notated, it will be represented as a single ternaria, in which case it is impossible to decide whether this ligature stands for three notes of the second mode or of the first mode. Then the proper reading can be made only by examining the context of the ligature. If the preceding or following ordines are first or second modes, the single ternaria will be transcribed in the same mode. The peculiarity of the ternaria of the second mode is that it is the only ligature used to represent the modal patterns that disobeys the rule that the penultimate note of a ligature must be a brevis and the final note a longa. Because of this fact it became the practice of pre-Franconian writers to distinguish this ligature from other ternariae by altering the form of the initial note, or in technical terminology to write it as a ligature sine proprietate. "In a ternary ligature without propriety and with perfection the penultimate note is said to be a longa and the two outer notes are breves," wrote the St. Emmeram Anonymous.[33] The premensuralist theorists, with the excep-

32. CS, *1*, 378b: "Quarta regula est quod in omnibus modis ordo debet teneri. Quilibet enim modus habet suum ordinem."

33. Sowa, p. 45, ll.6–9: "Alia regula: in figura ternaria sine proprietate et perfecta penultima dicitur esse longa et due exteriores sunt breves." Cf. Garlandia, CS, *1*, 100a and 178b; Anon. IV, CS, *1*, 341b; Pseudo-Aristotle, CS, *1*, 274b.

tion of the two earliest, the author of the *Discantus positio vulgaris* and Anonymous VII, all advocate the writing of the ternaria of the second mode as a ligature sine proprietate. This method of separating this ligature from all other ternariae of the modes, because of its deviation from the law of the penultimate and final notes of ligatures, offers still more conclusive evidence that this same law was one of the very first and most important precepts formulated at the beginning of the modal system. At the same time it speaks for the priority of the first mode, for it is from this mode that this law is derived.

In the preceding discussion the notation of the modes has been taken up according to their historical appearance in the manuscripts and it has been shown that the prior establishment of the notation of the first mode created certain rules and considerations that affected the notation of the succeeding modes. The conclusions reached are at many points divergent from the only other attempt that has been made to explain the modal system, that of Friedrich Ludwig.[34] It is necessary, therefore, that we pause at this point to examine Ludwig's position. He first of all illustrates the patterns of the six modes and then says, quite correctly, that the first composers did not represent the values of these patterns by specific note forms,

> but they found in the different methods of combining tone-groups in ligatures an actually complete means of solving the difficulties, a means which in spite of the complete similarity of the external signs indirectly but with absolute certainty suggests the underlying rhythm.[35]

He continues:

> They proceeded from the principle of representing a rhythm which moves in an alternation of arsis and one thesis by chains of binaria ligatures; and a rhythm which moves in an alternation of arsis and two theses by chains of ternary ligatures; and they always gave the binaria ligatura the meaning: short-long, which therefore corresponds in the first example [i.e., in the first mode] to the succession: thesis-arsis () and in the second example [i.e., second mode] to the reverse succession: arsis-thesis (); and they gave the ternaria ligature in the rhythm of the third example [i.e., third mode] the analogous meaning: two theses-arsis 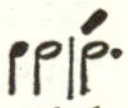).
>
> This meaning of the ligature forms of quadratic notation lasted, as is well known, as long as these ligatures were generally used in notation, therefore until the end of the sixteenth century. If the later notation—mensural notation—wished to represent values other than this by a binaria ligature (for example, two long or two short or two shorter notes, or the

34. Michalitschke's theories rest upon the assumptions first advanced by Ludwig and thus are only extensions of Ludwig's premises.

35. *Repertorium,* p. 44.

succession: long-short which is the opposite of its original meaning), it was obliged to alter the original forms and did this by the well known differentiation of the form of the ligatures of mensural notation, the ligatures sine proprietate—that is, the abrogation of the former characteristic meaning (the proprietas) of the initial note, therefore the short value of this note—cum opposite proprietate, sine perfectione, etc.

The regular successions of chains of binary or ternary ligatures described above now need in part to be supplemented further by other ligature forms either at the beginning or at the close of individual phrases, and particularly in three cases in quadratic notation these successions were interrupted or altered, so that four peculiarities of the use of ligatures are to be established here, the first two cases of which also bring an actual change of the meaning of the ligatures.[36]

Ludwig then goes on to explain the four exceptions or peculiarities of modal notation, but only the first of these need concern us here. The first exception, according to Ludwig, lies in the usage of the first and second modes, which begin and conclude respectively with a ternaria. These are exceptions to the basic principle of modal notation that a ternaria has the meaning ♩𝅗𝅥𝅗𝅥., for in the first mode the ternaria will be read 𝅗𝅥♩𝅗𝅥, and in the second mode ♩𝅗𝅥♩. But we have seen that for the pre-Franconian theorists a ternaria cum proprietate et perfectione was said first and foremost to be long, short, long, or arsis, thesis, arsis. In other words, the meaning of the ternaria in the first mode was considered to be the primary meaning and not an exceptional usage. In fact, it is not until the treatise of Franco that the ternaria of the first mode comes to be considered an abnormal ternaria and is consequently represented as a ligature sine proprietate. Furthermore the writing of the third mode in Leonin's *Magnus liber* suggests that the ternaria is to be read here as a ternaria of the first mode. It would seem then that the ternaria of the third mode complies with principles derived from the first mode, notably the rule that the penultimate note is a brevis, the final note a longa. If Ludwig's theory is true, that the ternaria of the first mode is an exception to the normal reading exemplified by the ternaria of the third mode, it is very difficult to see why the pre-Franconian theorists did not devise a special form for this ligature as they did for the ternaria of the second mode. But it is a fact that this ligature was always said to be cum proprietate et perfectione, and what is even more striking the theorists always define the normal ternaria, the ligature with propriety and perfection, in terms of its reading in the first mode [37] and not of the third mode.

Ludwig's theory of chain ligatures is a brilliant rationalization of the existing

36. *Repertorium,* pp. 44–45.

37. See above, p. 61, n. 4.

facts of modal notation, for it is true that the first, second, third, and fourth modes are notated in a series of binariae or ternariae, series which are differentiated one from another by their opening or closing ligatures. But his belief that modal notation began with such chains of ligatures as a first principle rests upon the assumption that the modal system was conceived as a unified whole from its inception. He assumes that the binaria and ternaria were first of all assigned specific values apart from any specific mode and that the individual modes were then created by modifying the series of binariae or ternariae with different opening and closing ligatures. But the modes were not created simultaneously, as is clearly evident from Leonin's *Magnus liber* where only the first mode has an autonomous existence. It is in relation to this mode that the binaria and ternaria were assigned the specific meanings which were to remain the primary ones in the evolution of the modal system. These ligatures were then adapted to the other modes. That the end result was a series of binariae or ternariae in the various modes is only natural, for only two types of ligature were employed and any repetition of the modal pattern would necessarily be accompanied by the repetition of one or the other of these ligatures. Such a chain of ligatures, however, is incidental to modal notation rather than being of central importance. Historically, the modal system started not from chains of ligatures but from the establishment of the first mode with its concomitant rule that the last note of a ligature is a longa and the penultimate a brevis. The ligatures of the modes which appeared after the formulation of the first mode either conform to this rule or reveal their violation of it by the position which they are given in an ordo. Thus while Ludwig's theory of chain ligatures is outwardly a plausible explanation of modal notation, it must be recognized as a theory which is not supported by the evidence of the manuscripts or of the theorists.

3. *Irregular Notation*

In the notation of the six rhythmic modes by means of ligatures and notae simplices arranged in a certain succession, the Notre Dame composers were provided with a clear, coherent method of representing the rhythmic patterns that underlie all compositions of the epoch. While furnishing the clue to the basic rhythm of a composition, these patterns of notation are at the same time subject to infinite variation. The normal arrangement of the ligatures is frequently disrupted by the repetition of a tone, by the substitution of other, equivalent values for values of the modal pattern, or by the appearance of a new syllable in the text. In addition to these phenomena the notation of the imperfect modes must also be taken into account. When one of these occurrences takes place, the notation itself must reflect it, thereby deviating from the normal modal pattern. Concerning the forms of notation used in such circumstances the theorists are surprisingly silent. Their uncommunicativeness, however, is probably attributable to the fact that by their time specific symbols had been created for the longa and brevis, and the various forms of the ligatures had unalterable temporal values, so that irregularities in the modal pattern could be notated by these exact symbols. In the Notre Dame manuscripts, however, all ligatures are written in their normal form, i.e., cum proprietate et perfectione, and the nota simplex, although appearing in the form of both the brevis and the longa, represents a brevis or longa value solely by context with a modal pattern. The exact meaning of the ligature or nota simplex in irregular notation is thus not revealed by the form of the ligature or note but is to be divined from the rhythmic and harmonic context. Despite the equivocal nature of such irregular notation, the existence of certain conventions in the treatment of it facilitates an understanding of its meaning. It is the purpose of this chapter to interpret and codify these usages.

Without doubt the most common exception to the usual patterns of ligatures is the separation of notes that would normally be grouped into a ligature because of the repetition of a tone. In the words of Johannes de Garlandia, "all tones which are of the same pitch cannot be joined together and cannot form a composite figure of notation, because every composite figure or ligature is ascending or descending; and whenever notes are of the same pitch, they neither ascend nor descend; therefore a ligature, that is a figure of notes joined together, cannot be made from these notes." [1] When such repeated notes occur they are most commonly represented by a nota simplex. Thus two notes which would normally be grouped into a binaria are written as two notae simplices, if these notes are of the same pitch, e.g., ■ ■. In the case of notes which would normally be grouped into a ternaria there are several possibilities of notation. If the first two notes are repeated, the first note will be written as a nota simplex, while the second and third notes are notated as a binaria (Ex. a). If the second and third notes are repeated, the three notes will be written as a binaria followed by a nota simplex (Ex. b). If all three notes are of the same pitch, each will be written as a nota simplex (Ex. c).

In general the scribes are careful to write such notes close to each other in order to indicate their relationship. These notes will, furthermore, receive the same value that would have been accorded to the ligature which they replace. "All notes which are not joined together must be reduced to a ligature by equivalence," states Garlandia; [2] they must be understood as the equivalent of a modal ligature.

When a nota simplex appears in the Notre Dame manuscripts it is written in the form of a brevis or longa more or less indiscriminately, no matter what value is to be assigned to it. Nevertheless Ludwig saw in such single notes used in place of a ligature the origin of the mensuralist system of equating the brevis value with the form ■ and the longa value with 𝆷. His theory, however, rests in part upon his belief that the normal ternaria ligature is to be read ♩𝅗𝅥𝅗𝅥.. Ludwig states [3] that if the initial note of a group is separated from the ligature because it is the first of two repeated notes, the scribes will usually write it ■; while if the final note of a group is separated, it will usually be written in the form of a longa. He then says that since in most cases the note ■ stands for a short value as in the binaria and "normal" ternaria, and the longa form represents a final long value in these ligatures, these notes gradually assumed a specific and permanent value of one tempus and two or three tempora respectively—the

1. CS, *I*, 181a: "Item omnes voces, que accipiuntur in eodem sono, non possunt ligari vel facere figuram compositam, quia omnis figura composita, vel ligata dicitur ascendendo, vel descendendo, et quecumque sunt in eodem sono, non ascendunt, nec descendunt; ergo ex iis non fit ligatura, id est figura ligata." Cf. Garlandia, CS, *I*, 103a,b; Anon. IV, CS, *I*, 342b; Sowa, p. 72.

2. CS, *I*, 181a: "Item, omnes figure non ligate debent reduci ad figuram compositam per equipollentiam."

3. *Repertorium*, pp. 46–48.

brevis note and longa note of the mensuralists. Ludwig observes, on the other hand, that the method of signifying such isolated notes differs somewhat in the various manuscripts. But an examination of the three principal Notre Dame manuscripts reveals that it is unsafe to assume that the note ■ is even generally associated with a short value. It is true that the initial note of two notes standing for a binaria is usually to be found in the form ■. But the initial note separated from a ternaria presents no such uniform treatment. In W_1 such an isolated initial note is almost always represented by the longa form, whether it is to be understood as part of a ternaria reading 𝅗𝅥♩𝅗𝅥, as it usually is, or as part of a ternaria reading ♩𝅗𝅥𝅗𝅥. . In the Florence manuscript the form ■ is usually chosen, but since the greatest proportion of ternaria ligatures are first mode ligatures, it means that this form is most commonly associated with a long value in this manuscript. W_2 is quite careful on the whole to write ▜ for a long value and ■ for a short value; but W_2 is a late manuscript showing definitely mensural characteristics, even to the admission of ligatures cum opposita proprietate. Under the circumstances Ludwig's hypothesis about the development of the mensuralist brevis and longa, logical as it may be, should be accepted only tentatively until a thorough, statistical examination has been made of all the manuscripts. It may well be that no such "natural" evolution is to be found at all.

There is yet another means of notating repeated notes. This occurs primarily in the first mode when a final, repeated note of a ligature group is not written as a nota simplex but is incorporated into the following ligature. Thus when the final note of an opening ternaria is a repeated tone, it is frequently added to the following binaria so that the ordo begins with a binaria followed by a ternaria:

In the case of a binaria of two repeated notes, the first will remain a nota simplex while the second is added to the following binaria, e.g.,

In both instances the resulting ternaria is the normal ternaria cum proprietate et perfectione of the first mode.

Another cause of irregular notation is the practice of substituting other equivalent values for the individual values of the modal pattern—the fractio and extensio modorum. The principles of the fractio modorum have already been discussed in connection with the sixth mode, which was shown to have originated in the practice of replacing the longa of the first mode by two breves.[4] This division of the longa was notated either by adding a plica to the final note of a ligature or by the use of ternary ligatures after the second or any ensuing longa. When the first longa of an ordo was to be replaced by two breves, the initial ternaria of the first mode was written as a quaternaria. It is possible, however, to substitute even smaller values than the brevis for the values of a modal pattern, for the brevis in turn may be divided into two or more semibreves. When this occurs new means of notation are required to represent these smaller notes. But before turning to the notation used for the fractio modorum it is necessary to establish the number of semibreves into which a brevis may be divided, for it would be difficult to interpret the notation without an understanding of the permissible limits of the division of the brevis into semibreves.

Up to the time of Franco of Cologne the theorists in general admit only a double or triple division of the brevis. Anonymous IV on the other hand mentions the possibility of writing as many as four semibreves for a brevis value. However, he restricts such a division to instrumental music, allowing no more than three semibreves in vocal music.[5] It is apparent then that polyphonic music at least until the middle of the thirteenth century confined itself to no more than a triple division of the brevis. Nevertheless, despite this seeming unanimity of opinion among the theorists, there is a certain amount of disagreement concerning the exact measurement of these semibreves. The point of dissension is this: if a brevis can be subdivided into three equal semibreves, how are two semibreves to be read? Are they to be considered as two equal halves of a brevis? Or does one of them have a value of one-third of a brevis and the other two-thirds, in the same manner that a ternary longa is divided into a brevis recta and a brevis altera?

Rather significantly this problem does not appear in the earlier theorists but only in the later ones. It is not until the treatise of Pseudo-Aristotle (mid-thirteenth century) that the reading of two semibreves as notes of unequal duration is established as a rule. From this time on the first of two semibreves was deemed to be the equivalent of one-third of a brevis, and the second, two-thirds of a brevis. But theorists whose teaching is closer to modal practices speak of two semibreves as being equal. Anonymous IV, in speaking of the semibrevis, which

4. See above, pp. 64 f.

5. CS, *I*, 338a: ". . . non ponimus quatuor [semibreves] pro brevi in voce humana, sed in instrumentis sepius bene fit." *Ibid.*, 341b: ". . . si quatuor currentes pro uno brevi ordinentur, sed hoc raro solebat contingere; ultimi vero non in voce humana, sed in instrumentis cordarum possunt ordinari."

he calls "Elmuahym," says: "Sometimes it is called a semibrevis [i.e., half a brevis], if it is before or after another similar note; but sometimes it is the third part of a brevis, and this is when three of these notes are written in the manner of currentes and thus there are three for a brevis."[6] From this statement it is obvious that for Anonymous IV the term semibrevis means literally one-half of a brevis. Similarly, two other theorists whose precepts are near to the early modal system recognize only the bipartite division of the brevis. Amerus, an Englishman writing in Italy in 1271, states that "two breves equal a longa and four semibreves equal a long,"[7] while Dietricus (ca. 1225?) maintains that two semibreves constitute a brevis.[8] The fact that earlier theorists mention only equal semibreves suggests that in early polyphonic music, that is in organum, no more than two semibreves were used as the equivalent of a brevis. This hypothesis is confirmed by Walter Odington in his statement that "the brevis was divided into two semibreves by earlier composers, but sometimes into three and sometimes into two by the moderns."[9] Accordingly it may be assumed that in the music with which we are dealing no more than two semibreves will replace a brevis and that these semibreves will have an equal duration. This is an important guide to the proper method of transcribing the series of semibreves in the form of currentes, sometimes as many as eleven, that are frequently to be found in the Notre Dame manuscripts.

To indicate the division of the longa or brevis of the modal pattern into semibreves two methods of notation were employed, ligatures and conjuncturae. In the first case composers substituted ligatures of more than the usual number of notes for the normal ligatures of the modal pattern. The principle behind this manner of notation is the same rule that governs the opening quaternaria of the sixth mode: "In every ligature with propriety and perfection, the penultimate note is said to be a brevis, and the final note a longa; if there are any notes preceding the brevis, they are all [in sum] equivalent to a long."[10] A ligature of

6. CS, *1,* 341a: "Quandoque dicitur semibrevis, si sit ante alteram consimilem vel post; aliter quandoque est tertia pars brevis; et hoc est quando tres per modum currentium ponuntur, et sic sunt tres pro brevi."

7. Joseph Kromolicki, *Die Practica Artis Musicae des Amerus und ihre Stellung in der Musiktheorie des Mittelalters* (Berlin, 1909), p. 9. "Nota, quod duae breves valent unam longam et quatuor semibreves valent unam longam."

8. Hans Müller, *Eine Abhandlung über Mensuralmusik* (Leipzig, 1886). This work was not available to me and I draw this information from J. Wolf, *Handbuch der Notationskunde,* p. 245.

9. CS, *1,* 235b: "Brevis vero apud priores resoluta est in duas semibreves; apud modernos, aliquando in tres, aliquando in duas."

10. CS, *1,* 99b, 100a.

five notes according to this rule would be read so that the first three notes are equivalent to a longa, the fourth note is a brevis, and the final note a longa. The specific value and the relationship of the three initial notes is explained by Anonymous VII: "Whenever three little notes are substituted for a longa in the first mode, the first two equal a brevis and the last then equals the two preceding ones." [11] In the case of ligatures larger than the quinaria each successive brevis will be divided into two semibreves. Thus a senaria is transcribed as four semibreves, a brevis, and longa (); and a septenaria equals six semibreves and a longa ().

Such a method of transcription does not conform to the teachings of the later theorists who, however, admit a ternary division of the brevis. They would here apply the rule: ". . . if there is a multitude of breves in any place, the more a brevis approaches the end, the longer must it be held." [12] According to this principle the individual notes of a quinaria would have the meaning of one-third of a brevis, two-thirds of a brevis, brevis, brevis, and longa (Ex. a); a senaria would equal three semibreves for a brevis, followed by two breves and a longa (Ex. b): [13]

a) 
b) 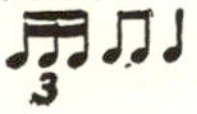

While such a division does not conform to the practices of the early composers, it would seem nevertheless to have some bearing upon the transcription of large ligatures which replace the ternariae of the third mode. If one applies the rule regulating a multitude of breves to a quaternaria or quinaria replacing a ternaria of the third mode, it is evident that the first two notes of the quaternaria and the first three notes of the quinaria should stand for a brevis recta, while the remaining two notes would be a brevis altera and longa perfecta: [14]

 and 

11. CS, *1*, 378b: "Quinta regula est quocienscunque tres notule in primo modo ponuntur pro una longa, prime due valent unam brevem, et ultima valet tunc sicut due precedentes."

12. Johannes de Garlandia, CS, *1*, 176a: ". . . si multitudo brevium fuerit in aliquo loco, quando brevis plus appropinquat fini, tanto debet longior proferri." The term brevis still retains something of its original meaning of simply a short value and thus includes semibreves as well. Cf. Garlandia, CS, *1*, 103b: ". . . brevium multitudo, id est semibrevium."

13. See the complete table of ligatures in Sowa, p. xli f.

14. Anon. VII says: "If three or four notes are found in place of two breves [of the third mode], the last note has two tempora and all the rest equals only one tempus." CS, *1*, 379a: "Si vero tres

But regarding the third mode one must keep in mind that in its primitive state it was undoubtedly related to the first mode and that the larger of the two breves preceded the smaller. Consequently larger ligatures in this mode would be read in the same manner as those employed in the first mode. A quaternaria is to be transcribed as three breves and a longa [15]; a quinaria equals two semibreves, two breves and a longa, etc.

Larger ligatures are also used to replace the binaria of the first mode and the ternaria of the sixth mode. When a ternaria appears in an ordo of the first mode after the initial ternaria, it is normally to be read as two breves and a longa, the first brevis being understood as part of the preceding longa. The same reading would apply when such a ternaria follows a nota plicata, for example,

Here the final longa of the first ligature has been divided into two semibreves and a brevis. Similarly when a quaternaria or quinaria is inserted in the modal series of the first or sixth mode, it is to be understood as having a value equivalent to a ternaria. Thus a quaternaria used in lieu of a ternaria will contain two semibreves, a brevis, and for the final note either a brevis or longa. A quinaria would contain four semibreves and a final brevis or longa.

The second means of notating the fractio modorum is the conjunctura or currentes. These are series of diamond-shaped notes added to a nota simplex or to the end of a ligature, e.g.,

The exact meaning of these symbols is frequently difficult to establish, because in the Notre Dame manuscripts the nota simplex followed by currentes is commonly used as the equivalent of a descending ligature. The conjunctura ternaria in particular is used as frequently as the ligature  to indicate three descending notes, and it is to be transcribed in the same manner that a ligature would be in the same context. In fact the conjunctura appears so often as a substitute for a descending ligature that one should first of all endeavor to read it according to the rules applicable to ligatures. However, the currentes have another

vel quatuor inveniantur pro duabus brevibus, ultima valet duo tempora et totum residuum non valet nisi unum."

15. J. Kromolicki, *Die Practica Artis Musicae,* p. ii: "Quando tres coniunctae sequuntur tres coniunctas, vel tres coniunctae quatuor conjunctas, vel e converso, vel quatuor coniunctae quatuor coniunctas, tenenda est ultima cuiuslibet coniuctionis, et omnes aliae de illis coniunctis sunt breves."

meaning which is analogous to that of the plica: the currentes are to be understood as values subtracted from the note which they follow, so that the note together with the currentes will occupy only as much time as the note by itself would have. Garlandia established the rule that "whenever there is a multitude of breves, i.e., semibreves, they always share in the value of the preceding note, because the preceding note together with these semibreves is understood to have only such a value as the preceding note represents." [16] In practice the preceding note will always be a longa in the Notre Dame manuscripts. This longa divided into smaller values by the currentes will then be read in the same manner as that described in the preceding paragraphs. That is, no more than two semibreves will replace a brevis and the larger value will be placed at the end of the series. For example,

If the longa is of three tempora, the following readings would result:

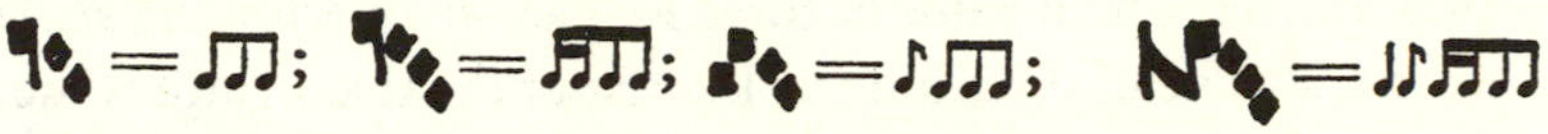

There is still another meaning for the conjunctura. In many cases it will be found that the currentes added to the final note of a ligature have a total value greater than a longa, that is, greater than the preceding note. For example,

In these examples the conjunctura is not so much employed as a symbol for the fractio of a longa but as a substitute for a ligature. In reality these currentes are a sort of shorthand, for the writing utensil used by the scribes tended to draw descending notes as diamonds more easily than to draw square notes in a descending ligature. Thus two ligatures are compressed into one form by writing the second in the form of currentes:

The frequency and undoubted authenticity of this usage of currentes in conjunction with ligatures serves as a clue to the proper transcription of series of more than six currentes added to a nota simplex. For example,

16. CS, *I*, 103b: "Item notandum est quod ubicunque invenitur brevium multitudo, id est semibrevium, semper participat cum precedente, quia precedens cum eis non reputatur in valore, nisi pro una tali, sicut et precedens."

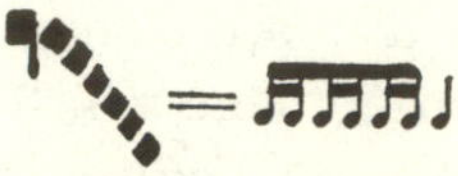

this form simply being read according to the rules for a ligature of more than three notes. But if one attempts to apply the same rules to an octonaria or novenaria conjunctura, it is apparent that this would entail a ternary division of the brevis. Thus an octonaria and a novenaria would have to be read as follows:

However, it has been shown that such a tripartite division of the brevis is highly improbable in the Notre Dame organum. On the contrary, we must assume that only a binary division of the brevis is permissible and that in the case of the octonaria and larger conjuncturae we are dealing with a shorthand method of writing two descending ligatures. In the same manner that a ligature together with currentes frequently stands in place of two ligatures so that a ternaria followed by currentes has a total value of three longae, so an octonaria replaces two ligatures and has a value of three longae. Instead of the two ligatures the simpler figure of a conjunctura octonaria is employed, but both the ligatures and the conjunctura are to be transcribed in the same way:

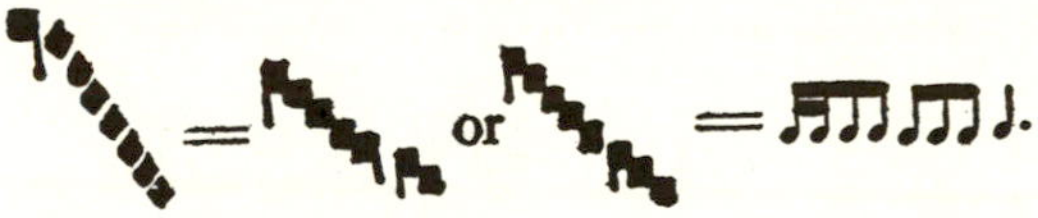

This reading for the octonaria is confirmed by two passages in three-voiced organa, where an octonaria in one part is combined simultaneously with modal ligatures in a second voice. In the *Alleluya. Dies sanctificatus* (F, f. 16) there occurs this passage just before the syllable "ra" of the versus (f. 17′):

This ordo occurs at the end of a clausula in the first mode so that there can be no doubt about the meaning of the ligatures [17] of the triplum and no other reading is possible for the octonaria of the duplum without making the most

17. The binariae on the syllable "ra" are used here as an appoggiatura. See below, p. 126.

willful distortions of the ligatures in the triplum. A similar example is encountered in the three-voiced setting of the Gradual *Judea et Jerusalem* (F, f. 46′). At the end of a section in the second and third modes just before the end of the piece there appears this passage:

These two clear-cut examples are sufficient evidence for the proper meaning of the conjuncturae of more than seven notes. It is possible that Garlandia recognized that groups of breves and semibreves could have a total value of more than one longa, for among the rules governing the modi in ultra mensuram he includes the following: ". . . if there should be a multitude of breves in any place, we must always make them equal to longs." [18] However, this statement is so contradictory to the other precepts of Garlandia concerning the value of the semibrevis that it seems probable that "longis" is either a careless slip or a misreading of "longae." On the other hand this sentence may be correct as it stands, thereby affording us evidence by a theorist that groups of breves and semibreves can have a value of more than one longa.

The notation employed for the extensio modi is by no means as complicated as that used for the fractio modi. In extensio modi a larger value replaces the lesser values of a modal pattern. In other words a single note, the ternary longa, replaces a longa and brevis of the first mode, a brevis and longa of the second mode, or the brevis notes of the third, fourth, and sixth modes. The most common expression of this rhythmic factor is the nota simplex. For example, a nota simplex written before the ternary ligature of the first mode indicates that the first note of the ordo has a duration equal to an entire foot of the mode:

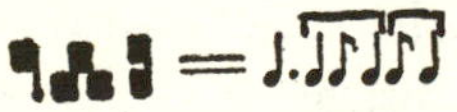

The nota simplex, when its appearance is not due to repeated notes which cannot be joined in a ligature, invariably has the meaning of a longa value. Consequently the final note of any ligature preceding a nota simplex in the first mode will always be a ternary longa, for the brevis note which separates any two

18. Cs, *I*, 176a: ". . . si multitudo brevium fuerit in aliquo loco, semper debemus facere quod equipolleant longis."

longae of the first mode has been suppressed and its value must be added to the preceding longa if the rhythm, indicated by the plausus, is to be maintained, e.g.,

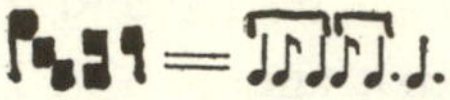

In the second, third, and fourth modes, however, the nota simplex itself is invariably a ternary longa which replaces the brevis and longa of the second mode or the two breves of the third and fourth modes. For example, in the following series

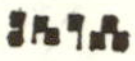

the nota simplex replaces the usual binaria of the second mode which would be read as a brevis and longa. These notes then have the meaning

Ligatures also play a part in the notation of extensio modi. In the first mode when any brevis but the first is suppressed the scribes, instead of writing a nota simplex, will join this longa value to the following binaria to form a ternaria which will have the normal meaning of a ternaria of the first mode, i.e., long, short, long. For instance,

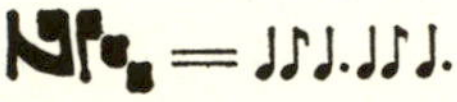

The brevis between the last note of the first ligature and the first note of the second ligature has been suppressed and its value added to the final longa of the opening ligature. The equivocal nature of the notation of irregular notes is here apparent, for the same two ligatures can have in fractio modi the meaning

The meaning of these ligatures is nevertheless usually easily discernible from their context with other voices either through harmonic concordance or through the values of the ligatures in other voices. In the second mode the scribes commonly write a ternary ligature instead of a binaria and nota simplex when a foot of the modal pattern has been replaced by a ternary longa. In this case the ternaria will have the meaning of a ternaria of the third mode, i.e., brevis recta, brevis altera, ternary longa. It is interesting to see that here the fine distinction between the brevis altera and the longa recta is done away with and that a theoretical brevis value replaces a longa.

A third cause of irregular notation is the appearance of a new syllable in the text. In organum all voices change to a new syllable simultaneously. Even though the words of the chant are written only below the original Gregorian melody of the tenor, the coincidence of all parts is carefully indicated by a little line drawn before the notes of the upper and lower voices which are to be sounded together with the new syllable of the tenor. This line, aptly called a *Silbenstrich* by Ludwig (*Repertorium,* p. 49), is explained by Anonymous IV in the following way: "Sometimes this line is large and sometimes small and it does not represent any temporal value; but it is written because of the division of syllables since it has one syllable on one side and another syllable on the other (whether these are parts of the same word or of different words), if at the same time these syllables should be joined together in ligatures in singing."[19] The Silbenstrich according to this definition is a convenient visual clue to indicate on what note within an ordo a new syllable is to be sung.

The appearance of a new syllable within an ordo results in the breaking up of the modal ligatures, for it is a rule derived from the notation of Gregorian chant that a ligature may have no more than one syllable. As a result of this, when two syllables are to be sung to values that would normally be grouped into a modal ligature, the notes belonging to the first syllable are placed on one side of the Silbenstrich and the notes of the new syllable on the other side. For example, if a new syllable enters on the second longa of an ordo of the first mode, the customary opening ternaria of this mode will be replaced by a binaria, followed by a Silbenstrich and a nota simplex, e.g.:

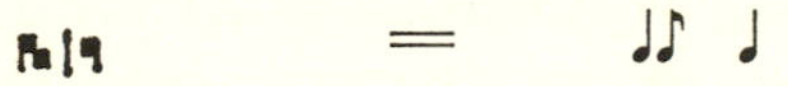

Al-le (*luya*) *Al—le*

This method of notation is essentially the same as that used for repeated notes which cannot be grouped into a ligature. In both cases a ligature is divided into smaller parts, but no special mark of division is required for the division of a ligature because of repeated notes, for the repeated notes in themselves are a sufficient indication that the two parts are to be understood as one ligature; whereas a Silbenstrich is almost mandatory if one is to understand that the two groups are in reality a substitute for a single ligature.

When the syllables change rapidly so that each syllable has at the most one or two notes, the whole system of modal ligatures breaks down. The resulting

19. CS, *I,* 350b: "Quandoque est major, quandoque minor, et nullum tempus signat; sed ponitur propter divisionem syllabarum, quoniam unam syllabam habet ex una parte, alteram ex altera, si fuerit ejusdem dictionis sive ex diversis dictionibus, si debeant simul copulari in cantando."

notation will be a series of notae simplices and ligatures having an appearance quite unlike normal modal notation. This occurs not infrequently in organum but is most commonly encountered in the motet and conductus, the former being completely syllabic, while the latter is syllabic at least in part. Such an "unmodal" notation, that is, not written in modal ligatures, is referred to as notation *cum littera* (with a text) in opposition to the notation of organum where the relatively small amount of text is set in a melismatic fashion so that each syllable has a great many notes which can be grouped into modal ligatures. This latter type of notation is spoken of by the theorists as notation *sine littera* (without a text). The term sine littera is by no means to be taken literally, for it represents a relative and not an absolute distinction from the term cum littera. It does not mean a complete absence of text but connotes a text which is set to music in a melismatic fashion so that there are relatively few syllables to a melody. Hence cum littera and sine littera are nearly synonymous with syllabic and melismatic style.

The terms cum littera and sine littera have caused an unnecessary amount of confusion among modern musicologists. Garlandia cited the motet as an example of notation cum littera, and the *neuma* of the conductus, that is the opening and closing phrases of conductus which are notated in ligatures, as an example of notation sine littera.[20] Since Garlandia does not refer to the main part of the conductus which is notated principally in notae simplices and binary ligatures, it has all too often been assumed by modern historians that the conductus, except in the caudae, is written in some sort of a free rhythm.[21] And those musicologists who have maintained that the conductus is to be read in modal rhythm have attempted to transcribe the notation either by taking each note and ligature at its face value or by interpreting the rhythm according to the metrical accent of the text. None of these methods is correct with the exception of the last which is in part correct, for the accent of the text may or may not coincide with the long and short values of the musical rhythm. In reality the texted part of the conductus is notated in a modal rhythm in the same manner that the early

20. CS, *1,* 177b: "Et sciendum quod hujus modi figure aliquando ponuntur sine littera: sine littera ut in caudis vel conductis; cum littera, ut in motetis." This definition is repeated by Pseudo-Aristotle, CS, *1,* 269b and in an expanded form by Franco, CS, *1,* 130a, and after him by Anon. I, CS, *1,* 302a. The St. Emmeram Anon. also relies upon this definition, Sowa, p. 14, l.2.

21. For a summary of prevalent theories see Apel, *Notation,* pp. 258–267. Two recent articles on the rhythm of conductus should also be consulted: Heinrich Husmann, "Zur Grundlegung der musikalischen Rhythmik des mittellateinischen Liedes," *AfMW, 9* (1952), 3–26; Jacques Handschin, "Zur Frage der Conductus-Rhythmik," *Acta Musicologica, 24* (1952), 113–130.

motet is, with the exception that the lowest part of a polyphonic conductus is notated cum littera instead of in modal ligatures as in the tenor of the motet. Furthermore the particular form of notation cum littera will appear whenever the modal ligatures are broken up because of a change in syllables, be it in the motet, the conductus, or organum. In all cases the rhythm will be a modal rhythm and only the form of the notation will change, the seemingly erratic notation cum littera replacing the customary modal ligatures.

That the terms cum littera and sine littera denote nothing but two different forms or methods of notating modal rhythm is clearly expressed by the theorists. Garlandia's definition may be quoted in this connection.

A sign of notation is the representation of a tone according to its measure. And you must know that sometimes signs of this sort are written without any text: sine littera as in the *caudae* of conductus; sometimes with a text as in motets. Moreover between figures which are written without a text and those with a text there is this difference: those that are without a text must be joined into ligatures as much as possible. But concerning signs of this sort, *whether they are associated with a text or not,* the following types and rules are given. [Italics mine.] [22]

He then proceeds to give a description of the various notae simplices and ligatures and the rules concerning their values. According to these statements it is obvious that the terms cum and sine littera simply mean notes which have a syllable under them or notes which have no syllable under them but which presumably are to be sung to the last preceding syllable of the text. The same forms of notes will be found in either case, but there will be more ligatures in notation sine littera than in notation cum littera, for notes which are to be sung to different syllables cannot be joined to form a ligature. These notes which represent long and short values will be organized into one or the other of the modal patterns whether they are cum or sine littera, for according to Garlandia, "Whatever proceeds in measured time, to wit in longae and breves, is called a mode [and] there are six types of modes." [23]

In organum the introduction of a new syllable in the text, thereby producing

22. CS, *I*, 177b: "Unde figura est representatio soni secundum suum modum. Et sciendum quod hujus modi figure aliquando ponuntur sine littera: sine littera ut in caudis vel conductis; cum littera, ut in motetis. Item inter figuras que sunt sine littera et cum littera, talis datur differentia; quoniam ille que sunt sine littera debent, prout possunt, amplius ad invicem ligari. Sed hujus modi figurarum tam littere associetarum quam non associetarum dantur divisiones sequentes, ac etiam regule."

23. CS, *I*, 175a: "Maneries ejus appellatur quidquid mensuratione temporis, videlicet per longas, vel per breves concurrit. Sunt ergo sex species ejus maneriei, . . ."

a note cum littera and a consequent breaking up of the pattern of modal ligatures, occurs at relatively infrequent intervals so that it is not difficult to interpret the meaning of the resulting irregular notation, since the modal rhythm has been firmly established by the preceding modal ligatures. In the earliest versions of the motet, which are notated by signs which had not as yet attained mensural significance, the problem of ascertaining the modal rhythm is more difficult, since the syllabic nature of the motet style prevents the notes from being grouped into modal ligatures. Nevertheless, the mode of the motetus and triplum can usually be established without any doubt by context with the tenor part, which with its relative paucity of text is notated in the usual modal ligatures. But in the syllabic portions of conductus, where all parts singing the same text simultaneously are notated cum littera, it is by no means a simple matter to discover the underlying modal rhythm. Nonetheless the theorists have left us some indications as to how this notation is to be interpreted. Although the questions of conductus notation lies outside the scope of this study, I shall take up one aspect of it, for one of its principles applies equally to organum.

A very significant passage in Garlandia together with its amplification in Anonymous IV has hitherto escaped particular notice and yet the doctrine contained there provides an adequate indication of the method to be followed in deciphering the notation of conductus. Garlandia is the first of the theorists to introduce the ligature sine perfectione as an accepted practice in notation. An imperfect ligature is one which alters the normal form of the final note. In a descending ligature the last note is drawn as an oblique line and in an ascending ligature the last note, instead of being drawn directly above the preceding note, is turned to the right:

According to Garlandia there are three types of ligatures sine perfectione or imperfecta: ligatures with propriety, i.e., in which the first note is drawn in the normal manner (Ex. a); ligatures sine proprietate, i.e., in which the form of the first note is altered (Ex. b); and ligatures with opposite propriety, i.e., in which an ascending line is prefixed to the initial note (Ex. c).[24]

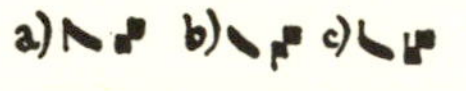

The meaning of this last form need not concern us here but regarding imperfect ligatures with and without propriety Garlandia makes the following highly

24. CS, *I*, 100b.

relevant remark: "The rule is that every imperfect ligature, if it is with propriety, extends throughout a perfection of the first mode up to the first longa that follows it. If it is without propriety, it extends throughout a perfection of the second mode up to the first brevis that follows. *And all this is understood in conductus when they appear with a text,* if they are notated in the proper manner. But if they are not notated properly, in general all ligatures are to be taken as being imperfect, and this is to be understood in discant and wherever correct measurement appears." [25] According to this statement the ligatures appearing in the syllabic portions of conductus are generally to be construed as imperfect ligatures, whether they are written in this form or not. Here is a most important clue to the proper meaning of conductus notation, but in order to comprehend its significance further amplification is required.

By perfection Garlandia means a complete foot of either the first or second mode. Anonymous IV uses a similar expression in his discussion of the notation of the third mode: "The principle [of the notation] of the third perfect mode proceeds by a longa and three [notes in a ligature], three, three, etc., but without a rest. The foot is completed [*perficitur*] in the penultimate [note of each ternary ligature]." [26] Turning to Garlandia's definitions with this fact in mind, we find that a binaria with propriety and without perfection represents a foot of the first mode, or a longa and brevis, while a binaria without propriety and without perfection stands for a foot of the second mode, or a brevis and longa. But if this is the case, why is there any need for imperfect ligatures? According to Garlandia's teaching a normal binaria, i.e., with propriety and perfection, has the meaning of a brevis and longa, and a binaria without propriety but with per-

25. This passage occurs in both versions of Garlandia printed by Coussemaker, but unfortunately neither version is wholly correct as it stands. In the compilation of Jerome of Moravia the text runs: "Regula est quod omnis figura imperfecta, si sit cum proprietate, extenditur quoad perfectionem primi modi usque ad primam longam sequentem; si sit sine proprietate, extenditur quoad perfectionem secundi modi, usque ad primam brevem sequentem. Et totum hoc intelligitur in conductis et in motetis, quando sumuntur sine littera vel cum littera. Si proprio modo figurantur, omnes figure fere accipiuntur imperfecte, et hoc intelligitur in discantu, et ubicumque rectus modus accipitur." (CS, *I*, 100b.) In the second version there is the following reading: "Regula est: omnis imperfecta figura, si sit cum proprietate, extenditur usque ad primam longam sequentem; si sit sine, intelligitur usque ad primam brevem. Et totum hoc intelligitur in conductis, quando sumitur cum littera, si proprio modo figurantur. Si improprio modo figurantur, fere omnes figure accipiuntur imperfecte, et hoc intelligitur in discantu et ubicumque rectus modus accipitur." (CS, *I*, 179a.) The italics are mine.

26. CS, *I*, 329b: "Principium tertii modi perfecti procedit per longam unam et tres, tres, tres, etc., sed sine pausatione. Pes perficitur in penultima . . ."

fection signifies a longa and brevis. The imperfect ligatures thus duplicate the more usual forms of the binariae. The only possible explanation for this usage is that ligatures without perfection are employed to represent parts of a modal ligature which has been broken up because of the appearance of a new syllable or because of repeated tones.

Anonymous IV abundantly illustrates this fact in his presentation of the ligatures without perfection. After describing the ligatures with opposite propriety and with perfection ( = two semibreves;  = two semibreves and a longa), he proceeds to an explanation of the imperfect ligatures.

Furthermore a ligature is said to be imperfect when it is drawn or formed in a manner other than as described above, and it possesses no rule except that it is to be reduced to a perfect ligature. Such a reduction sometimes occurs because notes are placed on the same pitch. But every ligature is said to ascend or descend . . . ; but those notes which are of the same pitch neither ascend nor descend. Therefore a real ligature cannot be made from these notes, but through the understanding alone they may properly be joined into ligatures by the reduction of the longae and breves according to their equivalence: wherefore such a ligature of two notes [i.e., with opposite propriety and imperfection] together with a separate longa coming after it is the equivalent of a ternaria such as mentioned above [i.e., with opposite propriety and perfection]; that is, the ligature of two notes equals a brevis and the single note, a longa, just as in a ternary ligature [with opposite propriety and perfection] two notes stand in place of a brevis and the last note is a longa.[27]

This paragraph reveals the fact that while a binaria cum opposita proprietate et imperfecta has the same meaning, as far as its value is concerned, as a binaria cum opposita proprietate et perfecta, it is nevertheless to be written as an imperfect ligature because it is to be understood as part of a ternary ligature cum opposita proprietate et perfecta which cannot be written as such because two of the tones which should be included in this ternaria are repeated notes.

In the next paragraph Anonymous IV explains the nature of the ligatures cum proprietate et imperfecta and sine proprietate et imperfecta following Garlandia's teaching, but relating their usage still to the fact that repeated notes

27. CS, *I*, 342b: "Iterato figura imperfecta dicitur que alio modo depingitur, vel figuratur quam sicut superius dictum est, et nullam regulam obtinet, nisi ad perfectionem supradictam reducatur. Que quidem reductio quandoque contingit quod soni ponentur in eodem sono, qui omnis ligatura dicitur ascendendo vel descendendo, ut superius dictum est; sed que sunt in eodem sono, non sunt ascendendo vel descendendo. Igitur ex ipsis non fit ligatura materialis, sed per reductionem longarum et brevium solo intellectu juxta equipollentiam bene ligantur, quare due ligate tales cum una longa disjuncta et postposita equipollent tribus, ut supradictum est, videlicet due pro brevi et una pro longa, sicut de tribus, duo pro brevi et ultima longa."

cannot be combined into a ligature.[28] He then turns his attention to the nature of notation cum littera.

In notation cum littera ligatures are indeed sometimes made, sometimes not; but for the most part the notes are separated more than they are joined together. Whence the rule: Every nota simplex, as it appears under its name [i.e., according to its form and meaning], is lengthened or shortened. The separation of notes is due to the syllables placed under them, since whenever a nota simplex is placed above any syllable, it is to be attributed to the same. And according to some people any note, by reason of the difference of syllables, is said to be absolute, according as it is not reduced to a ligature. [In other words, the forms of the longa and brevis in themselves denote an absolute value, and these notes do not have to be considered as part of a modal ligature.] To be sure, if a note is reduced, one alone is not, but it can be reduced with another one or with others. For example, a brevis recta over one syllable and a longa recta over another syllable next to it are the equivalent of a binary ligature with propriety and perfection following the aforesaid rule that every ligature with propriety and perfection [is to be understood in the following manner: the penultimate note is a brevis and the last note a longa].[29]

The author then continues to illustrate how various combinations of notes and ligatures with syllables under them are to be reduced to the equivalent of modal ligatures.[30]

In this highly important passage, which firmly establishes the principles to be followed in reducing notation cum littera to its equivalent in modal ligatures, it becomes clear that the ligatures used in this notation will be either cum proprietate et perfectione or imperfect. The ligature sine proprietate is not much used in notation cum littera, Anonymous IV informs us.[31] And from his de-

28. CS, *I*, 343a: ". . . et hoc dictum est propter plura puncta que non possunt invicem ligari, secundam materiam, nisi solo intellectu."

29. CS, *I*, 343a, b: "Cum littera vero quandoque fit ligatio, quandoque non; sed in majori parte plus distrahuntur, quam ligantur. Unde regula: Omnis simplex figura, prout se ostendit sub suo nomine, elongatur vel abbreviatur. Distractio est propter syllabas subpositas, quoniam supra quamlibet syllabam quandoque ponitur, una simplex sibi ipsi attribuitur. Et ratione diversitatis syllabarum, secundum aliquos, quilibet punctus absolutus dicitur, prout non reducitur ad figuram ligatam. Si vero reducitur, unus solus non reducitur, sed cum alio vel aliis potest reduci, sicut una brevis recta supra unam syllabam, et una longa recta supra alteram syllabam sibi conjunctam equipollent duabus ligatis cum proprietate et perfectione, juxta regulam supradictam, videlicet omnis figura cum proprietate et perfectione posita, etc."

The completion of this last sentence is drawn from Anon. IV's definition of the ligature cum proprietate et perfectione, CS, *I*, 341b.

30. CS, *I*, 343b through 345a.

31. CS, *I*, 343b: ". . . sine proprietate et cum perfectionem, quod quidem non solebatur multum uti, . . ."

scription of the various ligatures employed it becomes apparent that the ligature with propriety and perfection will have the same value that it would have in modal notation sine littera, while the imperfect ligature is used when the values in this ligature are considered to be part of a larger ligature with propriety and perfection which cannot be written as such because of the appearance of a new syllable.

A binary ligature with propriety and imperfection above one syllable with a longa following is to be reduced to a ternary ligature with propriety and perfection;

or with a brevis and longa following it is to be reduced to a ternary ligature in the same way.

[The quaternaria here has a value equivalent to a ternaria cum proprietate et perfectione according to the rule: "every ligature of more than three notes is to be reduced to a ternary ligature of the same species" (CS, *1*, 343a).] Likewise a ternary ligature with propriety and imperfection together with the next following longa is reduced to a ternaria with propriety and perfection.

[Again the quaternaria is equivalent to the value of a ternary ligature with propriety and perfection.] In a like manner we understand that ligatures of four, five, or six notes with propriety and imperfection together with the first longa following over another syllable are to be reduced to ternariae.[32]

There can be no doubt that notation cum littera whether it appears in the motet, the conductus, or organum is to be understood as the equivalent of the ligatures which express modal rhythm. The novel form of the imperfect ligature introduced by Garlandia is quite obviously intended to remove the ambiguity of the older notation of the conductus, etc., as well as of the former method of notating repeated tones which cannot be properly joined into normal ligatures. The imperfection of a ligature informs the singer that this ligature is in reality part of a larger ligature, the remainder of which is to be found in

32. CS, *1*, 344b: "Iterato due ligate cum proprietate et imperfectione supra unam syllabam cum longa sequenti reducuntur ad tres ligatas cum proprietate et perfectione, vel cum brevi et longa sequentibus simili modo reducuntur ad tres, etc.

"Iterato tres ligate cum proprietate et imperfectione, cum longa proxima sequente, ad tres reducuntur cum proprietate et perfectione.

"Sic etiam intelligimus de quatuor, quinque, vel sex, etc., cum proprietate et imperfectione, cum prima longa sequente, supra alteram syllabam, ad tres ligatas reducuntur."

the next following note; and the propriety or lack of propriety of an imperfect ligature tells us that this ligature is part of a ligature of the first mode or second mode. Both Garlandia and Anonymous IV acknowledge the modernity of the imperfect ligature and state that it will not be found in older manuscripts, examples of which have come down to us in W1, F, and W2, where ligatures sine perfectione are not to be found. "Nevertheless," adds Garlandia, "if the ligatures are not notated properly [that is, if they are perfect rather than imperfect], in general all ligatures [in conductus] are to be taken as being imperfect, and this is to be understood in discant and wherever correct measurement appears."[33] To which remark Anonymous IV adds the following condescending statements:

> Those ligatures which are said to be with propriety and without perfection were at first known in a confused manner. They were treated in an equivocal manner, which is really no manner at all. For in the old books the notes were too equivocal, because the simple note forms were all alike, and the singers worked solely through their understanding, saying: I understand this note to be long and that note to be short. And they labored for too long a time before they had mastered what is now easily perceived by all those who work in such matters by means of the above-said rules, so that today one accomplishes more in an hour than formerly they did in seven.[34]

The principles laid down by Garlandia and Anonymous IV provide the basis for the transcription of the conductus of the Notre Dame epoch. In all cases a modal rhythm is to be maintained. The various ligatures and notae simplices written above the syllables are to be construed within a modal pattern. In this connection two conductus to be found at the end of the fascicle of three-voiced conductus in the Florence manuscript (folios 252′–254′) are most enlightening. These compositions are presumably of a later date than the other pieces in the manuscript, for they are written throughout in mensural notation which of course makes their rhythmic meaning plain. Stylistically, however, they belong to the tradition of such conductus as the *Salvatoris hodie* of Perotin. Despite the fact that the text was never added, the appearance of the notation betrays the sections that are syllabic and those that are melismatic. In the first case, the notes

33. See n. 25, above.

34. CS, *I*, 344a: "Ea que dicuntur cum proprietate et sine perfectione, erant primo confuse quoad notitiam, sed per modum equivocationis accipiebantur, quod quidem modo non est, quoniam in antiquis libris habebant puncta equivoca nimis, quia simplicia materialia fuerunt equalia, sed solo intellectu operabantur dicendo: intelligo istam longam, intelligo illam brevem, et nimio tempore longa laborabunt, antequam scirent bene aliquid quod nunc ex levi ab omnibus laborantibus circa talia percipitur mediantibus predictorum, ita quod quilibet plus proficerit in una hora quam in septem ante quoad longum ire."

are widely spaced to accommodate the text and consist of notae simplices and small ligatures written in mensural forms. In the latter case, the notes are grouped into ligatures in the typical manner of notation sine littera. Of particular interest is the relationship of the text to the musical rhythm. The first ordo of the syllabic portion of the first conductus distributes the syllables one to each perfection of the third mode. The next ordo begins in the same way but halfway through changes this procedure and adapts each syllable to the individual values of the modal pattern. Later ordines are written entirely with one syllable to each of the longae and breves. It is apparent that the textual rhythm is subordinated to the modal rhythm and that the composer does not hesitate to violate the prosody of the text when he so desires. At the same time the modal rhythm itself is not rigidly adhered to, but freely admits fractio and extensio modi.

This concrete example of rhythmic practices in conductus substantiates the statements of the theorists that modal rhythm prevails in this category of composition. The proper approach to the conductus should accordingly be through the rhythmic modes. It should be generally assumed that the same mode is to be found in the syllabic portions as in the caudae. The value to be assigned to the notae simplices and ligatures will be determined by their position within the modal pattern. At the same time the ligatures must commonly be read as if they were imperfect ligatures. The total value of the ligature will depend upon whether the ligature represents two or more parts of the modal pattern or whether it stands for only one part. In the first mode, for example, a binaria above a syllable may stand for a complete foot, or it may be two breves equivalent to a longa recta, or two semibreves equal to a brevis recta. A ternaria, on the other hand, can represent only the value of a longa recta or longa ultra mensuram. It could not equal a brevis recta since the brevis was not divisible into three semibreves. I am well aware of the fact that the problems of the notation of conductus are by no means completely solved by this brief discussion. Nevertheless it seems certain that the conductus, at least of the Notre Dame epoch, can be transcribed only in terms of modal rhythm.

At its best, notation cum littera is never wholly unambiguous and one can easily understand the complacent attitude of Anonymous IV toward the recent innovations in notation that resolved all the complexities and doubts of the older method. The uncertainty of the original notation cum littera is strikingly revealed in a number of clausulae in the Florence manuscript. These substitute clausulae seem to be in notation sine littera, i.e., they are written primarily in ligatures. However, they do not lend themselves easily to transcription and one can only transcribe them by the most arbitrary distortion of the laws of modal ligatures. The problematic nature of these pieces arises from a not very successful attempt to convert motets into substitute clausulae by omitting the text of the motetus and changing the notation cum littera into the ligatures of notation sine littera. Often the individual notes and ligatures of the motet have been only partially reassembled into modal ligatures, and at times they have been converted into ligatures that are incorrect by the laws of modal notation. It is only by comparison with the original motet that the correct values of the notes may be determined. Evidently the scribe did not understand the original notation or he could not transliterate it into the more normal notation sine littera.

The number of such clausulae derived from motets, apparently in an attempt to enrich the stagnant repertory of organum, is relatively large. It includes *Domino* No. 12 (f. 88′) and the substitute clausulae Nos. 14, 41, 59–60, 61, 77, 85, 94, 105, 106, 131, 141, 150, 156, 163, 283.[35] In addition to these pieces there are four others that are written in the same irregular manner, although there is no known motet source for them. These are *Domino* No. 13 (f. 88′) and the substitute clausulae Nos. 50, 126, 146. In these derivatory clausulae the treatment of the text as well as the notation points to an origin in the motet. In the motet the text of the tenor is usually written at the beginning of the piece rather than placing each syllable under the note to which it properly belongs. Accordingly, in the process of converting the motet into a clausula it would be necessary to realign the syllables of the text under their proper notes. The scribe has endeavored to do this but oftentimes quite carelessly. For example, only the first syllable of *Domino* No. 12 has been written down and only the initial letter of *Flos filius ejus* (No. 166). It is also significant that the syllable marks, which are employed in organum but not in the motet, are often absent (Nos. 85, 94, 104, 150, 166). This process of enriching the repertory of organum from the motet is interesting proof of the reversal of the roles of organum and motet in the thirteenth century. Organum had once been the source from which motets were drawn. Now it is organum which draws upon the motet.

35. The related motets will be found listed in Ludwig, *Repertorium.* However, the following additions should be made: Nos. 59 and 60, listed by Ludwig as two clausulae, are in reality only one, which is derived from the motet *Quant li nouviaus tens* (W_2, f. 243); No. 77 = *Hui main* (W_2, f. 234′ — 235); No. 85 = *Quant froidure* (Mo, No. 221).

To return to the question of the notation cum littera in organum, it will be found that three methods of notation are used: the plica, the ligature which is to be understood as an imperfect ligature, and currentes. An excellent illustration of the use of the plica and the currentes is provided by the very first of the substitute clausulae in the Florence manuscript, *Et Jerusalem,* f. 147. In the first ordo the second syllable of the text is introduced, thereby disrupting the normal modal ligatures. The original notation of the ordo, together with the equivalent notation sine littera and the modern transcription, appear in the following example:

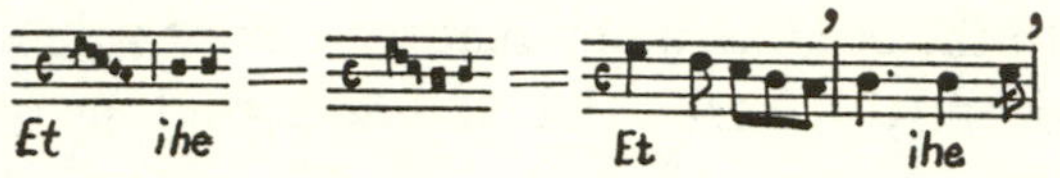

Both examples of modal notation have the same rhythmic meaning. The introduction of the syllable "ihe" on a longa value, which properly should be joined with the preceding brevis in a binaria, means that the binaria as such cannot be written. Therefore the composer has added the brevis to the preceding ligature and at the same time has replaced the plica with a regular tone, creating a conjunctura of two notes. The two currentes are thus to be understood as partaking of the value of the final note of the ligature which is a longa, in this case a ternary longa.

The use of the plica is to be seen in the same piece in the long ordo beginning with the syllable "sa." The notation is as follows:

The syllable "lem" on the fifth longa of the ordo breaks up the binaria which belongs here. In place of a ligature, the brevis has been added to the preceding ligature in the form of a plica and the longa has been grouped with the succeeding binaria to form a ternaria to be read as a ternaria with propriety and perfection. As for the use of ligatures in notation cum littera, the second ordo of the clausula *Dum loqueretur* (F, f. 181) may serve as an example. This phrase is written:

This clausula is in the first mode, so these notes must be read:

We have here an example of extensio modi in which ternary ligatures have been broken up by the appearance of new syllables. If written sine littera this ordo would be represented thus:

It will be noticed that the final ternaria may not be represented as such because of a repeated note.

Another cause of irregular notation are the imperfect modes. Although they are a legitimate part of the modal system, their notation is derived from that of the perfect modes with the consequence that ligatures and notae simplices are given new and unusual treatment. The only full discussion of the imperfect modes is to be found in Anonymous IV (CS, *1*, 329a–336b; 345b–347a). It is not necessary to repeat all the details given by him, but it is essential to outline the principles regulating them and their notation. It has been shown above (pp. 42 ff.) that an ordo of an imperfect mode must always be followed by another ordo beginning on the second part of the foot and terminating on the first part of the foot. As a result, the notation of these two ordines will differ even though they are both in the same mode. For example, the first ordo of the first imperfect mode together with its answering ordo would be notated in the following manner:

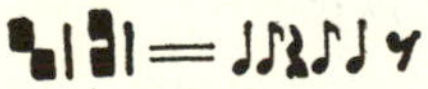

The first ligature must be written sine proprietate to signify the succession longa brevis, while the second ligature must be written cum proprietate. In the case of the third mode the first ordo with its answer would be written:

According to Anonymous IV the third imperfect mode is subject to almost infinite variation since he maintains that one or both breves may be omitted so that an imperfect ordo of this mode may consist of the initial longa alone, or only the first longa and brevis. This means that the answering phrases will also be varied in order to bring the mode back into balance. The notation for these ordines will differ of necessity for the initial ordo and the succeeding ones.

The notation of the imperfect modes as outlined by Anonymous IV presents no difficulties, since he uses notes and ligatures with mensural significance. However, the notation becomes very problematic in the modal system because the notes and ligatures receive a specific value, not from their forms but from their context in the modal pattern. It is undoubtedly for this reason that the imperfect modes are seldom encountered in the music of the Notre Dame era. Nevertheless, they do occur upon occasion, primarily in the realm of conductus. They are usually employed to produce a hocketing effect between two parts. To interpret the notation of the imperfect modes one must generally assume that a ligature is to be read as being imperfect. An example of the use of an imperfect mode is to be found in the conductus *Salvatoris hodie.* The end of the third line of text is as follows: [36]

A melisma begins on the final syllable and the ligatures in the tenor indicate that the first mode is being used. The triplum starts with a binaria followed by a rest. This must be interpreted as an imperfect ligature representing the end of an imperfect ordo. The following rest is a long replacing the first part of the foot; the nota simplex is a brevis, again followed by a long rest. At the end the two *c*'s must be construed as a binaria with the normal reading brevis, longa, thus restoring the mode. The second *c* is, of course, a ternary longa, since it is followed by a longa. A similar passage is to be found in the same piece in the melisma at the end of the first line of text of the second stanza in the top voice:

Again the first binaria is read as an imperfect ligature ending an imperfect ordo, while the next binaria is to be read in the normal way. Most of the examples of imperfect modes that I have encountered are as relatively simple as these. Despite their simplicity it is still important to recognize that they form an integral part of the modal system. And what is more, the examples from *Salvatoris hodie*

36. There is a minor discrepancy between the manuscripts for the penultimate note of the triplum. The version given above is that of W_2 (f. 31). W_1 has only one *c,* while Florence writes this note as a duplex longa.

prove that the imperfect modes were already in use at the time of Perotin and are not simply the hypothetical constructions of later theorists as has commonly been assumed. That the imperfect modes play a very minor role in modal rhythm must be admitted, but they must nevertheless be accepted as part of the system, for they do occasionally occur in practical musical examples. To the best of my knowledge the imperfect modes are not to be found in organum but only in conductus.[37]

To conclude this chapter on irregular notation mention should be made of several types of irregularities that occur frequently enough to indicate that they are part of the general practice of the time. These are deviations from the rules of ligature writing which are to be explained simply as orthographical usages. Perhaps the most common of these devices is the manner of writing an ascending quaternaria. The normal form of this ligature evidently was difficult to write in the cramped lines and spaces of the scores. Therefore it is frequently replaced by other forms:

Other exceptional ligatures occur when the scribe, for the sake of convenience, combines two ligatures into one larger ligature. It is not unusual to find the opening ternaria and binaria of an ordo of the first mode written as a quinaria to be read ♩♪♩♪♩ (see the clausula *Lux magna* at the end of *Alleluia. Dies sanctificatus*). Particularly frequent are quinariae which replace a binaria plicata and a binaria of the first mode. For example, in *Descendit de celis* (F, f. 14, third ordo) we find this notation:

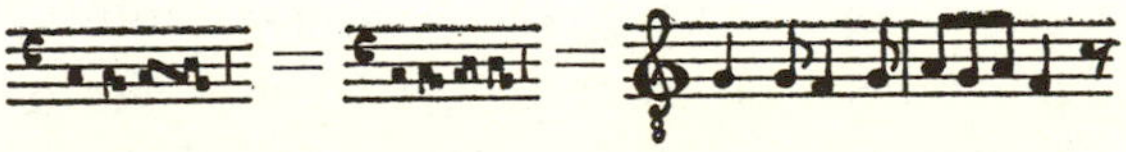

Another irregularity occasionally encountered is the use of a ternaria instead of a binaria plicata in the second mode. This ternaria will then have the value of three breves rectae. However, this usage is seldom encountered except when its context is made very clear by the surrounding ligatures or by the ligatures in the other voices.

37. A use of the hocket effect, somewhat similar to that produced by the imperfect modes, is to be found in the clausula "mea" of *Alleluya, Veni electa mea* (W_1, f. 40′).

4. *The Notation of Organum Duplum*

The discussion of the notation of Leonin's great volume of two-voiced organa has been reserved for this final chapter for two reasons. First of all, the very nature of organum duplum has never been fully understood. Misled by certain statements of the theorists and by the unusual groups of ligatures that appear in the great melismata of the upper voice, historians have assumed that organum purum represents a special category of composition in which the rhythm is markedly nonmodal. It is considered that the melismata are either to be sung in a free rhythm resembling the modern interpretation of Gregorian chant or are notated in a curious hodgepodge of long and short values representing a mixture of modal patterns.[1] Even when the modality of these compositions has been accepted the most willful transcriptions of the ligatures have been made. The second reason for deferring the discussion of the notation of organum duplum to the end of this study is that an understanding of the ligatures can only be reached upon the basis of the modal principles discussed in the preceding chapters. It is necessary therefore that we first establish the nature of organum duplum, whether it is modal or nonmodal. Then, having ascertained the nature of its rhythm, it will be possible to penetrate the mysteries of its notation.

The cloud of obscurity which surrounds the problem of the organum duplum is directly attributable to a general misapprehension of the stylistic distinctions of music set up by the thirteenth-century theorists. It is believed today that the music of the period with which we are dealing was divided into two antithetic categories. On one side is grouped the motet, the conductus, the hocket, and organa tripla and quadrupla, all of which are characterized by modal rhythm. Opposed to these types of composition is the organum duplum, characterized by a free rhythm. Midway between these two categories lies a mysterious style known as the copula. Recognizing that modal rhythm does nevertheless exist in organum duplum in the clausulae where the tenor moves more rapidly, historians have somewhat modified the rigidity of the above classification. It is assumed that both modal and nonmodal rhythm exist side by side in organum duplum and that the copula is a bridge passage of peculiar rhythmic qualities that links the modal and nonmodal sections of a piece. The schematization also

1. For a summary of current theories see W. Apel, "From St. Martial to Notre Dame," *Journal of the American Musicological Society, 2,* No. 3 (1949), 145 f.

has to be altered for the conductus, if the sections cum littera are to be considered nonmodal and the sections sine littera as modal.

The discrepancies in this system of classification are only too obvious and have made many a student of this period throw up his hands in despair. Considering the lack of clarity in the statements of the theorists, particularly of the post-Franconian generations, it is not surprising that this state of confusion should exist today. Nevertheless a careful reading of the pre-Franconian theorists will reveal that a coherent systematic doctrine of musical styles was taught and understood by writers before the time of Franco of Cologne. To comprehend the nature of these styles one must turn to the definitions of the theorists and endeavor to establish the correct significance of each style as well as the various categories of composition that are related to them.

Until the middle of the twelfth century polyphonic music was called by the theorists either organum or discantus (*diaphonia*). Jacques Handschin[2] has ably demonstrated that no clear-cut distinction was made between these terms before the appearance of the school of St. Martial with its advanced style of organum. Hitherto discantus had been only a rather loose equivalent of organum, both meaning simply the combination of melodies; but with the development of two distinct manners of combining voices in polyphonic compositions, the meanings of the two terms became more sharply distinguished. An anonymous *Tractatus de musica,*[3] obviously related to the St. Martial circle, for the first time clearly characterizes discantus as something different from organum. This treatise associates the term discantus with the combination of voices nota contra notam, reserving organum as the appellative for the increasingly prominent manner of composing long melismata in the upper part over the individual notes of the cantus firmus. "The difference between discantus and organum," writes the anonymous author, "is that discantus accords with its cantus firmus always through some consonance or unison and by means of an equal number of notes, while organum is made to agree with its cantus firmus not with an equal number but with an infinite multiplicity of notes and with a certain wonderful flexibility."[4] The author is acutely aware of the essential

2. "Zur Geschichte der Lehre vom Organum," *ZfMW, 8* (1926), 321.

3. In Juste Adrien L. de la Fage, *Essais de diphthérographie musicale* (Paris, 1864), *1,* 355 ff. Handschin, pp. 333–336, reprints part of this treatise.

4. "Inter discantum vero et organum hoc interesse probatur quod discantus equali punctorum numero cantui suo per aliquam semper consonantiam respondet aut compositionem facit unisonam; organum autem non equalitate punctorum, sed infinita multiplicitate, ac mira quodam flexibilitate cantui suo concordat." (Handschin, p. 335.)

differences between these two manners of composition. Even though both of them could exist side by side in the same composition, a fact attested to by the existing manuscripts of St. Martial organum, they should by no means be used indiscriminately. The author admits that it is possible to introduce passages in the style of organum within sections of discantus for aesthetic purposes (*ut discantus pulchrior et facietior habeatur et ab auscultantibus libentius audiatur*), but warns against an abuse of this practice. "When you wish to embellish the end of a section, beware lest you intermix too frequently too many flourishes of organum with the discantus; lest when you think you are writing discantus, you will be creating organum and destroying the discantus." [5]

The distinction drawn here between discantus (counterpoint nota contra notam) and organum (counterpoint with a melismatic upper part above sustained tenor notes) was to be retained by the theorists of the thirteenth century. Even though organum (i.e., the polyphonic setting of a responsorial chant) underwent a profound change in the last half of the twelfth century through the introduction of modal rhythm by the Notre Dame composers, these two techniques of composition were maintained throughout the first half of the thirteenth century. At the same time, however, the new rhythmic considerations necessitated still more precise definitions of these terms. In the middle of the century Johannes de Garlandia undertook this clarification, expanding the twofold characterization of musical styles by the addition of a third, the copula. Garlandia's classifications were accepted by later theorists, notably by Anonymous IV and the St. Emmeram Anonymous, but in the last part of the century they came to be misunderstood. The ascendancy of the motet, with its newly created system of mensural notation, gradually destroyed the older form of organum and its system of modal notation. Consequently Garlandia's definitions, which were based upon existing practice in organum, no longer were properly understood by the practitioners and theorists of mensural rhythm. In the treatises of Magister Lambertus (Pseudo-Aristotle) and Franco, the first advocates of a mensural system based upon a ternary long, the terminology of Garlandia has already lost something of its proper meaning. Franco's incorrect interpretation of copula and Pseudo-Aristotle's vague explanations of the three styles reveal that the musical culture which produced these styles has ceased to

5. "Proinde cum deflorere finem clausulae volueris, vice ne nimios modulos per nimium saepius discantui misceas; ne cum discantum facere putaveris, organum aedifices et discantum destruas." (*Ibid.*, p. 333.)

be a living force and that these terms have little or no significance for contemporary musical practice.

It is to Garlandia's treatise, then, that one must turn to gain an insight into the accepted musical practices of the Notre Dame epoch. Written in the middle of the century at a time when the author could look back upon the fully developed potentialities of Parisian organum, this treatise summarizes the musical achievements of the immediate past. Of particular interest is Garlandia's classification of music, for it enables us today to obtain a clear idea of the styles and rhythmic features of the music of Leonin's and Perotin's generations.

In conformity with the age-old tradition of a threefold division of music,[6] Garlandia divides music into three parts–in this case, *musica plana, musica mensurabilis,* and *musica instrumentalis:*

> Musica plana is that which was first brought forth by Saint Gregory in honor of God, of Mary the most glorious mother of God, and of all the saints of God. Afterwards it was corrected, collected, and organized by the monk Guido. Musica mensurabilis is that which is made in proportions according to a correct measurement by means of an appropriate mode correctly maintained. Musica instrumentalis is that which is performed on musical instruments.[7]

This classification is not wholly consistent, for the first two are based on the measurement or lack of measurement of temporal values, while the third depends upon the means of performance. Presumably, however, musica instrumentalis is also to be classified as musica mensurabilis. The principal distinction then is unmeasured music, i.e., the Gregorian chant on one side and measured or modal music on the other.

At the same time, musica plana and musica mensurabilis are differentiated as monodic and polyphonic music respectively. The Gregorian chant will always be monodic and unmeasured, while polyphonic music will always be measured. That for Garlandia polyphony, organum, and musica mensurabilis are synonymous terms becomes apparent in a later definition: "Having spoken of plainsong which is said to be unmeasured, I now intend to speak of musica men-

6. See Gerhard Pietzsch, *Die Klassifikation der Musik von Boetius bis Ugolino von Orvieto* (Halle, 1929).

7. "Musica plana est illa que ad honorem Dei nec non gloriosissime Dei genetricis Marie et omnium sanctorum Dei a beato Gregorio primo fuit edita, et postea a Guidone monaco fuit correcta, composita et ordinata. Musica mensurabilis est illa que proportionabiliter, secundum rectam mensuram et mensurabilem modo debito ac proprie observato efficitur. Musica instrumentalis est que instrumentis musicalibus exercetur. . . ." (CS, *I*, 157b.)

surabilis which is called organum, so that as far as we are concerned *organum generale* means all measured music. Whence organum is both the species of all measured music and at the same time, in a different sense, a genus." [8] The term organum generale accordingly is a generic term for all polyphonic music, one type of which is also called organum—*organum speciale*. Musica mensurabilis or organum generale is, like musica, subject to a triple division: "You must know that there are three generally accepted species of organum: discantus, copula, and organum." [9] These three varieties of measured, i.e., modal, music are then defined in turn:

Discantus is the simultaneous sounding [*consonantia*] of different melodies according to mode and according to the equivalence of one to another. And thus there are as many species of modes in the equivalent part, which is called the *secundus cantus* [i.e., upper voice], as there are in the tenor part, which is called the *primus cantus*. And there are six modes in discantus. You must know that three things are to be kept under consideration in connection with the tenor part, viz., *sonus, ordinatio,* and *modus*. Sonus here means musica [i.e., the pitch of a note]. Ordinatio means the number of notes before a rest. Modus means the quantities of the long or short notes. The same three things are similarly to be considered in connection with the secundus cantus. For this reason the primus and secundus cantus together are to be considered in relation to three factors, viz., number, mode, and consonance: in number, that there be as many equivalent notes in the secundus cantus as there are in the tenor part, or vice versa; in mode, that a longa shall be placed against a longa or breves equivalent to a longa; in consonance, that the tenor sounds well with the secundus cantus, and vice versa. Whence the rule: every odd note [i.e., the first, third, fifth, etc.] must form a consonance with every odd note [of the other part], whether they are in the first, the second, or the third mode. But in the third mode two notes will appear instead of one [i.e., two breves instead of a single longa] and sometimes one of these notes may form a dissonance to add color to the music. This dissonance may be formed by either the first or second note and this practise has been permitted and sanctioned by the fore-

8. "Habito de ipsa plana musica que immensurabilis dicitur, nunc est presens intentio de ipsa mensurabili, que organum dicitur, quantum ad nos prout organum generale dicitur ad omnem mensurabilem musicam. Unde organum et est species totius mensurabilis musice, et est genus diversimode tamen." (CS, *I*, 175a.)

9. "Sciendum ergo quod ipsius organi generaliter accepte tres sunt species: discantus, copula, organum, de quibus dicendum est per ordinem." (*CS, I,* 175a.) In connection with these definitions, cf. the St. Emmeram Anonymous: "[Musica] mensurabilis est illa, in qua sua quantitas temporum reperitur . . . Cuius mensurabilis musice tria sunt genera, scilicet discantus, copula et organum. Et est aliud organum, quod idem est quod musica mensurabilis et prout ita sumitur est genus generale ad tria genera supradicta. . . ." (Sowa, p. 5, ll. 5 ff.) Sowa incorrectly divides the last sentence into two: "Et est aliud organum, quod idem est quod musica. Mensurabilis [etc.]." I can see no reason for Sowa's statement: "Die musikalischen Formen der ars antiqua scheidet der anonyme Autor in zwei Formengattungen: (I) organum generale sive discantus; (II) organum speciale sive organum duplex" (p. xxvii).

most composers. This is to be found moreover in many places in organum and especially in motets. It is to be noted that there are three species of discantus: rectus modus against rectus, which is the first species; modus per ultra mensuram against modus per ultra mensuram, which is the second species; and rectus modus against modus per ultra mensuram, which is the third species.[10]

From the extensiveness of this definition it is possible to obtain precise knowledge of the nature of discantus. It is the combination of two voices, both of which are modally measured. Furthermore there is an exact correspondence of both parts in that each contains the same number of notes in an ordo or the equivalent of the same number of notes, as when the sixth mode is placed against the first or second mode so that there are two breves in one part against a longa in the other. In other words, discantus is essentially nothing but the nota contra notam style first clearly defined in the anonymous treatise printed by de la Fage. For each note of the tenor there will be a corresponding note in the other voice, and when the tenor has a rest at the end of an ordo, the other voice will also have a rest. Discantus is therefore a style, a specific manner of combining voices, and as a style it may appear in any of the various categories of composition: in the polyphonic setting of Gregorian chant (organum), in conductus, and in the motet.[11] Related to discantus, which by etymology implies the com-

10. "Discantus est aliquorum diversorum cantuum consonantia secundum modum, et secundum equipollentis equipollentiam. Et sunt tot species sicut et in modo a parte equipollentis qui dicitur secundus cantus, quot a parte tenoris qui dicitur primus cantus. Sunt autem sex species ejus, ut dicitur.

"Et sciendum quod a parte primi tria sunt consideranda; scilicet sonus, ordinatio et modus. Sonus hic accipitur pro musica. Ordinatio hic sumitur numerus punctorum ante pausationem. Modus pro quantitate longarum vel brevium notarum.

"Similiter eadem a parte secundi consideranda sunt. Propterea primus et secundus in tribus sunt considerandi, scilicet in numero, in modo et in concordantia. In numero, ut tot sunt puncti secundum equipollentiam a parte secundi, quot a parte primi, vel e converso. In modo, ut sit longa contra longam, vel breves equipollentes longe. In concordantia, ut primus bene concordet secundo, et e converso.

"Unde regula: omne quod fit impari debet concordari cum omni illo quod fit in impari, si sit in primo, vel secundo, vel tertio modo. Sed duo puncti sumentur hic pro uno, et aliquando unus eorum ponitur in discordantiam, propter colorem musice. Et hic primus sive secundus; et hoc bene permittitur ab auctoribus primis et licenciatur. Hoc autem invenitur in organo in pluribus locis et precipue in motetis.

"Et notandum quod sunt tres species discantus: aut rectus positus contra rectum, quod est prima species; aut modus per ultra mensuram ad modum per ultra mensuram, quod est secunda species; aut rectus contra per ultra mensuram, quod est tertia species." (CS, *I*, 106b–107a.)

11. The St. Emmeram Anonymous, who in the fifth chapter of his treatise presents Garlandia's definition of discantus almost word for word, writes at the beginning of the sixth chapter: "Note that the doctrine of the preceding chapter [i.e., on discantus] is extended to every kind of song in

bination of only two voices, are the terms triplum and quadruplum, which mean either the third and fourth voices added to the two voices of discantus or the resulting three- or four-part composition. The triplum and quadruplum will be in the same nota contra notam style.[12]

Passing by for the moment Garlandia's definition of copula, we shall now consider his exposition of the third variety of musica mensurabilis, organum:

Organum is spoken of in a number of ways: either generally or specifically. We have already spoken of organum generale previously; now, however, we are to consider organum speciale. Organum speciale is referred to in two ways: either per se [i.e., two-voiced organum or organum duplum] or with another [i.e., organum triplum]. Organum per se is said to be that which is produced in some rhythmic mode which is rectus or non rectus. A normal [rectus] mode here means that by which discantus is made. A mode is called non rectus because it differs from any normal mode in which the longae and breves are first and foremost used correctly in the proper way. In a modus non rectus a longa and brevis are, indeed, used in the first mode, though only incidentally. Moreover, organum non rectum is said to be that which is produced according to an abnormal measurement, as mentioned above. The upper part will be equivalent to a single note of the tenor up to the end of a *punctus* [a phrase or section within the piece], when the two parts will meet in some consonance.[13]

According to this definition, the characteristic feature of organum is that the nota contra notam style of discantus is here replaced by a measured upper part sounded against a single note of the tenor. The tenor part in organum style is thus unmeasured, in that it is not arranged in a modal pattern and each individ-

---

which correct proportion of measurement is maintained. . . . "Et nota, quod doctrina capituli precedentis ad omne genus cantuum se extendit, in quibus recta mensure proportio sit reperta . . ." (Sowa, p. 127, ll. 4–6.)

12. Garlandia defines triplum thus: "Triplum is the mixture of three tones according to the customary six consonances, viz., unison, octave, etc., in the same tempus. This is the common description, but a special sense of the word triplum is described thus: triplum is a melody in proportions which fits with discantus and is in consonance with it. Thus it is a third melody added to two others." "Triplum est commixtio trium sonorum secundum habitudinem sex concordantiarum, scilicet unisonus, diapason, etc.; et hoc in eodem tempore. Et ista est communis descriptio. Specialiter autem sic describitur: triplum est cantus proportionatus aliquis conveniens et concordans cum discantu. Et sic est tertius cantus adjunctus duobus." (CS, *1*, 114b.)

13. "Organum dicitur multipliciter: generaliter et specialiter. De organo generaliter dictum est superius; nunc autem dicendum est de ipso in speciali. Organum in speciali dicitur dupliciter: aut per se, aut cum alio. Organum per se dicitur id esse quidquid profertur secundum aliquem modum rectum, aut non rectum. Rectus modus sumitur hic ille per quem discantus profertur. Non rectus dicitur ad differentiam alicujus recte; que longe et breves recte sumuntur debito modo primo, et principaliter. In non recto vero sumitur longa et brevis in primo modo, sed ex contingenti. Organum autem non rectum dicitur quidquid profertur per non rectam mensuram, ut dictum est superius. Et ejus equipollentia tantum se tenet in unisono usque ad finem alicujus puncti, ut secum convenit secundum aliquam concordantiam." (CS, *1*, 114a.)

ual note receives its value not from its position within a modal pattern but from the number of notes in the duplum placed against it. Despite the fact that the tenor part is unmeasured, organum speciale is still to be classified as a species of organum generale, i.e., measured polyphonic music, because the upper voice is measured in modal rhythm. This particular style of a melismatic upper voice against a sustained note in the tenor is to be found primarily in organum, i.e., the polyphonic setting of a responsorial chant, and as a style it still lives today as organpoint (*punctus organi*). But organum as a style is not necessarily the only style employed in organum as a category of composition. The nota contra notam style of discantus occurs in sections where the tenor is modal,[14] and the copula as a style is also to be found.

The terms modus rectus and modus non rectus present some difficulties. It must not be assumed that the modus rectus is exclusively the property of discantus, as Willi Apel [15] has done in a recent article. Garlandia states explicitly that both the modus rectus and the modus non rectus are to be found in organum style. Garlandia is careful to explain that the term modus non rectus does not mean in this definition a modus per ultra mensuram (i.e., the third, fourth, and fifth modes, which contain long notes of three tempora and breves of two tempora). Modus rectus and modus non rectus simply refer to the manner of executing the long and short values of the modal pattern of the duplum. In modus rectus the longae and breves will be maintained in their exact mathematical relationships. In modus non rectus the normal value of the longa and brevis will be wilfully altered, but they will nevertheless remain in their characteristic modal arrangement. Anonymous IV informs us that in organum duplum there is a certain modus which is different from a true modus, "because the longs are too long and the breves too short, and it seems to be an irregular mode in comparison with the modes of discantus, although in itself it is regular." [16] The modus non rectus is thus an ad libitum performance of the duplum part by exaggerating the length or shortness of the individual notes.

14. Franco of Cologne confirms this in his definition of organum. "Organum properly speaking is a song which is not measured in every part. It is to be recognized that organum purum can exist only over a tenor where a single note is sustained, so that when the tenor has many notes all at once [i.e., in quick succession], it instantly becomes discantus." "Organum proprie sumptum est cantus non in omni parte sua mensuratus. Sciendum quod purum organum haberi non potest, nisi super tenorem, ubi sola nota est in unisono, ita quod quando tenor accipit plures notas simul, statim est discantus." (CS, *1*, 134b.)

15. W. Apel, "From St. Martial to Notre Dame," *JAMS, 2,* No. 3 (1949), 149.

16. "Est et sextum volumen de organo in duplo, ut: *Judea et Jerusalem, et Constantis;* quod quidem nunquam fit in triplo, velut potest fieri propter quemdam modum ipsum quem habet extraneum aliis. Et quia longe sunt nimis longe, et breves nimis breves, et videtur esse modus ir-

Anonymous IV devotes a lengthy passage to the description of the modi non recti, which he calls irregular or voluntary modes. The terminology applied to the longae and breves of these modes indicates the willfully arbitrary nature of their performance. The longa is variously referred to as a duplex longa or *nimis longa* (too long) in the first and second modes; and as a *minima longa* in the third, fourth, and fifth modes. The brevis is a semibrevis, a *brevis parva, brevis minima, longa tarda,* etc.[17] This irregular manner of performance is in no way indicated by the notation, which on the contrary consists of the usual modal ligatures.[18] In other words, the modus non rectus is still a mode, although its values are adjusted in various ways by the performer. Such a performance undoubtedly has nothing to do with the composer's original intentions, but depends solely upon the preference of the individual singer. There are, for instance, no less than three irregular manners of performing the third mode, none of which is indicated by the composer in his notation. This fact is of the utmost importance in the transcription of organum duplum, for it means that the transliteration of modal notation into its modern equivalent must, like its counterpart, present a modal picture. The transcriber needs only to present the modal values represented by the ligatures, leaving any alteration of the notes to the individual performer. For example, the transcription of a passage in the first mode would show a series of alternate quarter and eighth notes. These may be sung as they stand in modus rectus, or they may be executed in the manner of the irregular first mode by lengthening the quarter note and shortening the eighth note:

Having established that discantus is the combination of two parts, both of which are modal and have the same number of notes or their equivalent before a rest, and that organum is the combination of a modal voice (duplum) with

regularis quoad modos supradictos ipsius discantus, quamvis in se sit regularis . . ." (CS, *I*, 360b.). The St. Emmeram Anonymous makes substantially the same statement in his discussion of organum speciale: "Et nota quod licet rectam relinquat mensuram, cum habet modum et mensuram in se." (Sowa, p. 130, l. 4.)

17. See CS, *I*, 361b–362a.

18. Anon. IV states that the rules for the notation of the irregular modes are the same as those for the regular modes. "Iterato nota quod sufficit de modo figurandi juxta descriptionem eorumdem, ut superius plenius patet. Et est figuratio consimilis sicut in aliis regularibus, quamvis in aliquibus sit differentia, etc." (CS, *I*, 362a.) The notation given for the sixth irregular mode (ligatura quaternaria followed by ternariae), for example, differs in no way from that of the proper sixth mode.

a single note in the tenor, we are now in a position to understand Garlandia's definition of the third type of measured music, the copula:

The copula is of great value for discantus, because discantus is never fully known except by means of the copula. Whence copula is said to be that which is between discantus and organum. Copula may be described in another way: copula is that which appears in rectus modus equivalent to a single tone. And it may be defined in another way: copula is whever a number of puncti [i.e., signs of notation] are made. Punctus, as it is used here, means wherever there is a number of lines, and this part is divided into two equal parts; whence the first part is called the antecedent and the second, the consequence and each part contains a number of lines. Therefore a line is drawn wherever there is a number of intervals, such as the unison or other interval, according to the number required in the requisite ordo.[19]

The meaning of this passage is admittedly cryptic, but it is so only because a great amount of information has been compressed into a minimum number of sentences. By considering the individual sentences in conjunction with other passages it is possible to attain a complete understanding of the nature of the copula. It is to be noticed first of all that the copula is a variety of discantus, which means that it must consist of two measured voices.[20] But it is neither pure discantus (nota contra notam) nor is it pure organum (a modal duplum over a single note in the tenor). Instead it partakes of the nature of both styles (*quod est inter discantum et organum*), since within a discantus section one or more of the modal longae or breves are replaced by an equivalent number of notes of lesser value, with the result that several notes are now placed in one part against a single note in the other part, a relationship which is the distinguishing feature of organum. In other words, this is nothing but the device of dividing

19. "Dicto de discantu, dicendum est de copula que multum valet ad discantum, quia discantus numquam perfecte scitur, nisi mediante copula. Unde copula dicitur esse id quod est inter discantum et organum. Alio modo dicitur copula: copula est id quod profertur recto modo equipollente unisono. Alio modo dicitur: copula est id ubicumque fit multitudo punctorum. Punctus, ut hic sumitur, est ubicumque fit multitudo tractuum, et ista pars dividitur in duo equalia; unde pars prima dicitur aversus, secunda vero conversus; et utraque pars continet multitudinem tractuum. Unde tractus fit ubicumque fit multitudo specierum, ut unisoni aut soni, secundum numerum ordinatum ordine debito." (CS, *I*, 114a.) For Garlandia "species" is the synonym of "interval." Cf. CS, *I*, 163a. Simon Cserba in *Hieronymus de Moravia O.P. Tractatus de Musica* (p. 224) reads *aversus* as *antecedens* and *conversus* as *consequens*.

20. The St. Emmeram Anonymous confirms the relationship of discantus and copula when he says: "In hoc loco de quadam ipsius [discantus] specie sive membro que copula dicitur vult actor propositum declarare, . . ." (Sowa, p. 125, ll. 4–5.) He also indicates that both employ the same forms of notation and the same correct measurement: ". . . licet in figuris et rectitudine temporum sint eadem." (P. 126, l. 4.)

the individual values of the modal pattern into lesser values, which Anonymous IV refers to as fractio modi. A copula then is a variety of discantus, but it does not conform to the exact definition of discantus because some of the modal values are replaced by lesser values, so that we have several notes in one part against a single note in the other, a feature that belongs to organum speciale. At the same time it is not organum speciale, because both parts are modal, and the single note against which several other notes are placed is a modal, i.e., measured, and not an unmeasured value.

Garlandia explains how this is to be written: a copula is where there is a number of lines. Now a line in modal notation is used in two ways: it is either a plica, a line added to a note or to the final note of a ligature to indicate a division of the note into two notes, or it is a line placed after a note, indicating a pause or rest. Garlandia quite evidently has the plica in mind, for the plica would divide a modal longa or brevis into two breves or semibreves equivalent to a single longa or brevis in the other part. This is confirmed by both the St. Emmeram Anonymous and Anonymous IV. The St. Emmeram Anonymous takes his definitions of discantus, copula, and organum from Garlandia, repeating them almost verbatim. In his definition of the copula he adds this clarifying statement: "The punctus in this connection means wherever there is made a number of lines added individually to some end of the notes." [21] This sentence can apply only to the plica. The St. Emmeram Anonymous furthermore cites as specific examples of the copula two organa in the Notre Dame repertory. "A copula is wherever there is made a number of notes joined together by lines; and this appears in the Alleluia of *Posui* in both the triplum and duplum voices in the form of discantus in the first mode with its proper ligatures. It also appears according to the arrangement of organum speciale in the duplum part of *Judea et Jerusalem.*" [22] The passage referred to in the Alleluia of *Posui* can be located definitely, for Anonymous IV refers to the same copula, giving the specific notes in it. Citing this same passage as an example of the use of the irregular first mode, the anonymous author says: "This appears in the Alleluia *Posui adjutorium,* where it is set at the place of the copula in this form: [*f*] *duplex longa, f e con-*

21. "Punctus prout hic sumitur est illud, ubi fit multitudo actuum [tractuum] alicui punctorum termino singulariter attributa." (Sowa, p. 125, l. 22.)

22. "Copula est id ubique quod [fit] multitudo punctorum simul iunctorum per suos tractus, et hoc sub specie primi modi et sub recta serie figurarum sicut patet in Alleluya de 'Posui' tam in triplo cantu quam secundo, et hoc secundum dispositionem discantus, nunc autem secundum dispositionem organi specialis sicut patet in duplo de 'Iudea et Ierusalem.'" (Sowa, p. 125, l. 16.)

junctim, f d conjunctim, e c d f g f cum plica, d c cum plica, a duplex longa cum c conjunctim." [23]

This copula appears in the Florence manuscript on folio 36ᵛ.[24] It is given here in the original notation and in modern transcription.

It is immediately apparent that this copula is simply a passage in the first mode with several longae divided into two breves. It exactly fits Garlandia's description, for we have here a passage in discantus in the two upper voices, in which several notes are placed against a single note in the other part. In the second half of the third measure the duplum has two breves against the *e* of the triplum, while in the last half of the fourth measure the triplum has three notes against the single *a* of the duplum. This is notated in both cases by lines in the form of plicae.

This phrase is also an interesting example of the use of modus non rectus. Although Garlandia, the St. Emmeram Anonymous, and Anonymous IV state that the modus non rectus occurs only in organum duplum, Anonymous IV admits a limited application of it in organum triplum. One of the methods of setting an organum triplum, he says, is "with a single note in the tenor while the duplum and triplum have an unusual modus in that the first note may be too long and too short." [25] This occurs in the passage quoted above. Although

23. "Ut patet in *Alleluia; Posui adjutorium;* quoniam ibi ponitur loco copule sub tali forma: duplex longa [etc.]." (CS, *I*, 361b.)

24. E. de Coussemaker identified this passage many years ago in the mensural version of the Alleluya contained in the manuscript H 196 of the Faculté de Médecine de Montpellier. Cf. *L'Art harmonique aux xiie et xiiie siècles* (Paris, 1865), p. 272. The Montpellier version is to be found in facsimile and transcription in this same volume (Nos. 1 and 2) as well as in Yvonne Rokseth, *Polyphonies du xiiie siècle,* Vols. 1 and 2. I have used the original modal version in the Florence manuscript rather than the Montpellier variant, since the latter with its later form of notation does not conform to the precepts of the modal theorists.

25. "Tertia diversitas est cum eodem tenore, sed in duplo et triplo, per modum extraneum se habet, ut prima esset nimis longa et nimis brevis, . . ." (CS, *I*, 361a.)

the first note of the duplum part is written as an ordinary nota simplex, Anonymous IV speaks of it as a duplex longa, indicating that it is to be held beyond its normal length in the manner of the first modus non rectus. The first foot of the phrase is thus to be sung as a quarter note plus a sixteenth note, followed by another sixteenth note.

Garlandia's definition of the copula is not yet complete, for there is still another form of the copula. "There are two kinds of copula," he states, "one of which is between organum purum and discantus. The other is made by cutting away tones or by taking away a tempus after a tempus and tempora after tempora. And this style is called *flaiolis* [?], and some call this same style hocket." [26] The hocket, as is well known, is a form of music in which frequent rests replace the notes or part of the value of notes in the individual voices, so that one voice executes a note while the other voice rests, proceeding thus in a rapid alternation of notes and rests. The most extreme examples of hocket, those in which the individual values of the modal pattern are subdivided into tones and rests, occur only in pieces without a text and are presumably to be performed instrumentally. This is the *abscissio sonorum* of Garlandia. The most famous example of this practice is the hocket *In seculum,* which is cited frequently by the theorists and which exists in a number of manuscripts.[27] Much more common, however, is the substitution of rests for one or both values of a modal pattern (*sumendo tempus post tempus et tempora post tempora*) so that the two parts will dovetail with each other, one resting while the other sings. An example of this device is the substitute clausula *Tanquam* (F, f. 147′), shown in the following excerpt:

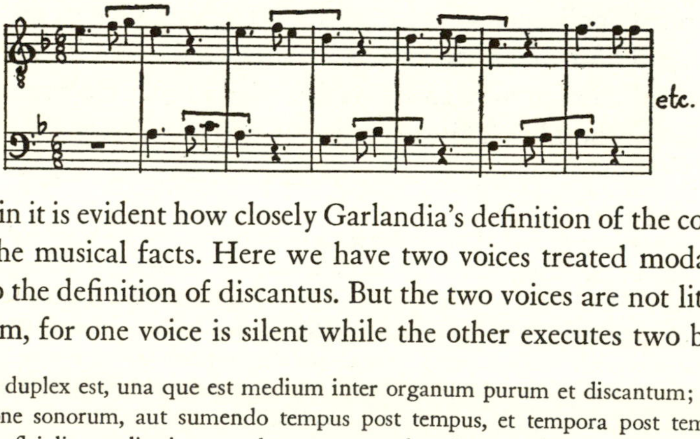

Once again it is evident how closely Garlandia's definition of the copula corresponds to the musical facts. Here we have two voices treated modally, which conforms to the definition of discantus. But the two voices are not literally nota contra notam, for one voice is silent while the other executes two breves. Nor

26. "Copula duplex est, una que est medium inter organum purum et discantum; altera est que fit in abscissione sonorum, aut sumendo tempus post tempus, et tempora post tempora. Et iste modus sumitur flaiolis; et aliqui vocant hoquetum modum istum." (CS, *1*, 116b.)

27. An easily accessible transcription of this piece is to be found in A. T. Davison and W. Apel, *Historical Anthology of Music* (Cambridge, Mass., 1946), *1*, 34–35.

do the two voices pause simultaneously at the end of each ordo, as is necessary in discantus. Therefore this particular style cannot properly be termed discantus, even though both parts are modally measured. Furthermore, this copula is "made by a number of lines," for this example and all others like it are written with many rests represented in modal notation by lines. One is also able to see here what Garlandia means by his statement that "the first part is called the antecedent and the second, the consequence," for the two parts proceed in alternation with one always preceding the other.

Further identification of the copula and hocket is to be found in a passage in Anonymous IV (CS, *I*, 332a). Writing about the third imperfect mode diminished by two of its values, he gives as the first ordo the series:

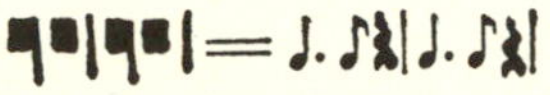

Then he adds a respondent to this phrase:

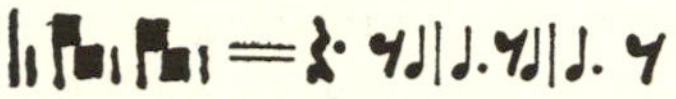

"It is to be observed," he continues, "that if this last ordo of two notes is sung with the other ordo of two notes, then a good copula will be made."[28] The combination of these two phrases will, of course, produce a hocket:

and the resulting hocket will once again be a copula made with a number of lines representing rests.

From the above definitions of discantus, copula, and organum it may readily be seen that one need not look for any strange rhythmic features in the polyphonic compositions of the Notre Dame school. In all cases modal rhythm will prevail. No longer need we accept the troubling hypothesis that a free, unmeasured rhythm and modal rhythm are to be found side by side in organum duplum in one and the same composition. No longer need we search for a fugitive passage, disguised as a copula, hidden between sections in discant and sections in organum. It is apparent from the preceding definitions that discantus, copula, and organum are styles differentiated one from another by the specific relationship of one voice to another rather than on the basis of any special rhythmic differences. In all three cases modal rhythm is maintained, although in or-

28. CS, *I*, 332a: "Notandum quod si ille ultimus ordo duorum punctorum cum reliquo duorum punctorum dicatur, bona copulatio fiet inde, . . ."

ganum style it is the duplum part alone which is modal while the individual notes of the tenor are sustained for long periods of time. Moreover, in organum style a certain liberty in the performance of the modes is admitted, for the individual notes of the modal pattern may be lengthened and shortened, while at the same time the essential outline of the pattern is preserved. This modus non rectus is an ad libitum performance, and it is in no way indicated by the notation itself. It is such a performance that the St. Emmeram Anonymous must have had in mind when he wrote, "[Organum] per se deviates from the precepts of the rules of art, for passing through various concords it neglects the usages of correct or regular measurement to attain sweetness of melody . . . And note that it is possible to relinquish correct measurement, since it has mode and measure in itself." [29]

Under the circumstances it is not surprising to find that the theorists devote but little space to a discussion of the notation of organum duplum. Nevertheless some guidance is necessary since the reading of the duplum rhythm is oftentimes difficult to establish when the usual modal ligatures are replaced by irregular groups of notes in fractio and extensio modi, repeated notes, etc. Since the tenor is not moving in modal measurement, the performer cannot be guided by the rhythmic and harmonic coincidence of the two voices that facilitates the rendition of similar passages in discantus and copula. In response to the need for some general rules of procedure in the performance of the duplum part Garlandia provided some rules of thumb. "The longae and breves in organum," he wrote, "are recognizable in the following manner, that is, by consonance, by the notation and by the penultimate note. Whence the rule: Everything that meets with another according to the virtue of consonances is said to be long. Another rule: Whatever is notated as a long according to organa before a rest or at a consonant place is said to be long. Another rule: Whatever appears before a long rest or before a perfect consonance is said to be long." [30] These same rules are

29. Sowa, p. 129, ll. 29–31; p. 130, ll. 4, 5: "Si per se regularum artis deviat a preceptis, nam per varias concordantias distributum recte mensure seu regularis habitudinem negligit dulcedine melodie . . . Et nota quod licet rectam relinquat mensuram, cum habet modum et mensuram in se." Cf. Anon. IV, CS, *1*, 360b: "Est et sextum volumen de organo in duplo . . . Et quia longe sunt nimis longe, et breves nimis breves, et videtur esse modus irregularis quoad modos supradictos ipsius discantus, quamvis in se sit regularis."

30. CS, *1*, 114b: "Longe et breves in organo tali modo dinoscuntur, scilicet per consonantiam, per figuram, per penultimam. Unde regula: omne id quod accidit in aliquo secundum virtutem consonantiarum, dicitur longum. Alia regula: Quicquid figuratur longum, secundum organa ante pausationem, vel loco consonantie, dicitur longum. Alia regula: Quicquid accipitur ante longam pausationem, vel ante perfectam concordantiam, dicitur esse longum."

repeated by the St. Emmeram Anonymous,[31] by Franco of Cologne,[32] and in a much expanded form by Anonymous IV.[33]

The three rules of consonance, notation, and the penultimate note are by no means absolute laws; rather they are general considerations to be kept in mind in evaluating the rhythmic meaning of certain notes in the duplum part. In reality these rules are nothing but restatements of general principles that have already been discussed in relationship to discantus. The rule of the consonance rests upon the same considerations that are applied to the combination of voices in discantus, namely, that the first note of a modal pattern must form a consonance with the tenor while the remaining note or notes of the pattern may form a dissonance. The earliest statement of this rule appears in the *Discantus positio vulgaris,* where it is said, "It must be observed that all odd notes when they are consonant should be more consonant than the even notes, and when they are dissonant they should be less dissonant than the even notes." [34] Garlandia's rule of the consonance has important implications that do not appear immediately. For if the duplum part is regulated by modal rhythm, and if the notes which form a consonance with the tenor are to be read as long notes, it follows that only two modes could be utilized in the duplum if consonances are to be formed by the first notes of the modal pattern: only the first and the third modes begin with longae. An examination of the practical sources reveals immediately that it is the first mode which prevails throughout in the duplum.

The second of Garlandia's three rules is also related to ordinary practice in modal notation. Since organum is always notated in modal ligatures and never by means of mensural forms, Garlandia in all probability was not referring to the specific note form of the longa when he states that "whatever is notated as a long is said to be a long." What Garlandia had in mind undoubtedly was the modal ligature, the last note of which must be a longa, and in which all the notes before the penultimate brevis stand in the place of a longa value. Garlandia's qualification of this rule by establishing the places where such a longa is to be read as notated, namely, before a rest and where a consonance is formed, again indicates a relationship to the first mode. Obviously the last note of a ligature before a rest will be in general a longa in the first mode, and equally ob-

31. Sowa, p. 130, l. 31: ". . . organum speciale cognoscitur per penultimam, per concordantiam, per figuram."

32. CS, *1,* 135a: "Ipsius organi longe et breves tribus regulis cognoscuntur," etc.

33. CS, *1,* 362b–363b.

34. CS, *1,* 95a: "Sciendum infra quod omnes note impares, he que consonant, melius consonant, que vero dissonant, minus dissonant, quam pares."

vious is the fact that the coincidence of a longa value and a consonance appears at the beginning of each foot of the first mode. Thus by implication the first two of Garlandia's rules substantiate the evidence of the manuscripts themselves that it is the first mode which underlies the seeming irregularities of duplum notation.

In the application of these rules to duplum notation a certain freedom of interpretation is necessary, for the rule of the consonance is by no means an absolute one. It is a characteristic of organum style, be it organum duplum, triplum, or quadruplum, that the upper voices pursue their own melodic direction oftentimes without regard for the possible dissonances that they may be forming with the sustained tenor note. Perotin's great organum quadruplum, *Viderunt,* for example, dwells on the dissonance of a major seventh in the opening fourteen measures.[35] In organum duplum there constantly appear passages written in unequivocal modal notation or in which the melody is constructed in sequences. When dissonances occur in such passages it is clear that the principle of consonance is being forfeited for the sake of the melody. It is to this practice that Anonymous IV was referring when he wrote, "There are sometimes many longs for the sake of the color or beauty of the melody, whether they be consonant or not, and this appears in the course of performance."[36] The rule of consonance then is not to be applied indiscriminately to the notes of the duplum melody but is to be used as a guide in passages where the notation is irregular and is consequently not immediately clear in its rhythmic meaning. In such passages the longa value is usually to be associated with the note or notes of a ligature which form consonances with the tenor.

That the rule of the consonance has only a limited applicability is evident from the number of consonances permitted in the polyphony of this period. With the exception of the *Discantus positio vulgaris,* which admits only the unison, fifth, and octave as consonances, all theorists state that there are no less than six consonant intervals, the unison, major and minor third, fourth, fifth, and octave. Since the same ligature often contains three or more notes forming consonances with the tenor note, it is obvious that one cannot rely upon consonance alone as a criterion for determining whether a note is to

35. Printed in G. Adler, *Handbuch der Musikgeschichte* (Frankfurt, 1924), p. 195. Also accessible in H. Gleason, *Examples of Music before 1400,* Eastman School of Music Series (New York, 1945), p. 36.

36. CS, *I,* 363b: "Iterato sunt quandoque longe plurime ratione coloris vel pulchritudinis melodie, sive fuerint concordantes, sive non, quod quidem per se patet in operando."

be read as a longa or brevis. For this reason it is the second rule of Garlandia that is most essential for deciphering duplum notation. It may here be stated as a general observation that in most cases the ligatures in organum duplum are to be read according to the rules for ligatures cum proprietate et perfectione. If the ligatures are read in this manner it usually happens that those notes which are to be read as longae according to the rules of modal ligatures will at the same time form consonances with the tenor. In the matter of establishing the correct value of a note the two rules of Garlandia actually complement one another. When, for example, a ternaria ligature is inserted within a series of binariae in an ordo of the first mode, both rules must be brought to bear to determine the value of the notes in the ligature. Such a ternaria could be read either as fractio or extensio modi with the values ♫♩ or ♩♪♩.[37] The decision as to whether the first note of the ternaria is to be read as a brevis or longa will be determined by the harmonic interval formed by this note with the tenor note. If it forms a dissonance this note is presumably to be read as a brevis in fractio modi; if it forms a consonance it is probably to be read as a longa in extensio modi. Even this procedure is not the final determinant, for one must also consider such factors as melodic sequence and symmetry of phrase. Like discantus the organum style tends to move in ordines of even numbers of feet, so that an irregular ligature must often be interpreted so as to preserve the symmetry of the ordines.

To a large extent the notation of organum duplum presents a straightforward modal picture. Most of the irregularities in the writing of ligatures are attributable to such factors as fractio modi, repeated notes, etc., and in general organum duplum utilizes the same methods of notation in these passages that were discussed in the previous chapter in relation to discantus. However, there exist in organum duplum certain clichés of notation for such passages that appear less often in discantus writing. It is necessary, therefore, to point out the meaning of these irregular usages.

One of the most frequent irregularities is the use of a single, large ligature in place of two ligatures. By far the most common is the quinaria used as a substitute for a ternaria and binaria of the first mode. Since this practice is also frequently encountered in discantus writing, it requires no special discussion here. A related usage is the senaria which replaces a ternaria plicata and binaria of the first mode. This senaria consequently has the meaning, ♩♪♫♪|♩. Such a ligature is akin to the quinaria used in lieu of a binaria plicata and another binaria

37. See above, p. 90.

of the first mode.[38] An example of this ligature appears in the *Gloria patri,* F, f. 74′:

The last of the ligatures of this type is the quaternaria which replaces two binariae of the first mode. The versus, *Constantes* (F, f. 65) provides an illustration of this ligature:

One of the most striking features of organum duplum is the repetition of certain melodic clichés, a surprisingly limited stock of melodic formulas that are used over and over again throughout the compositions of the *Magnus liber.* Among these formulas are certain brief phrases which appear at the end of a clausula just before the final note of the tenor. These same cadential formulas are also employed in the substitute clausulae as well as in organum triplum. Due to the fact that a change of syllable almost always follows these phrases and that a repeated note also appears in the melody, the notation presents a rather irregular appearance. The first of these formulas has the following form (from the *Gloria,* F, f. 65′ [*spiri*]*tui*):

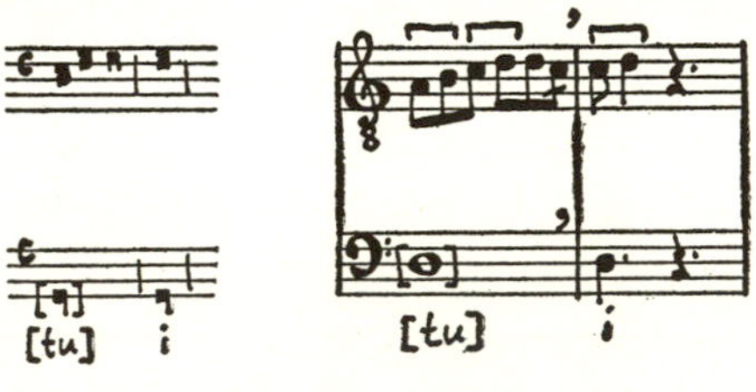

The two binariae stand for an ascending quaternaria, which is a common form of notating such a quaternaria in all the Notre Dame manuscripts. These two ligatures are to be read as all breves like the opening quaternaria of the sixth

38. See above, p. 105.

mode. The two remaining notes of the measure, which have the value of breves, cannot be written in any of the customary ways because the first brevis is a repeated tone and the second brevis is separated from the following note or notes by a change in syllable, as well as by a repeated note. Consequently they have been notated as a longa plicata, which quite exceptionally is used here to fill out the last two thirds of the modal pattern rather than the first two thirds. The correctness of this transcription is verified by several passages where the formula is accompanied by a modal tenor. For example, the end of the substitute clausula *Domino quoniam* employs this same formula with a modal tenor (F, f. 156):

A similar cadential formula is the following:

In this case the quaternaria is written in the conventional manner, which makes this phrase less ambiguous than the previous example.

In addition to these irregular forms of notation there are also certain conventional manners of opening and closing the various sections of organum. At the beginning of a piece of organum there frequently occur two longae of the same pitch, the second of which is commonly a longa plicata. At times the two single notes are replaced by a duplex longa with a plica. These notes, which are separated from the following notes by a line representing a breathing point,[39] are called by Anonymous IV "the beginning before the beginning" and apparently are to be performed with some sort of vocal flourish. "There is a certain *duplex longa florata*," he writes, "and this is placed at the beginning in the name of the most sacred Alpha, and it is called the beginning before the beginning and it will always form a consonance [with the tenor]." [40] The manner in which the

39. CS, *I*, 350b: "Est et alia pausatio que videtur esse pausatio et non est, et vocatur suspirium; nullum vero tempus habet de se, sed capit suum tempus ex diminutione alicujus soni ante immediate."

40. CS, *I*, 363b: "Iterato quedam est duplex longa florata, et illa ponitur in principio In nomine sanctissimi alpha, et dicitur principium ante principium et semper erit concordans."

longa florata is to be performed is somewhat uncertain, although Jerome of Moravia describes these "flowers" as trills. In an extensive passage Jerome presents several variations of the trill, with a whole tone or a half tone, at various speeds, etc.[41] The number of possibilities of execution, however, once again points to an improvisatory performance, which is by no means indicated by the notation itself. For this reason I have not deemed it necessary to add a sign of ornamentation, a method of transcription adopted by Kuhlmann in his edition of motets from the Montpellier manuscript.[42] The longa florata almost invariably has a total value of three tempora or six tempora. At the beginning of a composition, where the two single notes are frequently written as a duplex longa with a plica, it should be read, . Elsewhere it will be given either three tempora, , or six tempora, depending upon the context.

One final characteristic of organum style is the use of an appoggiatura on the first and last notes, as well as on the first notes of new syllables. Instead of a single note forming one of the accepted consonances with the tenor, the note is frequently preceded by a tone a second higher or lower. These two notes are written in the manuscripts as an ordinary binaria and are transcribed as an eighth note and quarter note. This ligature has no modal significance but is of an ornamental nature. In this ligature the introductory longa of an organum or the final longa of a section or of the piece, which would normally have the value of three or six tempora, is preceded by an ornamental brevis and this brevis value is subtracted from the value of the longa. Occasionally two notes precede the initial longa of an organum, approaching the consonant note from a third below. In this case the two initial notes are to be considered as breves which take two tempora from a duplex longa and are to be transcribed,

According to Anonymous IV the tenor is to be silent at such points until the consonant note of the duplum part is sung.[43]

With these special usages of organum our discussion of the rhythm and notation of the Notre Dame organum comes to a close. It has been demonstrated

41. CS, *1*, 91b.

42. G. Kuhlmann, *Die zweistimmigen französischen Motetten des Kodex Montpellier, Faculté de Medecine H196, in ihrer Bedeutung für die Musikgeschichte des 13. Jahrhunderts.* Literarhistorisch musikwissenschaftliche Abhandlungen, Band I (Würzburg, 1938), p. 111.

43. "The tenor begins with the second note if it forms a consonance, or with the third." CS, *1*, 363b: ". . . et tenor incipit cum secundo, si fuerit concordans vel cum tertio."

that the notation of this epoch is based throughout upon the system of six rhythmic modes. By establishing the theoretical background of the modal system the problems associated with the transcription of the notation have largely been resolved. There is in fact a most intimate relationship between modal rhythm and the notation which expresses it, for the various combinations of ligatures and notae simplices used to symbolize the modes are concrete, visual images of a rhythm built upon the repetition of a metrical pattern. Without a thorough comprehension of the rhythmic theory it would be impossible to understand many aspects of the practical art of notation, for the union of theory and practice is one of the most characteristic features of medieval thought, an attitude which is expressed in the following lines of an anonymous poet:[44]

> Musicorum & cantorum magna est distantia,
> Isti dicunt, illi sciunt, quae componit Musica.
> Nam qui facit, quod non sapit, diffinitur bestia.

In the case of modal notation it has been shown that the notation is the result of the adaptation of existing Gregorian forms to a theory of rhythm derived from St. Augustine. This achievement, probably to be attributed primarily to Leonin and Perotin, is one of the most important moments in the history of music, for it turned the course of European music into wholly new channels. It is to be hoped that this study has been a contribution to our knowledge of this moment and to the general knowledge of that marvelous flowering of the human mind which, rightly or wrongly, has been named the Renaissance of the Twelfth Century.

44. Gerbert, *Scriptores,* 2, 25.

Bibliography

Abert, Hermann. *Die Musikanschauung des Mittelalters und ihre Grundlage.* Halle, 1905.

Adler, Guido. "Die Wiederholung und Nachahmung in der Mehrstimmigkeit." *VfMW, 2* (1886), 271.

Amerio, Franco. *Il "De Musica" di S. Agostino.* Biblioteca del "Didaskaleion," *4.* Torino, 1929.

Anglès, Higini. *El Còdex musical de Las Huelgas (Musica a veus dels segles XIII–XIV).* 3 vols. Barcelona, 1931.

—— *La Música a Catalunya fins al segle XIII.* Barcelona, 1935.

Apel, Willi. "From St. Martial to Notre Dame." *JAMS,* 2 (1949), 145.

—— *The Notation of Polyphonic Music, 900–1600.* 4th corrected edition. Cambridge, 1949.

Aubry, Pierre. *Cent motets du XIIIe siècle publiées d'après le manuscrit Ed. IV. 6 de Bamberg.* 3 vols. Paris, 1908.

Augustine, St. *De musica libri sex.* Texte de l'édition Bénédictine, intro., tr. et notes de G. Finaert et F.-J. Thonnard. Oeuvres de Saint Augustine, 1re Série, VII, IV. Bruges, 1947.

Baxter, J. H. *An Old St. Andrews Music Book (Cod. Helms. 628).* Facsimile edition. London, 1931.

Besseler, Heinrich. *Die Musik des Mittelalters und der Renaissance.* Leipzig, 1931.

——"Studien zur Musik des Mittelalters. II: Die Motette von Franko von Köln bis Philippe von Vitry." *AfMW, 8* (1927), 137.

Blanchard, D. P. "Alfred le musicien et Alfred le philosophe." *Rassegna Gregoriana, 8* (1909), 419.

Bohn, Peter. "Die Plica im gregorianischen Gesange und im Mensuralgesange." *MfMG,* 27 (1895), 47.

Bonvin, Ludwig. "Der gregorianische Rhythmus nach den Forschungen Dom Jeannins." *KJ,* 25 (1930), 31.

—— "Dom Jeannins Schrift: 'Kurzer Akzent oder longer Akzent in gregorianischen Gesang?' " *KJ,* 25 (1930), 48.

Brewster, J. S., ed. *Fr. Rogeri Bacon Opera quaedam hactenus inedita. Vol. I. Rerum Britannicarum Medii Aevi Scriptores.* London, 1859.

Bruyne, Edgar de. *Études d'esthétique médiévale.* 3 vols. Brugge, 1946.

Coussemaker, Edmond de. *Histoire de l'harmonie au moyen âge.* Paris, 1852.

—— *Scriptorum de musica ineditì aevi novam seriem a Gerbertina alteram collegit nuncque primum edidit.* 4 vols. Paris, 1864–76.

Cserba, Simon. *Hieronymus de Moravia O.P. Tractatus de Musica. Freiburger Studien zur Musikwissenschaft, Heft 2.* Regensburg, 1935.

—— "Über den Vortrag des Gregorianischen Chorals im Mittelalter." *KJ,* 29 (1934), 32.

David, Lucien. "Les signes rythmiques d'allonguement et la tradition grégorienne authentique." *Revue du chant grégorien, 41–42* (1938–39), 180.

Doren, Rombaut van. *Étude sur l'influence musicale de l'Abbaye de Saint-Gall (VIIIe au XIe siècle)*. Louvain, 1925.

Faral, Edmond. *Les arts poétiques du XIIe et du XIIIe siècle. Recherches et documents sur la technique littéraire du moyen âge.* Bibliothèque de l'École des Hautes Études. Paris, 1923.

Fellerer, Karl Gustav. "Zur Kirchenmusikpflege im 13. Jahrhundert." *KJ,* 28 (1933), 7.

Ficker, Rudolf. "Der Organumtraktat der Vaticanischen Bibliothek (Ottob. 3025)." *KJ,* 27 (1932), 65.

—— "Polyphonic Music of the Gothic Period." *MQ, 15* (1929), 483.

—— "Probleme der modalen Notation. (Zur kritische Gesamtausgabe der drei- und vierstimmigen Organa)." *Acta, 18–19* (1946–47), 2.

—— *Musik der Gotik (Perotinus, Sederunt principes)*. Vienna, 1930.

Gennrich, Friedrich. "Perotins Beata Viscera Mariae Virginis und die 'Modaltheorie.'" *Die Musikforschung, 1* (1948), 225.

—— "Trouvèrelieder und Motettenrepertoire." *ZfMW, 9* (1926), 8.

Gerbert, Martin. *Scriptores ecclesiastici de musica sacra potissimum.* 3 vols. 1784.

Gerold, Théodore. *Histoire de la musique des origines à la fin du XIVe siècle.* Paris, 1936.

—— *La musique au moyen âge.* Paris, 1932.

Gröninger, Eduard. *Repertoire-Untersuchungen zum Mehrstimmigen Notre Dame-Conductus.* Regensburg, 1939.

Handschin, Jacques. "Gregorianisch-Polyphones aus der Handschrift, Paris, B.N. lat. 15129." *KJ, 25* (1930), 60.

—— "Zur Geschichte der Lehre vom Organum." *ZfMW, 8* (1926), 321.

—— "Zum Crucifixum in carne." *AfMW, 7* (1925), 161.

—— "A Monument of English Mediaeval Polyphony: The Manuscript Wolfenbüttel 677." *Musical Times, 73* (1932), 510; *74* (1933), 697.

—— "The Summer Canon and Its Background." *Musica Disciplina, 3* (1949), 55; *5* (1951), 65.

—— "Notizen über die Notre Dame-Conductus." *Bericht über den musikwissenschaftlichen Kongress der deutschen Musikgesellschaft in Leipzig (1925)*. Leipzig, 1926.

—— "Zur Geschichte von Notre Dame." *Acta, 4* (1932), 5, 49.

—— "Was brachte die Notre Dame-Schule Neues?" *ZfMW, 6* (1924), 545.

—— "Die Rolle der Nationen in der mittelalterlichen Musikgeschichte." *Schweizerisches Jahrbuch für Musikwissenschaft, 5* (1931), 1.

—— "Ein wenig beachtete Stilrichtung innerhalb der mittelalterlichen Mehrstimmigkeit." *Schweizerisches Jahrbuch für Musikwissenschaft, 1,* (1924), 56.

—— "Über den Ursprung der Motette." *Bericht über den musikwissenschaftlichen Kongress in Basel (1924)*. Leipzig, 1925.

—— "Über Voraussetzungen sowie Früh- und Hochblüte der mittelalterlichen Mehrstimmigkeit." *Schweizerisches Jahrbuch für Musikwissenschaft, 2* (1927), 5.

—— "Die mittelalterlichen Aufführungen in Zürich, Bern und Basel." *ZfMW, 10* (1927), 8.

—— "Zur Frage der melodischen Paraphrasierung im Mittelalter." *ZfMW, 10* (1928), 513.
—— "Zur Notre Dame-Rhythmik." *ZfMW, 7* (1925), 386.
—— "Conductus-Spicilegien." *AfMW, 9* (1952), 101.
—— "Réflexions sur la terminologie (à propos d'une rectification)." *Revue Belge de Musicologie, 6* (1952), 7.
—— "Zur Frage der Conductus-Rhythmik." *Acta, 24* (1952), 113.
Husmann, Heinrich. "Die Motetten der Madrider Handschrift und deren geschichtliche Stellung." *AfMF, 2* (1937), 13.
—— "Die Offiziumsorgana der Notre Dame-Zeit." *JMP, 42* (1936), 31.
—— "Die musikalische Behandlung der Versarten im Troubadourgesang der Notre Dame-Zeit." *Acta, 25* (1953), 1.
—— *Die dreistimmigen Organa der Notre Dame-Schule, mit besonderer Berücksichtigung der Handschriften Wolfenbüttel und Montpellier.* Leipzig, 1935.
—— *Die drei- und vierstimmigen Notre Dame-Organa. Kritische Gesamtausgabe.* Publikationen älterer Musik, XI. Jahrgang. Leipzig, 1940.
—— "Zur Grundlegung der musikalischen Rhythmik des mittellateinischen Liedes." *AfMW, 9* (1952), 3.
Jacobsthal, Gustav. *Die Mensuralnotenschrift des XII. und XIII. Jahrhunderts.* Berlin, 1870.
Kromolicki, Joseph. *Die Practica artis musicae des Amerus und ihre Stellung in der Musiktheorie des Mittelalters.* Berlin, 1909.
Kuhlmann, Georg. *Die zweistimmigen französischen Motetten des Codex Montpellier, Faculté de Médecine H196, in ihrer Bedeutung für die Musikgeschichte des 13. Jahrhunderts.* 2 vols. Würzburg, 1938.
Laloy, Louis. *Aristoxène de Tarente et la musique de l'antiquité.* Paris, 1904.
Ludwig, Friedrich. *Repertorium organorum recentioris et motetorum vetustissimi stili.* 2 vols. Halle, 1910.
——"Die geistliche nichtliturgische/weltliche einstimmige und die mehrstimmige Musik des Mittelalters bis zum Anfang des 15. Jahrhunderts." *Handbuch der Musikgeschichte.* Guido Adler, ed. Frankfurt am Main, 1924. Also, 2d revised edition. Berlin, 1930.
—— "Die mehrstimmige Musik des 11. und 12. Jahrhunderts." *Bericht über den III. Kongress der Internationalen Musikgesellschaft (1909).* Leipzig, 1910, 101.
—— "Die Quellen der Motetten ältesten Stils." *AfMW, 5* (1923), 185, 273.
—— "Musik des Mittelalters in der Badischen Kunsthalle Karlsruhe." *ZfMW, 5* (1923), 434.
—— "Die 50 Beispiele Coussemakers aus der Handschrift von Montpellier." *SIMG, 5* (1904), 177.
—— "Die liturgischen Organa Leonins und Perotins." *Riemann-Festschrift. Gesammelte Studien.* Leipzig, 1909.
—— "Über die Entstehung und die erste Entwicklung der lateinischen und französischen Motette in musikalischer Beziehung." *SIMG, 7* (1906), 514.
—— "Über den Entstehungsort der grossen 'Notre Dame-Handschriften.'" *Studien zur Musikgeschichte; Festschrift für Guido Adler zum 75. Geburtstag.* Vienna, 1930.
—— "Perotinus Magnus." *AfMW, 3* (1921), 361.

Mari, Giovanni. *I trattati medievali di ritmica latina.* (Memorie del R. Istituto Lombardo di scienze e lettere. Volume XX.–XI della serie III.– Fascicolo VIII ed ultimo). Milan, 1899.

Meyer, Wilhelm. *Gesammelte Abhandlungen zur mittellateinischen Rhythmik.* Berlin, 1905.

Michalitschke, Anton Maria. "Zur Frage der longa in der Mensuraltheorie des 13. Jahrhunderts." *ZfMW, 8* (1925–26), 103.

—— "Studien zur Entstehung und Frühentwicklung der Mensuralnotation." *ZfMW, 12* (1930), 257.

—— *Die Theorie des Modus. Eine Darstellung der Entwicklung des musikrhythmischen modus und der entsprechenden mensuralen Schreiben.* Regensburg, 1923.

Mocquereau, André. *Le nombre musical grégorien, ou rythmique grégorienne, théorie et pratique.* 2 vols. Rome, 1908–27.

Niemann, Walter. *Über die abweichende Bedeutung der Ligaturen in der Mensuraltheorie der Zeit vor Johannes de Garlandia. Ein Beitrag zur Geschichte der altfranzösischen Tonschule des XII. Jahrhunderts.* Publikationen der Internationalen Musikgesellschaft. Beihefte, Heft VI. Leipzig, 1902.

Paetow, Louis John. *Two Medieval Satires on the University of Paris: La Bataille des VII Ars of Henri D'Andeli and the Morale Scolarium of John of Garland.* Memoirs of the University of California, *4,* Nos. 1 and 2. Berkeley, 1927.

Pietzsch Gerhard Wilhelm. *Die Musik im Erziehungs- und Bildungsideal des ausgehenden Altertums und frühen Mittelalters. Studien zur Geschichte der Musiktheorie im Mittelalter, 2.* Halle, 1932.

—— *Die Klassifikation der Musik von Boetius bis Ugolino von Orvieto.* Halle, 1929.

Reese, Gustave. *Music in the Middle Ages. With an Introduction on the Music of Ancient Times.* New York, 1940.

Riemann, Hugo. *Geschichte der Musiktheorie im IX–XIX Jahrhundert.* Leipzig, 1898.

Roger, M. *L'enseignement des lettres classiques d'Ausone à Alcuin. Introduction à l'histoire des écoles carolingiennes.* Paris, 1905.

Rokseth, Yvonne. *Polyphonies du XIIIe siècle.* Le manuscrit H196 de la Faculté de Médecine de Montpellier. 4 vols. Paris, 1939.

—— "Danses cléricales du XIIIe siècle." *Mélanges, 3* (1945): Études historiques. Publications de la faculté des lettres de l'Université de Strasbourg. Fascicule 106. Société d'Edition: Les Belles Lettres. Paris, 1947.

—— "Le contrepoint double vers 1248." *Mélanges de musicologie offerts a M. Lionel de la Laurencie.* Paris, 1933.

Ronca, Umberto. *Cultura medioevale e poesia latina d'Italia nei secoli XI e XII.* Roma, 1892.

Royer, L. "Catalogue des écrits théoriciens de la musique conservés dans le fonds latin de la Bibliothèque Nationale." *Année Musicale, 3* (1913), 208.

Sachs, Curt. *Rhythm and Tempo, A Study in Music History.* New York, 1953.

Sasse, Götz Dietrich. *Die Mehrstimmigkeit der Ars antiqua in Theorie und Praxis.* Diss. Berlin. Leipzig, 1940.

Schäfke, Rudolf. *Aristeides Quintilianus: Von der Musik.* Berlin, 1937.

Schmidt, Helmut. *Die drei- und vierstimmigen Organa.* Kassel, 1933.

—— "Zur Melodiebildung Leonins und Perotins." *ZfMW, 14* (1931), 129.

Schneider, Marius. "Der Hochetus." *ZfMW, 11* (1929), 390.

—— "Zur Satztechnik der Notre Dame-Schule." *ZfMW, 14* (1932), 398.

—— *Geschichte der Mehrstimmigkeit. Historische und phänomenologische Studien. Zweiter Teil: Die Anfänge in Europa.* Berlin, 1935.

Schrade, Leo. "Political Compositions in French Music of the 12th and 13th Centuries. *The Coronation of French Kings.*" *Annales Musicologiques,* Société de Musique d'Autrefois. Paris, 1953, 9–63.

Sowa, Heinrich. *Quellen zur Transformation der Antiphonen. Tonar- und Rhythmusstudien.* Kassel, 1935.

—— "Zur Weiterentwicklung des modalen Rhythmik." *ZfMW, 15* (1933), 422.

—— *Ein anonymer glossierter Mensuraltraktat 1279.* Königsberger Studien zur Musikwissenschaft, 9. Kassel, 1930.

Spanke, Hans. "St. Martial-Studien. Ein Beitrag zur frühromanischen Metrik." *Zeitschrift für französische Sprache und Literatur, 54* (1930–31), 282, 385; *56* (1932), 56.

Steglich, Rudolf. *Die Quaestiones in Musica. Ein Choraltraktat des zentralen Mittelalters und ihr mutmasslicher Verfasser Rudolf von St. Trond* (1070–1138). Publikationen der Internationalen Musikgesellschaft. Beihefte, Zweite Folge, Heft X. Leipzig, 1911.

Suñol, Gregorio Maria. *Introduction à la paléographie musicale grégorienne.* Paris, 1935.

Tischler, Hans. "New Historical Aspects of the Parisian Organa." *Speculum, 25* (1950), 21.

Ursprung, Otto. *Die Katholische Kirchenmusik.* Leipzig, 1931.

—— "Die Ligaturen, ihr System und ihre methodische und didaktische Darstellung. Zugleich ein Beitrag zur Geschichte des Musikunterrichts." *Acta, 11* (1939), 1.

Vivell, Coelestin. "Zur Musik-Terminologie 'Planus.' " *ZIMG, 15* (1914), 319.

Wagner, Peter. *Einführung in die Gregorianischen Melodien. Zweiter Teil: Neumenkunde.* 2d revised edition. Leipzig, 1912.

—— "Über die Anfänge des mehrstimmigen Gesanges." *ZfMW, 9* (1926), 2.

Wolf, Johannes. "Die Musiklehre des Johannes de Grocheo. Ein Beitrag zur Musikgeschichte des Mittelalters." *SIMG, 1* (1899–1900), 65.

—— "Ein Beitrag zur Diskantlehre des 14. Jahrhunderts." *SIMG, 15* (1913–14), 504.

—— *Geschichte der Mensural-notation von 1250–1460. Nach den theoretischen und praktischen Quellen bearbeitet.* 3 vols. Leipzig, 1904.

—— *Handbuch der Notationskunde.* 2 vols. Leipzig, 1913–19.

—— "Die Musiktheorie des Mittelalters." *Acta, 3* (1931), 53.

Wooldridge, H. E. *The Oxford History of Music.* Vol. 1, The Polyphonic Period. Part I, Method of Musical Art. 2d edition, revised by Percy C. Buck. London, 1929.

THE TRANSCRIPTION

MAGNUS LIBER ORGANI DE GRADALI ET ANTIPHONARIO

WOLFENBÜTTEL 677, OLIM HELMSTADT 628

Prefatory remarks

The following transcription of the *Magnus liber* of Leonin has been made from the facsimile edition of W_1 published by J. H. Baxter with the title *An Old St. Andrew's Music Book* (London, 1931). The version of W_1 has been carefully compared with the versions of F and W_2, but no attempt has been made to indicate the variant readings of the three manuscripts. Desirable as such an editorial practice would be, it is not feasible in the case of the Notre Dame organum, where totally different versions of sections of one and the same composition are to be found in the various manuscripts. Only in the case of obvious errors, such as the omission of notes or the misplacing of tenor notes, have readings from the other manuscripts been introduced. The editor has endeavored to indicate the appearance of the original notation through the use of certain devices. Ligatures are represented by square brackets, and the same sign is also employed for a group of currentes attached to a nota simplex. Currentes appended to a ligature are indicated by a slur. A plica is signified by an oblique line drawn through the stem of the note. Lines in the manuscript other than rests, i.e., the Silbenstrich and the suspiratio, have been rendered as breath marks above the staff. As for the vexing problem of accidentals, the editor admits to having chosen the path of discretion rather than of valor. The manuscripts present such contradictory evidence in the use of signatures and incidental accidentals that it has been deemed best to introduce only those signs that appear in the version of W_1.

In the following list of compositions the system of numbering employed by Ludwig in his *Repertorium* has been retained. The number assigned to each piece indicates its numerical position within the most complete version of the *Magnus liber* contained in the Florence manuscript. The letters O and M prefixed to the numbers tell whether the chant is drawn from the Officium or the Mass. Wherever they are known, the original chant melodies are referred to in one of the four following books.

GR. *Graduale Romanum,* Desclée & Socii, Paris, 1924.

Gr. Sar. *Graduale Sarisburiense.* A reproduction in facsimile of a manuscript of the thirteenth century, with a dissertation and historical index . . . by Walter Howard Frere. The Plainsong and Mediaeval Music Society. London, 1894.

LG. *Liber Gradualis juxta antiquorum codicum fidem restitutus.* Solesmes edition. 1895.

Pro. *Processionale monasticum ad usum congregationis gallicae ordinis Sancti Benedicti.* Solesmes edition. 1893.

References to editorial emendations in the compositions are made through a system of three numbers. The first number refers to the page, the second to the system and the third to the measure. Thus 42, 3, 4 means page 42, system 2, measure 4.

Magnus liber organi de antiphonario

page

O35. Vir perfecte. Imitator Jesu. Gloria patri. 50

O36. Vir iste. Pro eo ut. 55

M37. Propter veritatem. Audi filia. 60

GR., 561. This version of a chant from the proper of the Mass appears at the end of the fascicle devoted to pieces from the Officium. Although it is out of place here, it seems best to retain it in its original position in the manuscript.

Magnus liber organi de gradali

M1. Viderunt omnes. Notum fecit. 67

GR., 33.

M2. Alleluya. Dies sanctificatus. 74

GR., 34. (81,4,4–5) Two measures missing in MS supplied from F, f. 106v.

M3. Sederunt. Adiuva me. 82

GR., 36. The first 22 measures in the duplum on f. 27 are written a third too low in the MS. (83,3,2) Syllable written incorrectly under this note in MS.

M5. Exiit sermo. Sed sic eum. 88

GR., 39.

M8. Laus tua. Herodes iratus. 94

(96,1,1) The missing note is supplied from F and W2; also from the same phrase in Veni electa mea (184,5,2). (99,5,1–2) The notes *a* and *b* are missing in the MS and have been added by the editor from the context.

M9. Omnes. Surge. 100

GR., 51v.

M11. Suscepimus deus. Sicut audivimus. 107

GR., 411.

M12. Alleluya. Adorabo ad templum. 114

GR., [73].

M13. Hec dies. Confitemini. 120

GR., 221.

M14. Alleluya. Pascha nostrum. 126

GR., 222.

M15. Alleluya. Epulemur in azimis. 131

Gr. Sar., f. 117. (132,5,7) The passage from this measure through the first four notes of 133,3,3 is a marginal insertion in the MS.

page

M17. Alleluya. Surrexit dominus. 135
Gr. Sar., f. 120.

M22. Alleluya. Dulce lignum. 144
GR., 468. (147,3,1) Tenor note supplied from the substitute clausula No. 119 (F., f. 160^{v}).

M23. Alleluya. Ascendens Christus. 150
Gr. Sar., f. 135.

M27. Alleluya. Veni sancte spiritus. 157
GR., 272. The versus is incomplete in MS.

M31. Alleluya. Tu es Petrus. 161
GR., 513. A fragment from the end of the versus.

M32. Benedicta. Virgo dei genitrix. 162
GR., [98].

M33. Alleluya. Assumpta est Maria. 169
Gr. Sar., f. 195.

M34. Alleluya. Hodie Maria. 175
Gr. Sar., f. 195.

M54. Alleluya. Veni electa mea. 183
Gr. Sar., f. 227. The notation of the first four lines of the versus should be compared with the identical passage on pp. 195–96.

M37. Propter veritatem. Audi filia. 189
GR., 561. (191,2,4) The notation of this passage seems to indicate the third mode, but F employs a number of plicae clearly signifying the sixth mode.

M38. Alleluya. Nativitas. 195
LG., 556.

M39. Alleluya. In conspectu angelorum. 204
GR., 592.

M40. Timete. Inquirentes autem. 209
GR., 596. (211,4,7) Second note written *g* in W_1, but *f* in F.

M42. Alleluya. Judicabunt sancti. 214
Gr. Sar., f. 199.

M48. Domine. Vitam petiit. 221
LG., [46]. (225,3,2) The first note of duplum supplied by conjecture.

M49. Alleluya. Letabitur justus. 225
Gr. Sar., f. 207. (231,1,3) There is a superfluous *d* in the tenor in the MS.

O 1. Judea et iherusalem.

℣. Constantes.
Con-
stan-
tes
e-

sto-
te
vi-
de-
bi-
tis
au-

xi-
li-
um
do-
mi-

ni
su- per
vos.
f 17'
2. Descendit
de celis.
Des-
cen-

dit
de
ce-
lis.

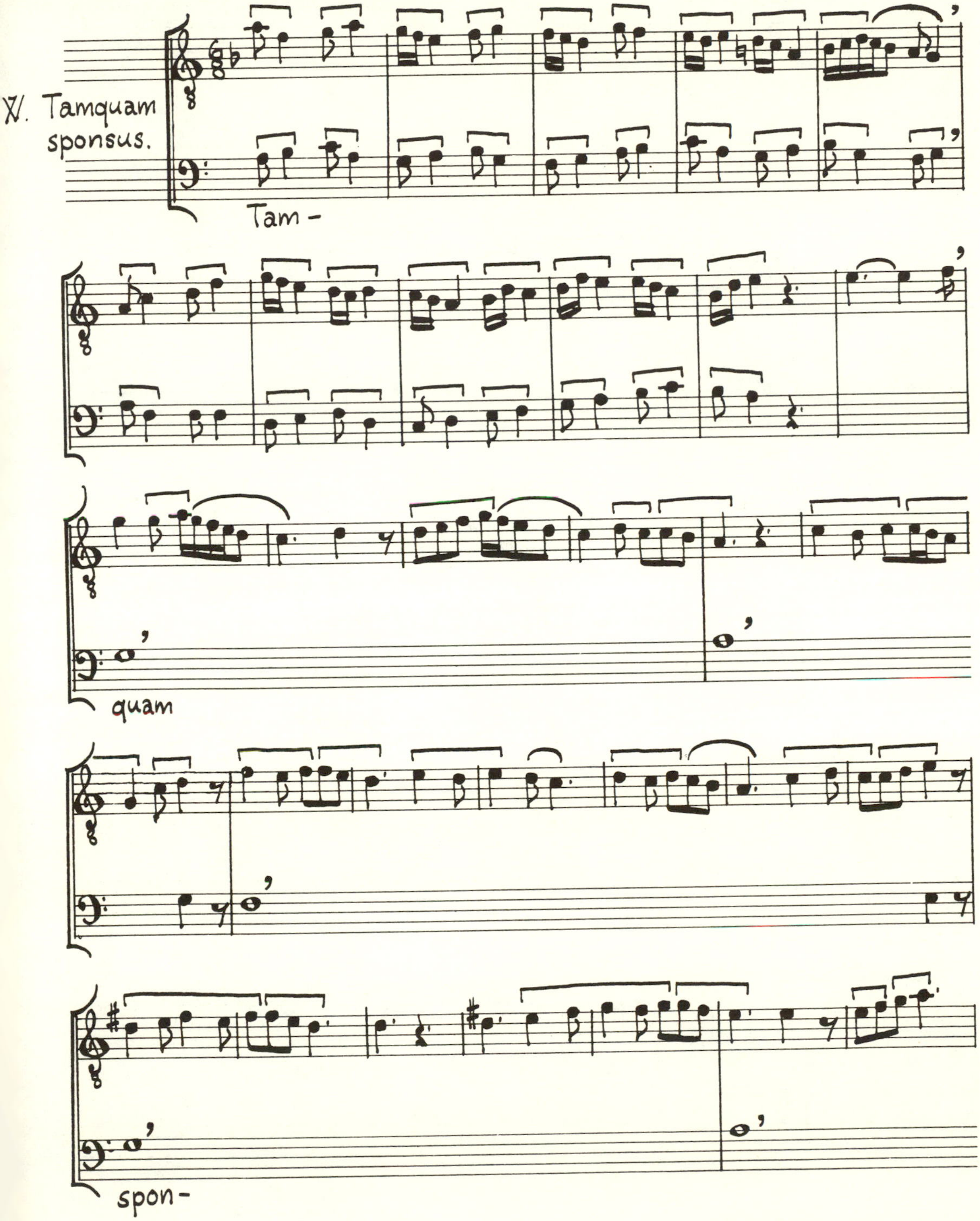
V̸. Tamquam sponsus.
Tam -
quam
spon -

sus
do-
mi-
nus
pro-

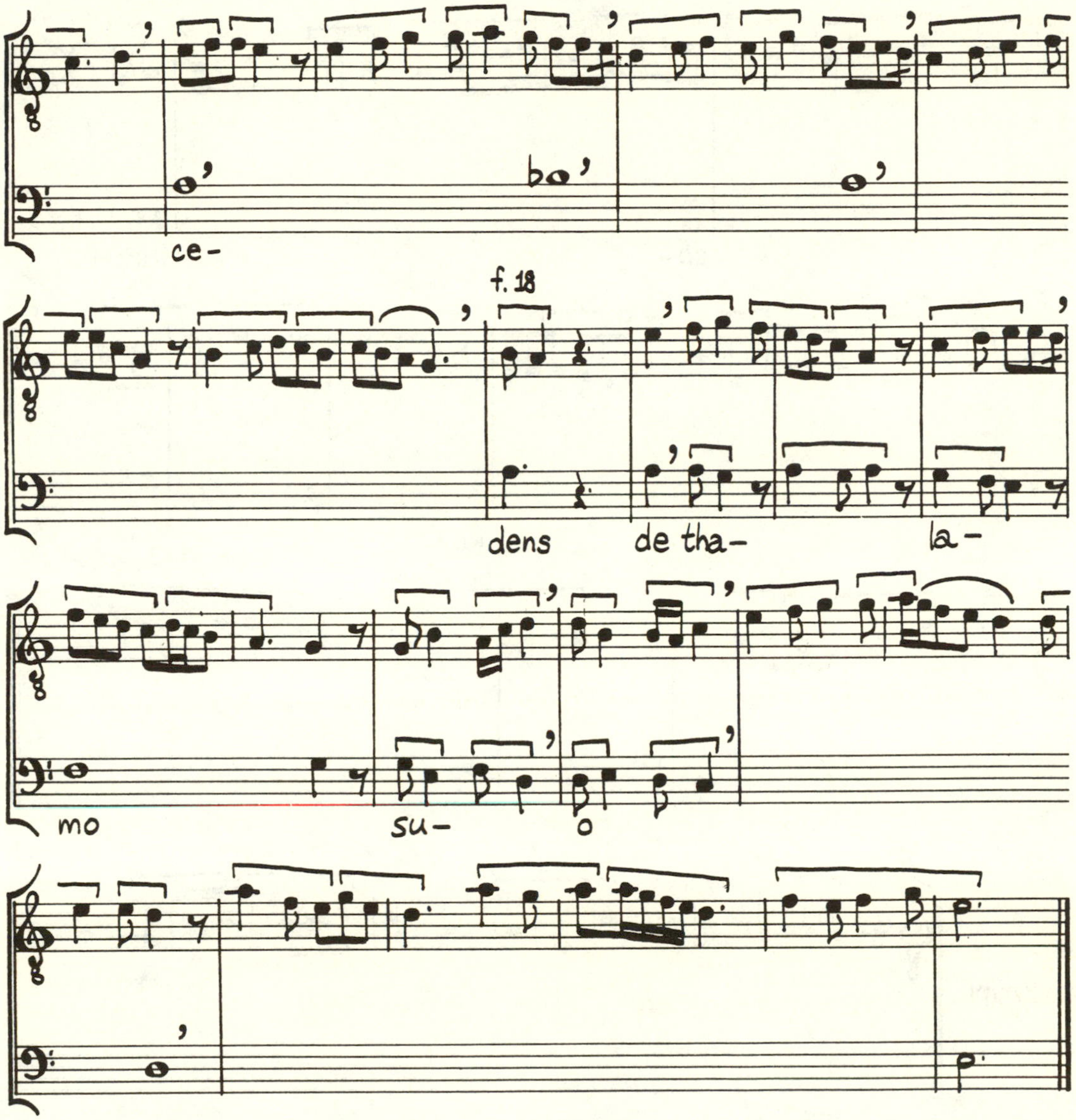
ce-
f. 18
dens de tha- la-
mo su- o

O4. In columbe.

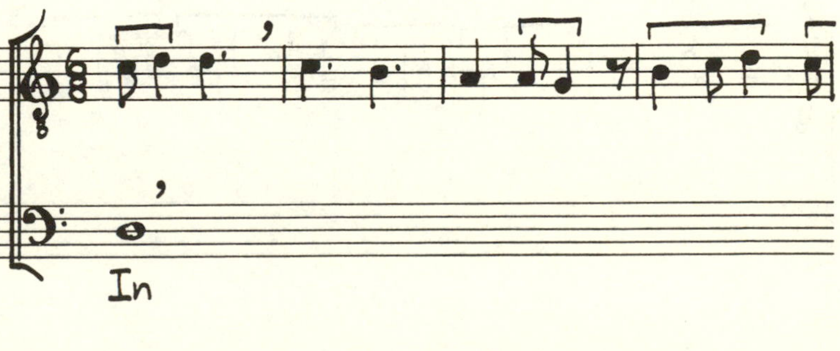
In

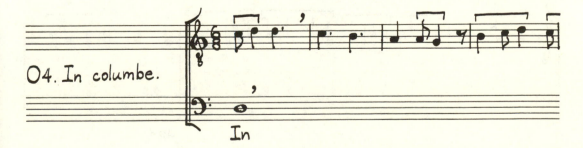

co-
lum-
be.
℣. Vox domini.
Vox
do-

mi -
ni
su-
per
a-
quas
de -

us
ma-
ie-
sta-
tis
in-
to-
nu-
it

do-
mi-
nus
su-
per
a-
quas
mul-
tas.

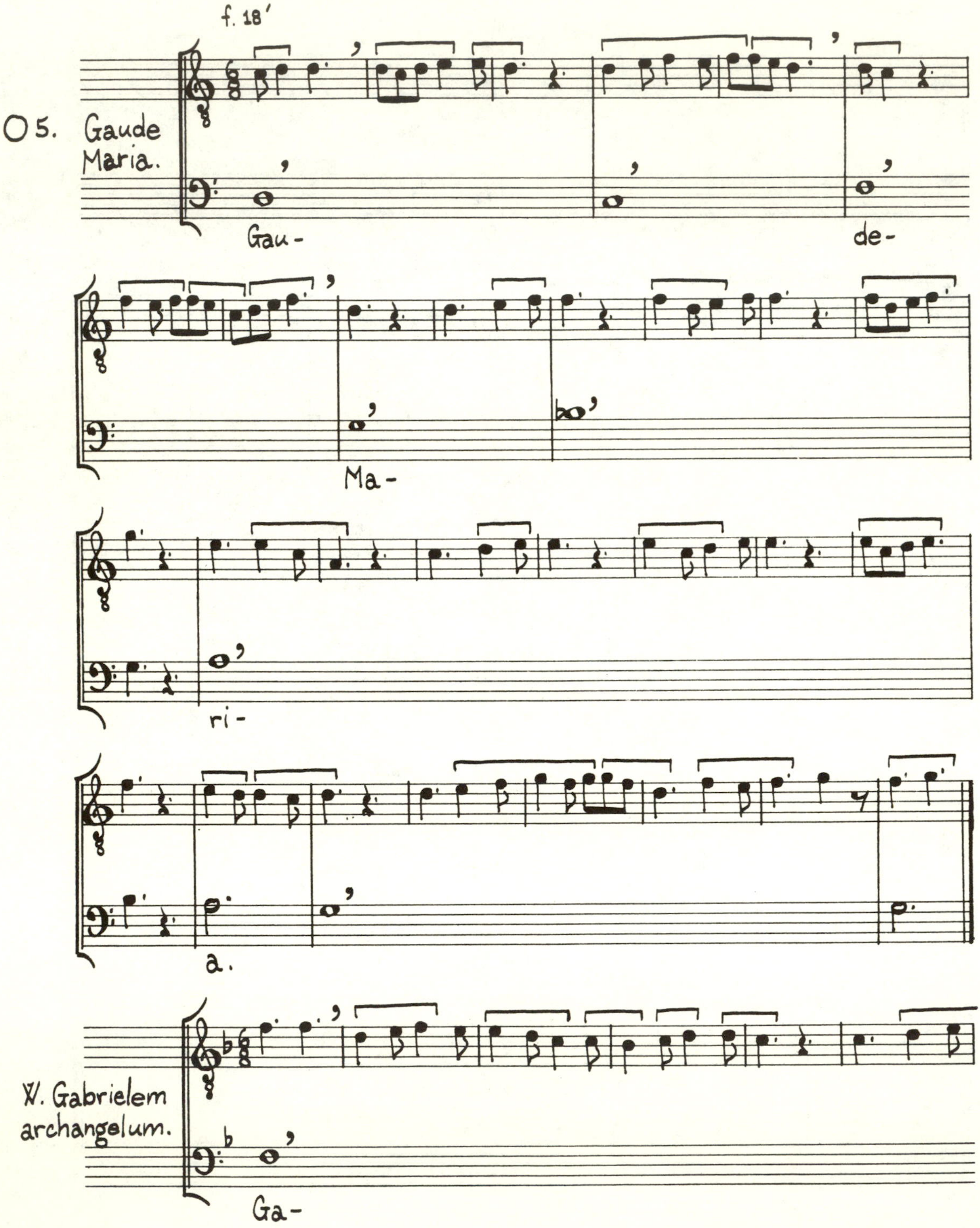
f. 18′
O5. Gaude Maria.
Gau-
de-
Ma-
ri-
a.
V. Gabrielem archangelum.
Ga-

bri-
e-
lem
ar-
chan-
ge-

lum sci- mus di- vi-
ni- tus te es- se af-
fa- tum:
u-

te-
rum tu-
um de spi- ri- tu san-
cto cre- di- mus im-
pre- gna-

tum: e- ru- be-
scat Ju- dae- us in-
fe- lix qui
di- cit xri- stum
f. 19
ex Jo- seph se- mi-

ne es- se na-
tum.
O 10. Non conturbetur.
Non
con-

tur -
be-
tur.
℣. Ego rogabo.
E -
go

ro-
ga-
bo
pa-
trem
et

a-
li-
um
pa-
ra-
cli-
tum
da-
bit
vo-

bis.
O 11. Dum complerentur.
Dum
com-
ple-
ren-
tur

℣. Repleti sunt.
Re-
ple-
ti
sunt

om-
nes
spi-
ri-
tu
san-

cto
et ce-
pe-
runt
lo-

qui.
O 13. Inter
natos.
In-
ter
tos.

f.20
℣. Fuit homo.
Fu-
it

ho-
mo mis-
sus
a
de -

o
cu-
i
no-
men
Jo-
han-
nes
e-

rat.
O24. Concede.
Con-
ce-
de.

℣. Adiuvent nos.
Ad- iu- vent nos
f. 20'
e- o- rum me-

ri -
ta, quos pro
pri - a im - pe -
di - unt sce - le -
ra, ex -

cu-
set
in-
ter-
ces-
si-
o,
ac-
cu-
sat

quos
ac- ti-
o: et qui
e- is tri- bu- i-
sti ce- le-

stis pal- mam
tri- um-
phi, no- bis
f.21
ve- ni-
am non de- ne-

ges pec-
ca ti.
O25. Ex eius tumba.
Ex e-
ius tum-
ba.

V. Catervatim ruunt.
Ca-
ter-
va-
tim
ru-
unt

po- pu-
li,
cer-
ne- re
cu-

pi-
en-
tes
quae
per
e-
um
fi-
unt
mi-
ra-

bi-
illegible
li-
a.
f. 21'
O28. Sint lumbi.
Sint
lum-
bi.

V. Vigilate ergo.
Vi-
gi-
la-
te
er-

go,
qui -
a
ne -
sci -

tis
qua
ho-
ra
do -

mi- nus ve-
ster ven- tu-
rus
sit
f. 22
29. Regnum mundi.
Reg-

num
mun -
di.

℣. Eructavit
cor meum.
E-
ru-
cta-
vit

cor me-
um ver
bum bo-
num, di-
co

e-
go
o-
pe-
ra

O 35. Vir perfecte.

per-
fec- te.
℣. Imitator ihesu.
I -

mi-
ta-
tor ihe-
su xri-
sti
sub
cunc-
tis
pa-
ti-
bu-
lo
nos
An-
dre-
a

fac con- for- tes ce- li con-
tu- ber- ni- o..
Gloria patri.
Glo-
ri- a
pa- tri et

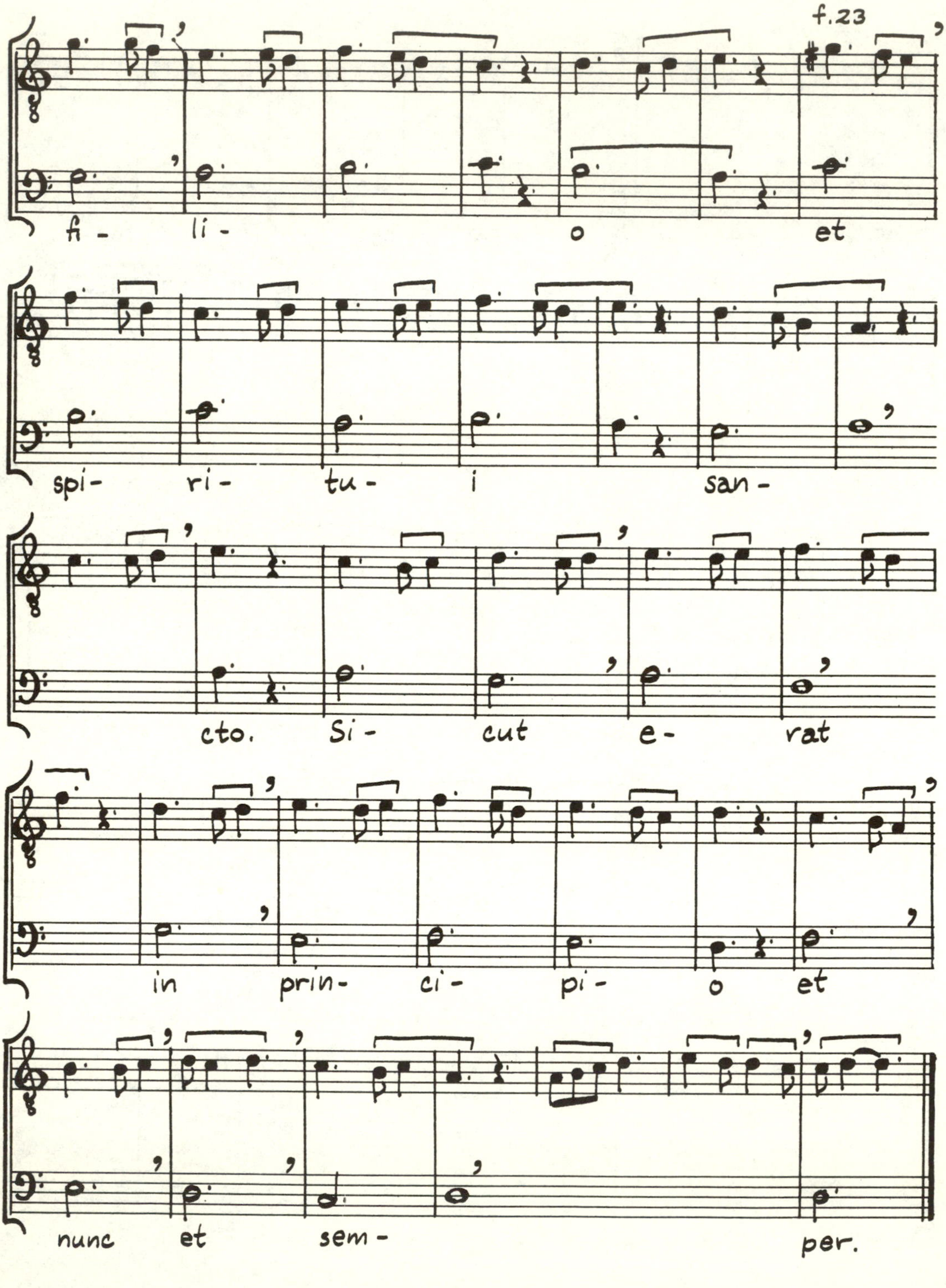
f.23
fi - li - o et
spi - ri - tu - i san -
cto. Si - cut e - rat
in prin - ci - pi - o et
nunc et sem - per.

O 36. Vir iste.

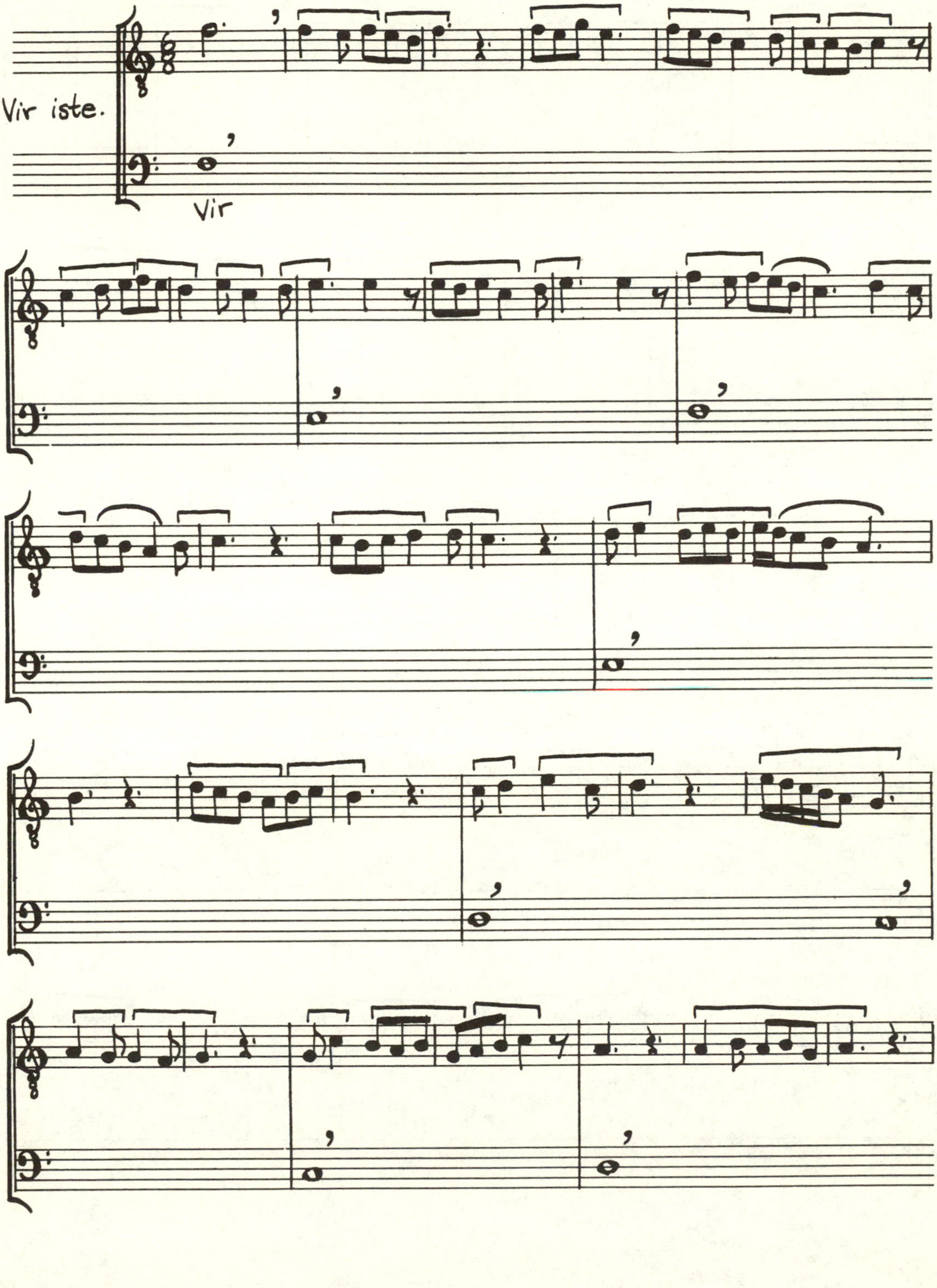

i-
ste
℣ Pro. eo ut.
Pro
e-
o

ut
me
di-
li-
ge-
rent,
de-
tra-
he-
bant
mi-
chi
f. 23′
e-
go
[au-

tem
o-
ra-

[o]
bam.]
M 37. Propter
veritatem.
Prop
ter
ve -
ri -

ta-

tem.
℣. Audi filia.
Au-
di
fi-
f. 24

li-
a
et
vi-
de

et
in-
cli-
na
au-
rem
tu-
am

au-
rem
tu-
am
qui-

a con- cu- pi- vit
rex.

f. 25
M 1. Viderunt omnes.
Vi -
de -
runt

om-
nes.
N. Notum fecit.
No-
tum

fe-
cit
do-

mi-
nus
f. 25'
sa-
lu-

ta-
re
su-
um

an-
te
con-
spec-
tum
gen-

ti-
um
re-
ve-la-
vit.

Mz. Alleluya.
Al-
le
lu-
ya.
℣. Dies Santificatus.
Di-

f. 26
es

san-
cti - fi-
ca-

tus
il-
lu-
xit
no-

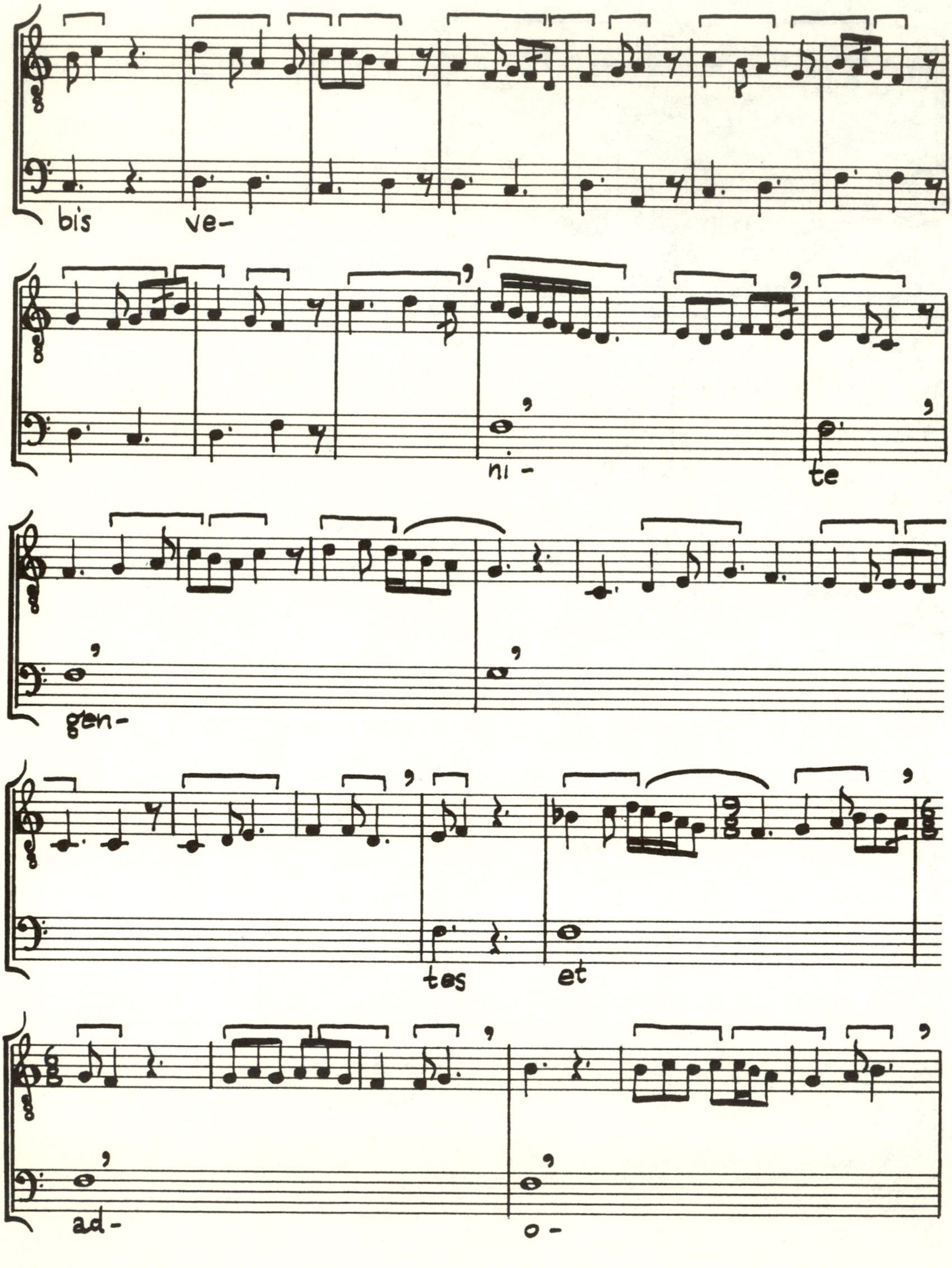
bis
ve-
ni -
te
gen-
tes
et
ad-
o -

ra-
te
do-
mi-
f. 26'
num
qui-

a
ho-
di-
e
de

scen-
dit
lux ma-
gna.

M3. Sederunt.
Se-
de-
runt.

℣. Adiuva me
Ad-
iu-
va
f. 27
me
do-
mi-
ne

de-

us
me-

us

sal-
vum
me
fac
prop-
f.27'
ter
mi-
se-
ri-
cor-

di-
am.
M.5. Exiit sermo.
Ex-

i-
it
ser-
mo.

℣. Sed sic eum
Sed
sic
e-
um
vo-

lo
ma- ne- re

f. 28
do-
nec

ve-
ni-
am.

Ms. Laus tua.
Laus
tu-
a

de-
us.
V. Herodes iratus.
He-
ro-

des
f. 28'
i-
ra-

tus
oc-
ci-

dit
mul-
tos
pu-
e-

ros
In beth- le-em

M9. Omnes.

nes.
℣. Surge.
Sur-
ge

et
il-
lu-
mi-
na-

re
ihe-
ru-
sa-
lem

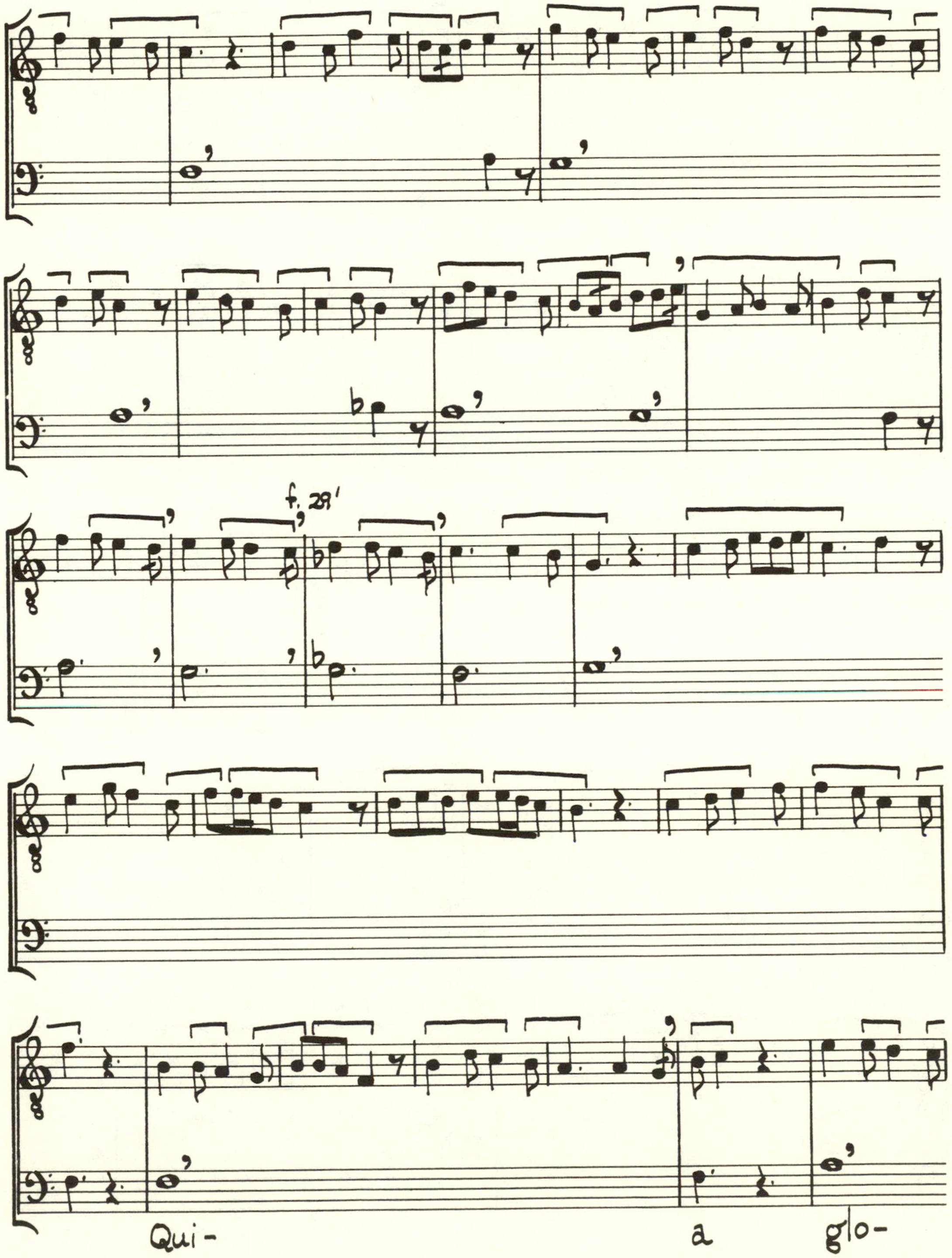
f. 28'
Qui-
a
glo-

ri-
a
do-
mi-

M 11. Suscepimus deus.

ce-
pi-
mus
de-
us.

℣. Sicut audivisimus.
Si-
cut
au-
di-
vi-

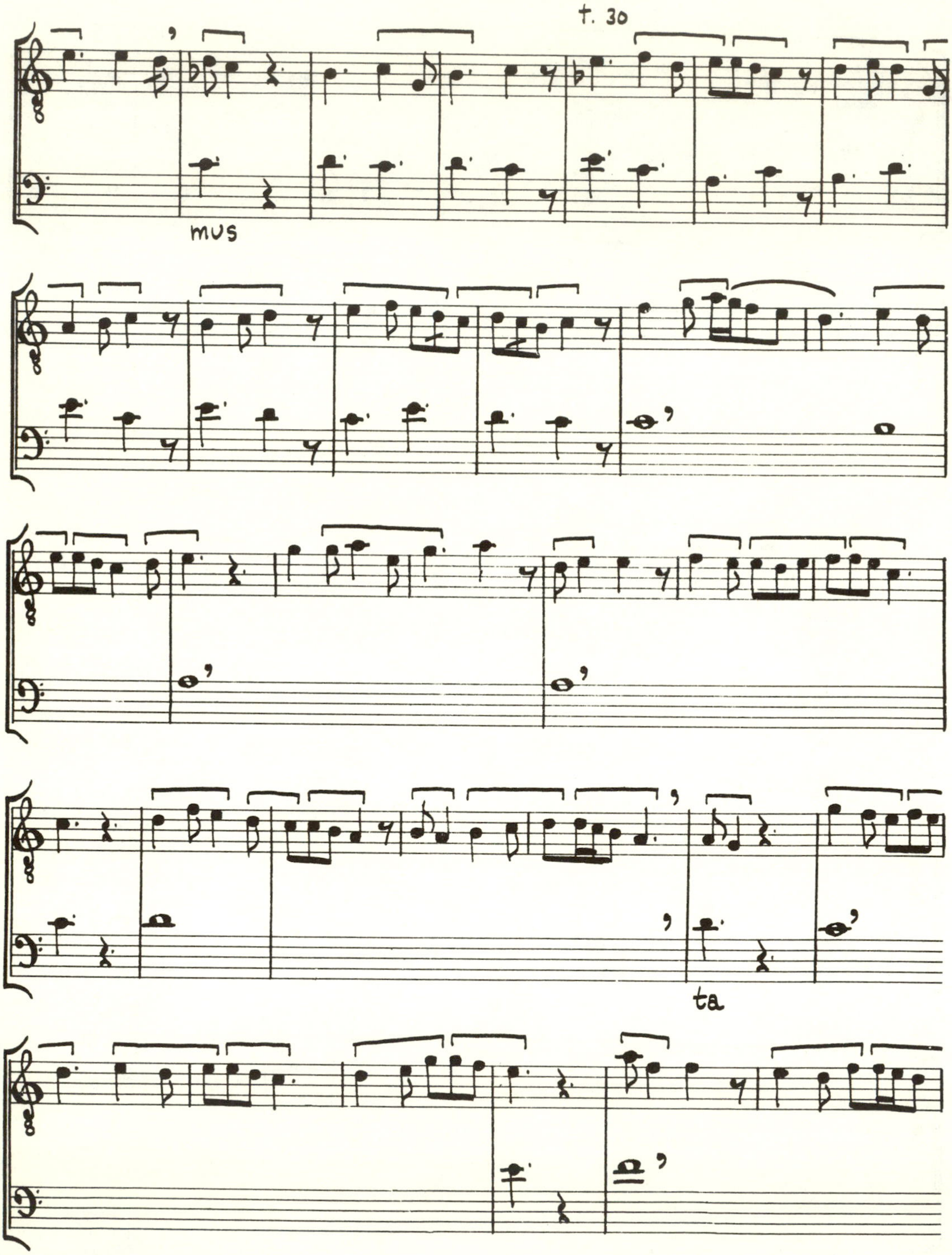
t. 30
mus
ta

et
vi-
di-
mus

in ci- vi- ta-

te de-
i no-
stri in mon-
te san-

cto.
M12. Alleluya.
Al-
f. 30'
le-
lu-

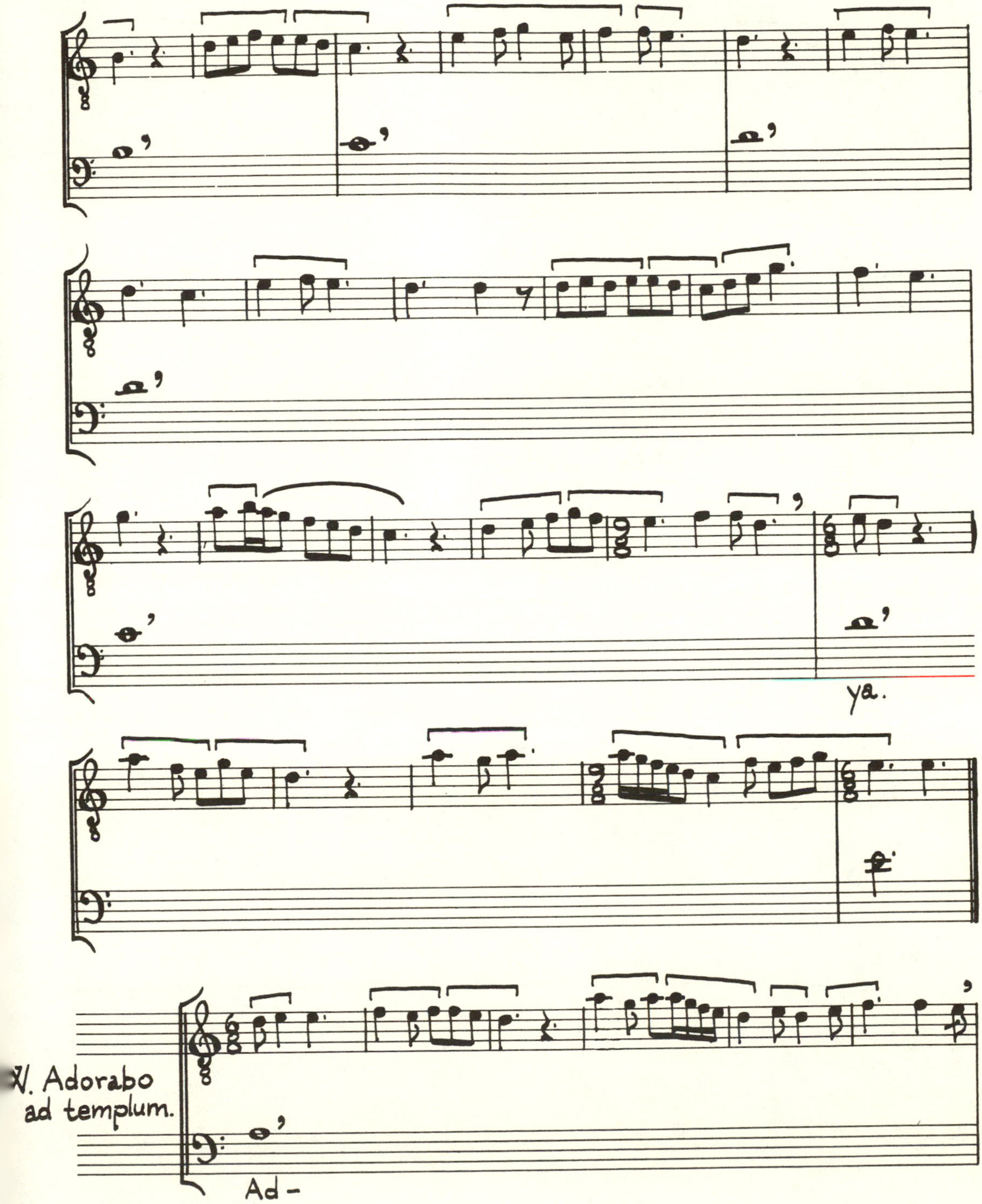
ya.
V. Adorabo ad templum.
Ad –

o-
ra-

bo
ad
tem-
plum
san-

ctum
tu-
f. 31

um et con- fi- te-

M. 13.
Hec dies.

di

es.
V. Confitemini.
Con-
fi-
f. 31'
te-

mi
ni
do-
mi-
no
quo-

ni
am
bo-

nus quo-
ni-
am
in se

M.14. Alleluya.

f. 32
ya.
V. Pascha
nostrum.
Pas-
cha
no-

strum

im-
mo-
la-

tus

est,
f. 32′
M 15. Alleluya.
Al-
le-
lu

ya.
℣ Epulemur in azimis.
E-
pu-
le-

mur
in
a-

zi –
mis
sin –
ce –

ri-
ta
tis.
1.17. Alleluya.
Al-
le-

lu
ya.
f. 33
V̸. Surrexit dominus.
Sur-
re-

xit
do-

mi –
nus
et
oc-
cur –

rens
mu-
li-

e-
f. 33′
ri-

bus
a-
it: a-
ve

te
tunc
ac-
ces-

se-
runt
et te- nu- e-

runt.
M22. Alleluya.
f. 34
Al-
le-
lu-

ya.
℣. Dulce lignum.
Dul-
ce
li
gnum
dul-
ces

cla-
vos
dul-
ci-
a-

fe-
rens pon-
de-
ra que so-

la
fu-
i-
f.34'
sti
di[g]-

na
su- sti-
ne-
re
re-
gem

ce-
lo-
rum.
M.23 Alleluya.
Al-
le

lu-

ya
℣. Ascendens Christus.
As-
cen-
f. 35
dens

xri –
stus
in
al–
tum

cap-
ti-
vam
du-
xit,

cap- ti- vi-
ta-

tem
de-
dit
do-
na.

M.27 Alleluya.

V. Veni sancte spiritus.
Ve-
ni
san-
cte

spi –
ri –

tus,
re -
ple -

tu-
o-
[rum corda fidelium: et tui amoris in eis.]
f. 38
M.31. Alleluya. ℣ Tu es Petrus
(Fragment from end of ℣).
[pe-]
tram
e- di- fi- ca-
bo.

M.32. Benedicta
Be-
ne-
di-

cta
V. Virgo dei genitrix.
Vir-
go

de-
i
ge-
ni-
f. 38′
[trix]

quem
to-

tus non
ca-
pit or-
bis,

in
tu-
a
se
clau-
sit
vi-

sce-
ra.
M.33. Alleluya.
Al-
le-

f. 39
ya.
℣ Assumpta est Maria.
As-
sump-

ta
est
Ma-
ri-
a-
in

ce- lum: gau-
dent
an- ge-

li
et
col -
lau -
dan-

f. 39'

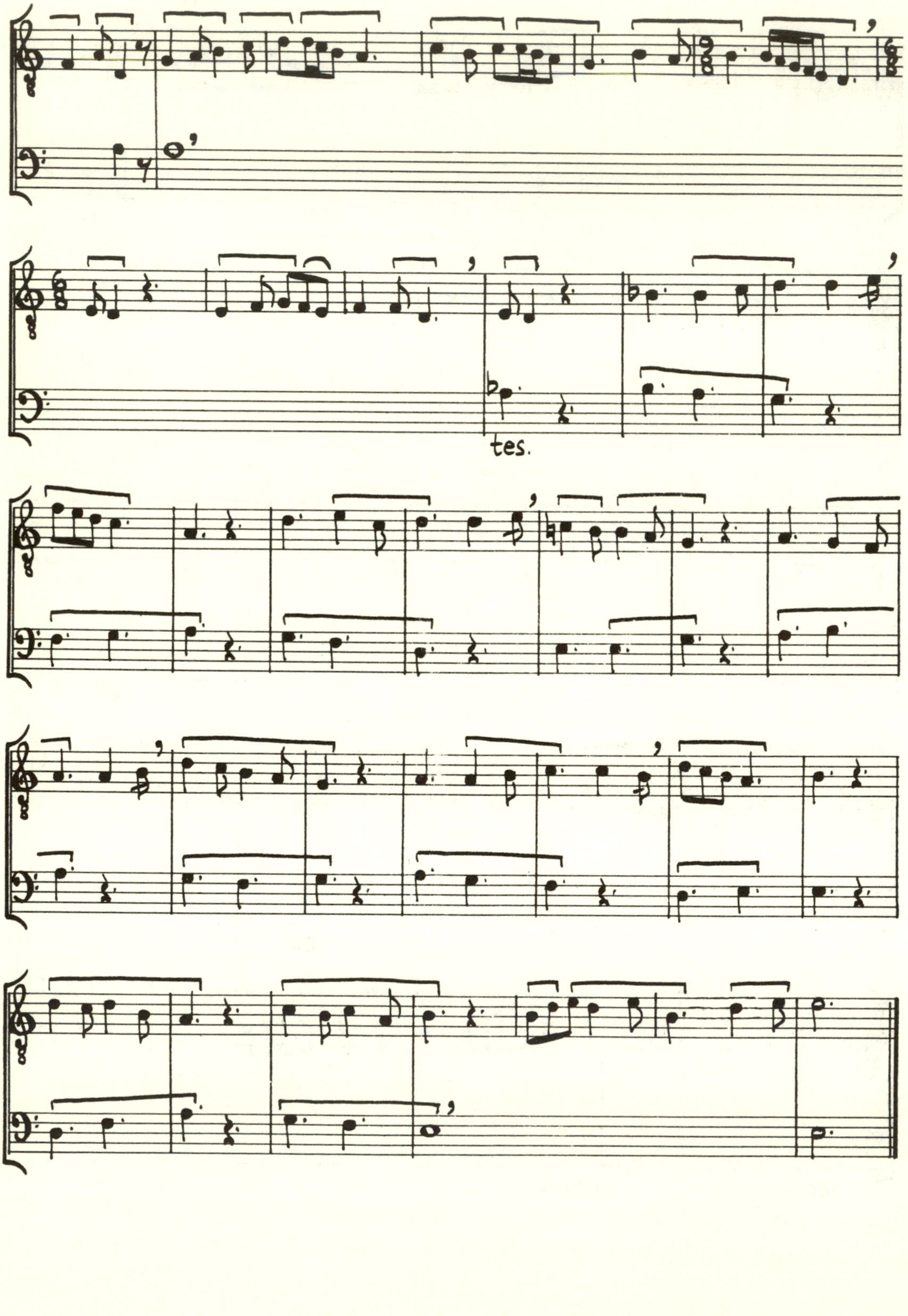

M34. Alleluya.
Al-
le-
lu-

ya.
℣ Hodie Maria.
Ho-
di-

[𝄾]
e
Ma-
ri-
a

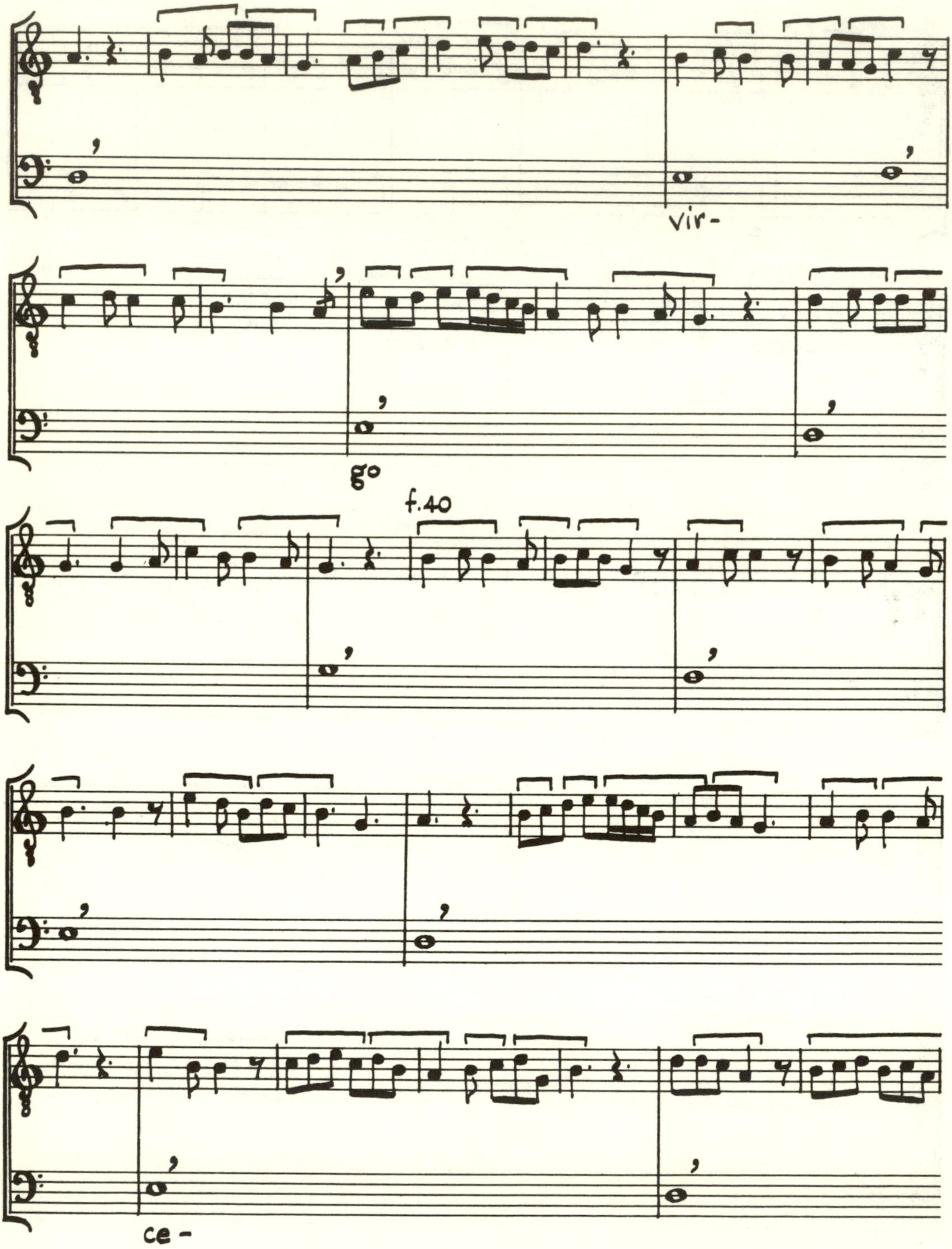
vir-
go
f.40
ce -

los
as-

[s]cen-
dit; gau-
de-
te

qui -
a
cum
xri -

sto
reg-
f.40'
nat.

M.54. Alleluya.
le -
lu-

ya.
℣ Veni electa mea.
Ve–

ni e- le-
cta me-
a

et
po-
nam
f. 41
te
in

thro-
num
me-

um qui-
a con- cu- pi-
vit
rex.

M 37. Propter veritatem.
Prop-
ter
ve- ri-

ta-
tem.
℣ Audi filia.
Au-
f. 41′
di
fi-

li
[9]
a
et
vi-
de

et
in-
cli-
na

au-
rem
tu-
am
qui-

[a]
a con- cu-
pi- vit
f.42
[vit]

M 38. Alleluya.
Al-
le-

lu-
ya.

℣ Nativitas.

tas glo- ri- o-
f. 42'
se Vir- gi-
nis Ma-

ri-
e
ex se-
mi-
ne

A-
bra-

he or- ta
de tri-

bu
Ju-
da.
f. 43
M 39. Alleluya.
Al-
le-

lu-
ya.
℣. In conspectu angelorum.
In
con-

spe-

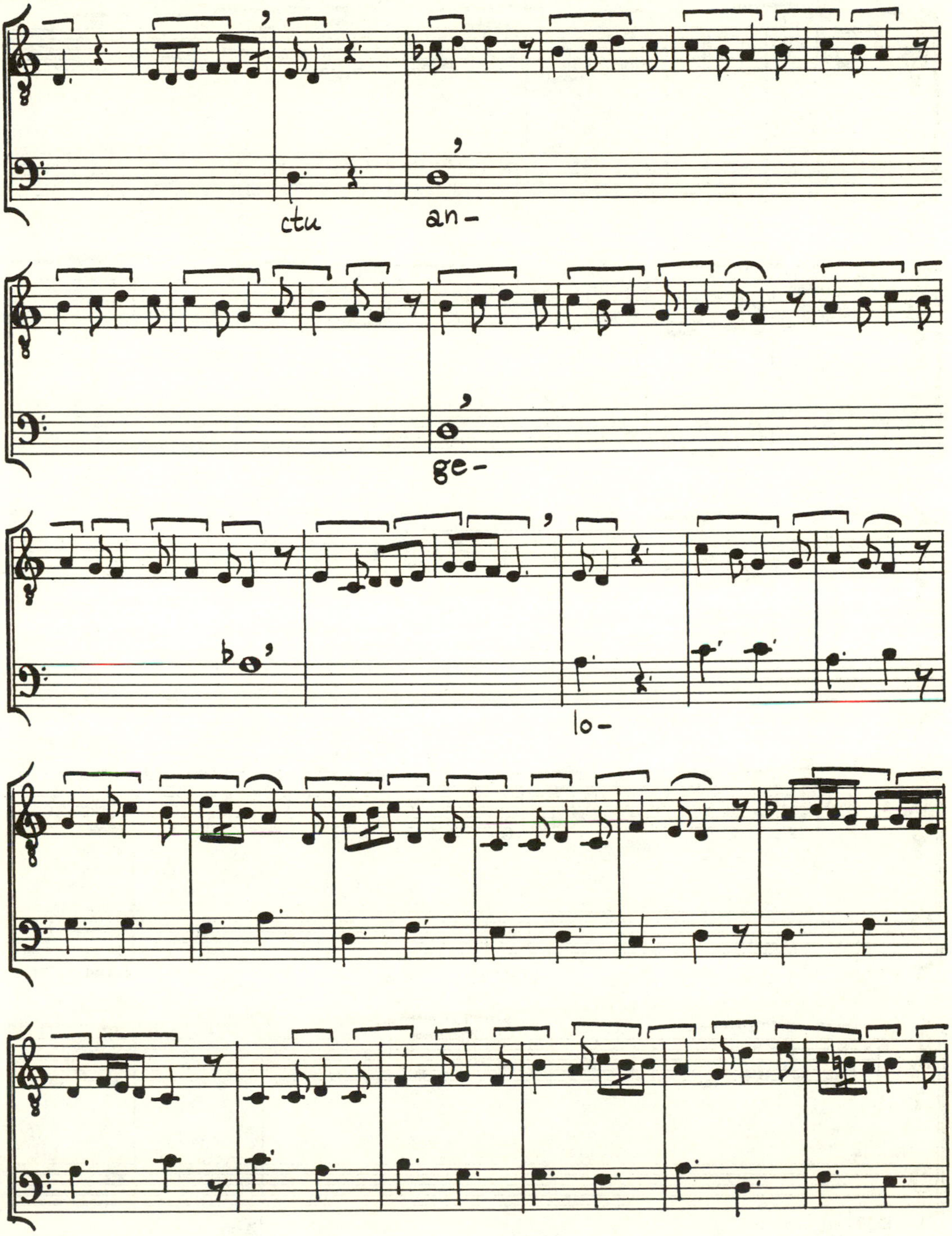
ctu
an-
ge-
lo-

f. 43'
[rum]
rum
psal-
lam

ti –

bi, Do-
mi-
ne De-

M.40. Timete.

me-
te
Do-mi-
f.44
num

℣. Inquirentes autem.
In-
qui-
ren-
tes

au-
tem

Do–
mi–
num
non
de–
fi–
ci–

M42. Alleluya.

f.43'
Iu-
ya.
℣ Judicabunt sancti
Ju-

di-
ca-
bunt

san–
cti na - ti - o-
nes
et
do–

mi-
na-
bun-
tur
po-

pu-
lis
f. 44
et
re[g]-
na-

bit il- lo-
rum rex.

M48. Domine.
Do-
mi-
ne.

℣. Vitam petiit.
Vi-
tam

pe-
ti
it et tri- bu-
i- sti
e-

i lon- gi- tu-
f. 45'
di-
nem di- e-

rum
in se-
cu- lum.
M49. Alleluya.
Al-

le-
lu-

ya.
℣ Letabitur justus.
Le-
ta-
bi-

tur ju-
f. 46
stus in do-
mi
no et

spe- ra-
bit
in
e-

o
et
lau-
da-

M50. Ecce sacerdos.

ce
sa-
cer-
dos.
℣. Non est inventus.
Non

est
in-
ven-
tus
si-
mi-
lis
il- li

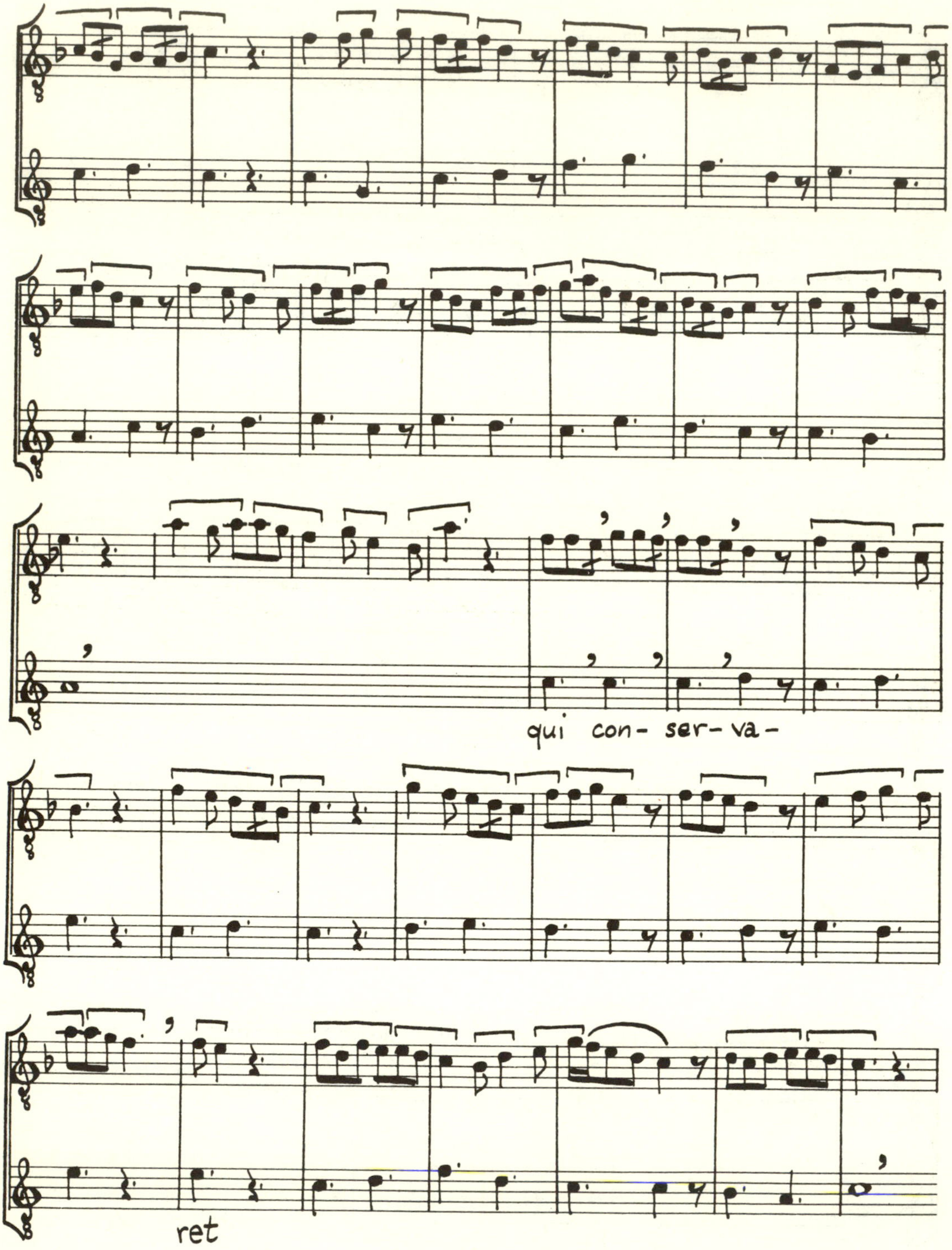
qui con- ser- va-
ret

su-
i
ad-
ju-
to-
ri-
um

su-
per po- ten- tem
et ex- al- ta-

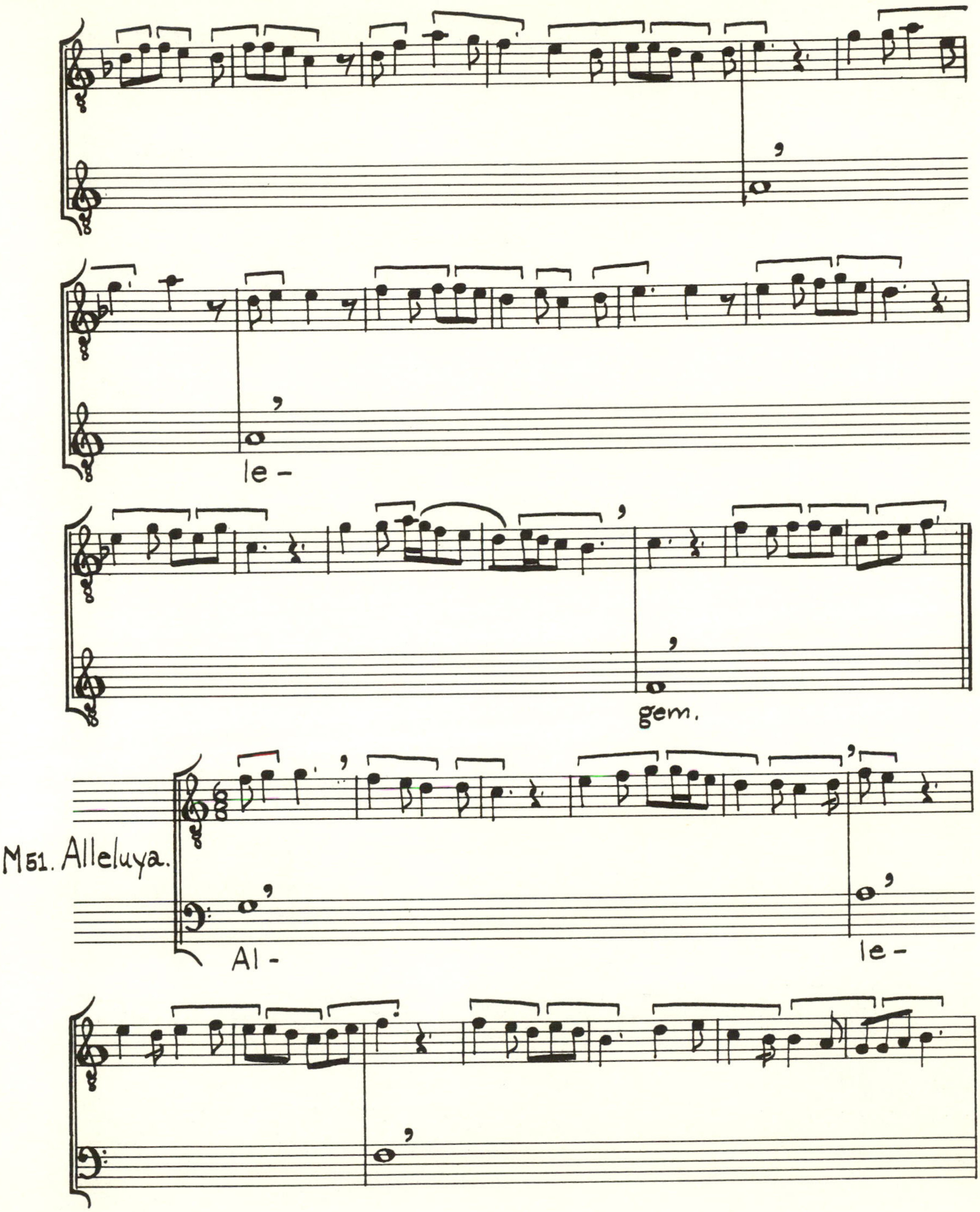
le -
gem.
M51. Alleluya.
Al -
le -

lu-
ya.
f. 47
℣ Posui adjutorium.
Po-

vi
e-
le-

ctum.
M53. Alleluya.
Al-
le-
lu-
ya.

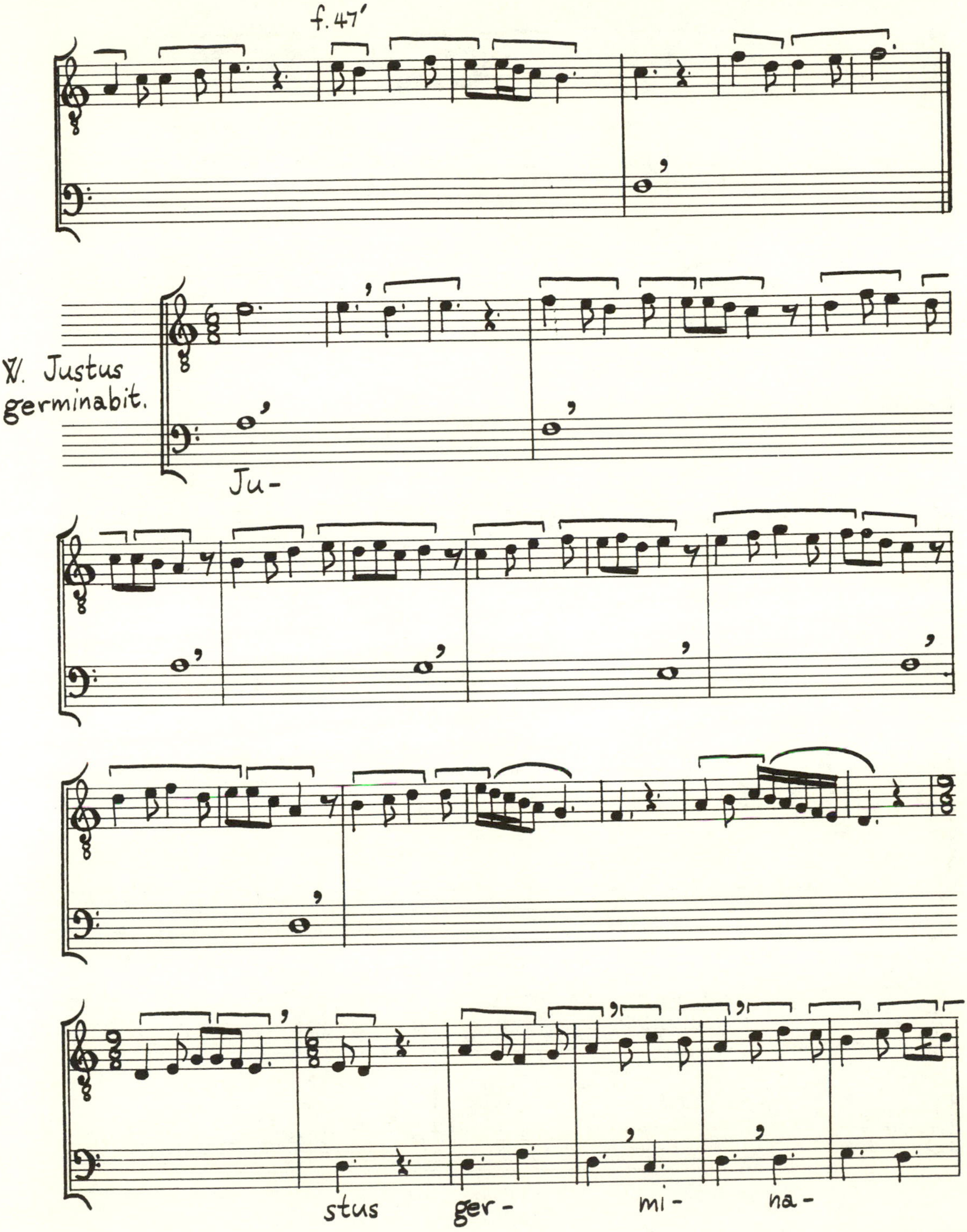
f. 47'
V. Justus germinabit.
Ju-
stus ger- mi- na-

bit
si-
cut
li-
li-

um
et
flo-

re-
bit
in

f.48
e-
ter-
num.
M58. Locus iste
Lo-

cus
i-
ste.
℣ Deus cui adstant.
De-

us cu-
i a-
stant an- ge-
lo- rum cho-

ri
ex-

au-
f. 48'
di
pre-
ces.

M46. Alleluya.
Al-
le
lu-
ya.

℣. Per manus autem.
Per
ma-
nus
au-

tem a- po- sto-
lo-
rum fi-
e-
bant sig-

na
et
pro–
di -
gi -
a.